A Country Garden
for Your Backyard

A Country Garden
for Your Backyard

Projects, Plans & Plantings for a Country Look

MARNY SMITH

with NANCY DUBRULE

Photographs by KAREN BUSSOLINI

RODALE PRESS
Emmaus, Pennsylvania

Printed in the United States of America on acid-free ∞ paper.

Library of Congress Cataloging-in-Publication Data
Smith, Marny.
    A Country garden for your backyard : projects, plans, & plantings for a country look / Marny Smith with Nancy DuBrule : photographs by Karen Bussolini.
        p. cm.
    Includes bibliographic references and index.
    ISBN 0-87596-135-5 hardcover
    1. Landscape gardening. 2. Gardens ~ Designs and plans. 3. Garden structures ~ Design and construction. 4. Gardening. I. DuBrule, Nancy. II. Title.
    SB473.S564 1992635—dc20   92-25963
                                                                                       CIP

Smallwood & Stewart Staff:
Text and Cover Design: Dirk Kaufman
Illustration: Wendy Frost, Elayne Sears
Managing Editor: Robin Haywood
Associate Editor: Kim Horstman
Woodworking Projects: Ken Burton, Jr.
Consultants: Ruth Lively, Sarah Price

Rodale Press Staff:
Senior Editor: Barbara W. Ellis
Editor: Ellen Phillips
Associate Editor: Deborah L. Martin
Copy Editor: Barbara M. Webb
Copy Manager: Dolores Plikaitis
Senior Book Designer: Linda Jacopetti

If you have any questions or comments concerning this book, please write to
Rodale Press, Book Readers' Service, 33 East Minor Street, Emmaus, PA 18098

Distributed in the book trade by St. Martin's Press

2 4 6 8 10 9 7 5 3 1   hardcover

CONTENTS

PART I

A GALLERY OF COUNTRY GARDENS

Six country gardens from concept to completion

Country Garden Style

A country garden brings to mind spring bulbs and appleblossoms, old-fashioned roses and peonies in June, the sound of bees on a hot summer day busying themselves among the purple coneflowers, Queen-Anne's-lace and cosmos, or shiny tomatoes, peppers, and eggplant hanging heavy, ready to be picked. If you have dreams about a country garden and yearn to have one of your own, this book is for you. Included in Part One are six real gardens that have evolved out of each gardener's creative taste and values to inspire you. In Part Two there are plans for other gardens that can be adapted to your own circumstances, and step-by-step instructions on how to implement these plans. The common thread running throughout the book is a commitment to gardening without synthetic chemicals ~ to working with nature to build the soil and control insects and diseases. By using soil amendments in their natural, slow-release form, by composting waste materials and recycling them back into the soil, by using natural pest and disease controls, and by using more disease-resistant, hardy cultivars in their appropriate zones, it is possible to have a garden that is every bit as beautiful as one that is constantly being fed and sprayed with petroleum-derived synthetic chemicals.

There are common features in some of the landscapes described here in Part One that may strike a familiar chord with regard to your own property. Lucie Carlin and Linda Jones live on the shore with wonderful water views, but with all the attendant problems of exposure to harsh weather. Susan Morgenstern, Janie McCabe, and my husband Fred and I live on heavily traveled suburban or country roads and have devised different ways to buffer ourselves from the traffic. Susan, Janie, Lucie, and Martha Paul have each shown that sloping land can be a positive rather than a negative feature. Shade cast by tall trees was a major factor in the development of Susan's garden and my own.

On a more personal note Janie and Linda are careful planners and record keepers; Lucie Carlin and I are more casual about the names and details, and move plants around according to how we think their colors and forms will look together. Janie and Martha have professions involving plants, and have extensive knowledge of how plants behave. Linda and Lucie employ the expertise of Nancy DuBrule (who designed the garden plans in Part Two) to help with their garden plantings. Susan is an amateur horticulturist who is always seeking new plants to fit the circumstances of her landscape. While every one of us is a convert to organic methods of gardening, Fred and I are the only ones who give equal time and attention to growing food as well as flowers.

It is our hope that this book will inspire and help you to create or improve your own country garden in a way that sustains the natural environment.

A "WILD" COTTAGE GARDEN

 Lucie Carlin lives on a quarter of an acre of mostly sloping land that faces southwest across a picturesque seaside cove. (Photographs on pages 17–21.) She tends a garden originally planted by her aunts over 50 years ago with hardy, old-fashioned plants which have continued to thrive without too much attention: Oriental poppies, 'Golden Glow' coneflower (*Rudbeckia laciniata* 'Golden Glow'), Jerusalem artichokes, 'The Fairy' roses, common lilacs, and forsythia.

This is neither a typical cottage garden nor a typical seaside garden. With native plants like swamp milkweed (*Asclepias incarnata*), bouncing bet (*Saponaria officinalis*), hollyhock mallow (*Malva alcea*), and Queen-Anne's-lace (*Daucus carota* var. *carota*), it looks more like a country meadow ~ a "wild" cottage garden.

It is also spared many of the problems of seaside gardening. A major cause of damage in seashore gardens is salt water, which kills most plants when it reaches their roots. But because this garden is on high ground, it does not have the drawbacks of lower-lying shore gardens. Lucie's garden is never flooded, even during severe storms. Some plants do get burned occasionally from salt spray and from the strong, salty wind. When this happens,

Pink honeysuckle, roses, clematis, and foxgloves create a colorful frame to an entrance on Lucie Carlin's property.

their leaves have to be removed.

The soil is not as sandy as most land near the water, although it does contain lots of seashells, and is therefore nearly neutral on the pH scale. (Rhododendrons and other acid-loving plants are fed an acid pH 5.5 compost or plant fodder each spring.) Although there are outcroppings of rock ledge, which often preclude seashore gardening, there are enough deep, soil-filled pockets to support abundant gardens.

The challenge for Nancy DuBrule, who works with Lucie to maintain the plants, is keeping the 50-year-old cottage garden vigorous and well-balanced. If left alone, the invasive plants ~ Jerusalem artichokes, forsythia, and Mexican bamboo (*Polygonum cuspidatum*) ~ that Lucie planted to create privacy would begin to take over the whole property within a year. So, during the summer, Nancy cuts these plants back, and takes some of them out. At the same time, Lucie wants abundance and color every day of the growing season, to remind her of the way the garden looked when she was a young woman. To achieve this, she and Nancy add plants throughout the summer when there is a gap in a border or color is lacking.

Lucie has an artist's sense of color, and she looks at the garden as a painting in progress, choosing plants purely for the color they bring. The color scheme of the garden is pale pink, blue, and white. But she has included splashes of orange, yellow, red, and some purple to add vibrancy to the pale palette. She avoids a clash between pinks and yellows by choosing only pinks that are pale, with no magenta or purply shades.

Because Lucie loves fullness and color, she allows most flowering plants that appear in her garden to grow, even if to most other people they are considered weeds. She doesn't pull dandelions out of her lawn until after they have gone to seed. And rather than use a high-nitrogen fertilizer on her lawn to encourage quick grass growth, she leaves the lawn alone. The lean soil seems to provide the perfect growing medium for the "weeds" she wants, such as clover, ajuga (*Ajuga reptans*), ground ivy (*Glechoma hederacea*), purple- or red-flowered lamium (*Lamium purpureum*), and other low-growing wildflowers. Lucie encourages the wild yellow buttercups (*Ranunculus* spp.) and white- and blue-flowered bluets (*Houstonia* spp.). She has added purple grape hyacinths (*Muscari armeniacum*) to fill in empty spaces in the lawn, then waits to cut the grass in spring until after all of them have finished blooming.

In a cottage garden like Lucie's, where conventional spacing rules are ignored and plants are much closer together than is usually recommended, there is an ongoing battle for elbow room between plants that have finished flowering and those that haven't. It takes an experienced gardener to create order out of the chaos of so many plants.

For example, the lush foliage of the Oriental poppies could easily smother the perennial ageratum (*Eupatorium coelestinum*) and mallow (*Malva alcea*) if Nancy didn't thin out the large leaves all spring to give the underlings some light and air. She removes the yellowing poppy foliage shortly after the last flower fades in late June to give the other flowers a chance to grow up and bloom later in the season.

Two strong growers for this garden are an 'Anthony Waterer' Bumald spirea (*Spiraea × bumalda* 'Anthony Waterer'), a shrub with pink flowers that bloom the entire month of June, and spiderwort (*Tradescantia virginiana*), which blooms in July. Both are cut back after blooming in the summer and revive to bloom again in the fall.

Good soil husbandry is important in a garden like Lucie's, where the beds, which have always been full of plants, haven't been fully renovated for at least 50 years. Fortunately, the soil is extremely rich, because Lucie has used seaweed as a mulch for decades. As long as it has been composted for several months, seaweed makes a very effective mulch. Otherwise, it's liable to add salt to your garden soil. In early spring, the only time the garden is bare, Nancy dresses the soil with plenty of compost and a balanced organic fertilizer. Every time she digs a new planting hole, she replenishes the soil with compost and organic fertilizer.

The best way to make a garden like Lucie's ~ one that is based solely on color, and not on form, shape, or other basic design principles ~ is to start small and let it evolve over a period of years. This is not a garden to be designed all at once by a beginner. It is an ongoing process that can take years to complete.

Begin with a small space ~ 150 to 200 square feet ~ and determine flower place-

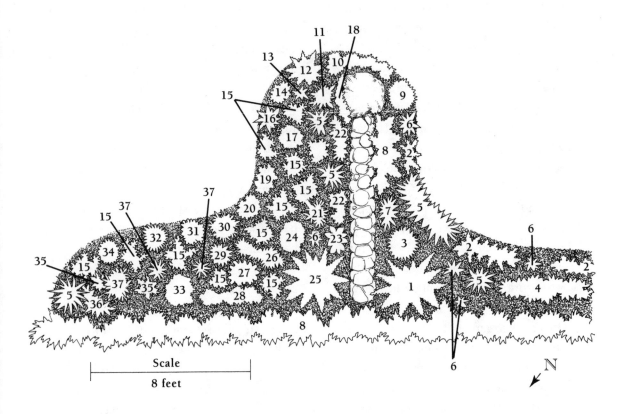

Scale

8 feet

N

A "Wild" Cottage Garden

1. *Buddleia davidii* 'Pink Profusion' (buddleia) 2. *Papaver orientale* (oriental poppies) 3. *Miscanthus sinensis* 'Zebrinus' (zebra grass) 4. Jerusalem artichoke 5. *Hemerocallis fulva* (orange daylilies) 6. *Iris sibirica* (Siberian iris) 7. *Valeriana officinalis* (valerian) 8. Forsythia 9. *Dianthus plumarius* (cottage pink) 10. *Chrysanthemum morifolium* (pink daisy mum) 11. *Paeonia lactiflora* (peony) 12. *Spiraea japonica* 'Little Princess' (dwarf pink spirea) 13. Bearded iris (yellow cultivar) 14. *Sedum* x 'Autumn Joy' (sedum) 15. *Rosa* 'Simplicity' (rose) 16. *Physostegia virginiana* 'Rosea' (obedient plant) 17. *Boltonia asteroides* 'Snowbank' (boltonia) 18. *Lonicera* sp. (honeysuckle) 19. *Chrysanthemum superbum* (shasta daisy) 20. *Chrysanthemum morifolium* (white daisy mum) 21. *Phlox paniculata* (lavender phlox) 22. *Delphinium* 'Blue Jay' (delphinium) 23. *Alcea rosea* 'Single Pink' (hollyhock) 24. *Cosmos bipinnatus* 'Sensation' (cosmos) 25. *Buddleia davidii* 'Empire Blue' (purple buddleia) 26. *Lysimachia clethroides* (gooseneck loosestrife) 27. *Malva alcea* (hollyhock mallow) 28. *Aster novae-angliae* 'Harrington's Pink' (pink aster) 29. *Tradescantia virginiana* (spiderwort) 30. *Daphne cneorum* (rose daphne) 31. *Sedum spectabile* 'Brilliant' (showy sedum) 32. *Coreopsis verticillata* 'Moonbeam' (coreopsis) 33. *Achillea millefolium* (white yarrow) 34. *Lysimachia punctata* (circle flower) 35. *Papaver* 'Pink Beauty' (pink poppies) 36. *Eupatorium purpureum* (Joe-Pye weed) 37. *Lilium tigrinum* 'Splendens' (orange tiger lily)

ment with a plan of the garden, sketched with color pencils, to see how the colors look next to one another and how they flow through the garden. Use a limited number of easy-to-grow "cottage plants": roses, poppies, mallows, coneflowers, lilies, cosmos, and spider flowers (*Cleome hasslerana*). Add annuals and perennials to the garden as the season progresses, buying mature plants that are already in bloom so you can make sure their color and shape are just right for filling empty spaces. With a few seasons' experience, you will develop the knack of envisioning what the garden will look like during the next succession of bloom and the ability to keep invasive plants under control so that you can maintain the lushness of a cottage garden.

A WOODLAND GARDEN

Susan Morgenstern's property, a 100 by 350-foot lot that slopes gradually downhill for almost its entire length, was originally covered with a dense woods of deciduous trees, shrubs, and vines. (Photographs on pages 22–27.) The overgrowth casts shade for much of the day. In this challenging setting, Susan has managed to create a charming woodland garden, with garden beds connected by meandering pathways.

Initially, Susan spent several years just cleaning away debris and removing obviously dead trees, tangled shrubbery, and vines. She felled some of the living trees ~ there were so many that some just had to go ~ and pruned the remaining ones. Then, tired of mowing the thin grass up and down the sloping, shaded lawn while ducking under and around the trees, Susan decided to replace much of it with woodland garden beds.

Even if you have only one large tree in your garden, you probably know how difficult it can be to garden under it. The branches and leaves block out sunlight, and the roots suck up water and nutrients at amazing rates. Finding a patch of soil where tree roots haven't already staked their claim sometimes seems impossible. Gardening on a property that is covered with trees takes ingenuity, persistence, and ~ in some cases ~ a willingness to do things that fly in the face of conventional horticultural wisdom.

When Susan was ready to plant her garden, she first removed some of the lower limbs from the remaining trees, both to allow more light in and to give her access to the ground beneath them. She then tilled the area with a small rotary tiller, which effectively tore out small roots. Susan used a grub-hoe to remove larger roots when necessary. She incorporated lime (to raise the pH, since woodland soil is usually acidic) and other soil amendments into the tilled earth. Then she mulched the beds thickly with composted sheep manure and shredded bark.

Today, Susan Morgenstern's backyard looks like a lovely park, with well-spaced trees surrounded by flower beds, and pockets of sunlight falling in between. Despite competition from tree roots, her beds are brimming over with healthy plants, thanks to heavy mulching, a lot of watering, and regular additions of composted sheep manure.

As you walk through her garden, you'll see sun-loving plants growing in dappled shade. She often experiments with pushing her favorite plants to their limits, in hopes that she will find non-conformists that will grow well in her less-than-ideal circumstances. For example, common lilacs (*Syringa vulgaris*)

Hostas and irises spill onto a stone path that leads from the house to the wooded area.

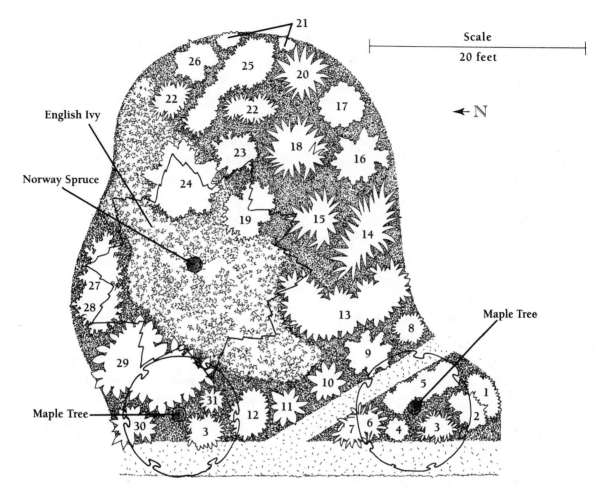

English Ivy

Norway Spruce

Maple Tree

Maple Tree

Scale
20 feet

← N

A Woodland Garden

1. *Veronica incana* (woolly speed-well) 2. *Astrantia major* (great masterwort) 3. *Rhododendron* cv. (azalea) 4. *Dicentra eximia* (fringed bleeding heart) 5. *Phlox stolonifera* (creeping phlox) 6. *Rhododendron* cv. (rhododendron) 7. *Endymion hispanicus* (Spanish bluebells) 8. *Campanula glomerata* (clustered bellflower) 9. *Aster × frikartii* (Frikart's aster) 10. Digitalis

ambigua (yellow foxglove) 11. *Di-gitalis lanata* (Grecian foxglove) 12. *Tradescantia × andersoniana* (blue spiderwort) 13. *Lobelia siphi-litica* (blue lobelia) 14. *Hemero-callis lilioasphodelus* (lemon daylily) 15. *Iris ensata* (white Japanese iris) 16. *Perovskia atriplicifolia* (Russian sage) 17. *Phyteuma heterofolium* (horned rampion) 18. *Iris ensata* (Japanese iris) 19. *Aquilegia × hy-brida* (hybrid columbine) 20. *Iris sibirica* (blue Siberian iris) 21. *Myosotis* spp. (forget-me-nots)

22. *Platycodon grandiflorus* (bal-loonflower) 23. *Dicentra spectabilis* 'Alba' (white bleeding heart) 24. *Salix discolor* (pussy willow) 25. *Aquilegia × hybrida* 'Raspberry Treat' and 'Nora Barlow' (hybrid columbines) 26. *Achillea mille-folium* (common yarrow) 27. *Di-centra spectabilis* (bleeding heart) 28. *Ceratostigma plumbaginoides* (blue plumbago) 29. *Hosta* cv. (hosta) 30. *Anemone blanda* (white windflower) 31. *Tricyrtis hirta* (hairy toad-lily)

grow along the north side of the house and still bloom obligingly. She has replanted purple coneflower (*Echinacea purpurea*) for two years in a row because she really wants it in a particular place, even though there isn't enough sun there.

Other plants that prefer more sun, but that are making do with only an hour or two here and there throughout the day, include 'Moonshine' yarrow (*Achillea* × 'Moonshine'), Russian sage (*Perovskia atriplicifolia*), catmint (*Nepeta mussinii*), and speedwells (*Veronica* spp.). Perhaps their colors are slightly less vivid, or they have fewer blossoms than their peers growing in the sun, but each makes a contribution of color, foliage texture, or shape to the garden that Susan finds pleasing.

You might expect to find lots of hostas growing in a woodland garden, and Susan's is no exception. But she's found an unusual way to put these plants to work as stump removers. She plants hostas all around a stump, as close to it as possible. The big hosta leaves shade it and keep it moist ~ pretty soon it begins to rot. In a couple of years she can usually take the stump out in pieces.

Susan is an avid reader of gardening books and catalogs, and her woodland beds are filled with unusual, often difficult-to-find plants. She enjoys raising many plants from seed under fluorescent lights; it's a good way to start plants that aren't available locally.

Susan swears by the self-watering, insulated foam growing trays she uses. She's found that it is possible to be gone for as long as a week without worrying that the seed-starting medium will dry out, and germination rates are high ~ even with hard-to-germinate species. The only problem she's had with them is that the foam melts when it comes into contact with soil-heating cables. She solved this problem by laying out the heating cables, covering them with sheets of glass, and setting the trays on the glass.

Susan's woodland garden proves that trees and flowers can exist in the same space. By clearing out, limbing up, and using plants in unusual ways, she has made the most of her property. The trees now stand surrounded by beds of flowers and foliage plants, a testimony to the power of ingenuity, determination, and patience.

Luxurious plant combinations create an almost wild feeling in this cottage garden. A large island bed partially hides the house, adding a sense of mystery to the property. It contains a mix of perennials, shrubs, and vegetables including 'Autumn Joy' sedum, 'Simplicity' roses, perennial ageratum, 'Snowbank' boltonias, asters, pansies, delphiniums, and Jerusalem artichokes. ➤

A "Wild" Cottage Garden

A "Wild" Cottage Garden

In June, the garden is bursting with orange Oriental poppies, buttercups, sweet rocket, and purple bearded iris. The poppies are summer-dormant, so as the foliage dies down, room is made for other plants ~ like 'Autumn Joy' sedum and perennial ageratum.

By October, perennial ageratum has filled in where the poppies were, the sedum has turned a deep bronze, and 'Marguerite' daisies, 'Grenadine' chrysanthemums (Chrysanthemum frutescens), and pink geraniums have been added for a final burst of color.

Self-sowing plants and flowers that can withstand competition are encouraged in this cottage garden. Purple larkspur (Delphinium ajacis) self-sows throughout the garden, while yellow loosestrife (Lysimachia punctata) and common yarrow (Achillea millefolium) are not disturbed by the crowding.

←

Joe-Pye-weed (Eupatorium purpureum) *contributes to the country feeling in this garden by attracting monarch butterflies. In this early fall picture, it is surrounded by blue mist* (Caryopteris × clandonensis) *and white-flowering gaura* (Gaura lindheimeri).

↑

Even the foundation plantings on this property are unconventional and give the impression of abundance barely held in check. In September, Jerusalem artichokes grow thickly around a rhododendron. Beneath, an aster spills over the edge of the bed, surrounded by a border of violets.

21

↑

Now that the trees have been limbed up, shade-tolerant plants, such as this naturalized checkered lily (Fritillaria meleagris), *can thrive.*

← *Most of the trees were on this property when the owner bought it, but they had to be thinned selectively to allow enough light for a woodland garden. Some of the lower branches were pruned from this magnificent saucer magnolia* (Magnolia × soulangiana).

Although this woodland garden was planned, the paths were allowed to meander informally to invite the visitor to walk from bed to bed. A beautiful pink weigela provides a focal point at the corner of this bed.

Foxgloves (Digitalis purpurea) enjoy the moist, humusy soil of a woodland garden. As long as the soil is well-drained, they will self-sow vigorously, producing clumps of pink and purple spikes in early summer.

Because so many woodland plants bloom briefly, foliage textures are a central feature of woodland gardens.

A mix of shade-loving hostas is combined effectively with the airy foliage of self-sown columbines and bowman's root (Gillenia trifoliata).

↑

In another part of the property,
Christmas fern (Polystichum
acrostichoides), European wild
ginger (Asarum europaeum),
and 'Palace Purple' heuchera
create a contrast in textures,
colors, and shapes in front
of an arborvitae.

The owners of this garden created a friendly, welcoming country tone with a white picket fence and arbor draped with fragrant flowers. In June, hardy, disease-resistant pale pink 'New Dawn' roses intertwine with deeper pink 'Viking Queen' roses on the arbor. White honeysuckle (Lonicera halliana) and beach peas (Lathyrus littoralis) mingle with the roses for additional summer color.

Planters are used throughout the property to add color where it is needed ~ on the patio, near the front door, even hanging on the fence.

Pinks, lavenders, and whites dominate this garden's color scheme, with a little blue as an accent. A close-up of the border by the picket fence shows pink 'New Dawn' roses, blue flax (Linum perenne), *and lavender dame's rocket* (Hesperis matronalis).

↑

*Inside the garden, a thickly
planted raised bed hides an
old oil tank. White flowering
tobacco peeks from behind the
foliage of obedient plant*
(Physostegia virginiana)
and blue Serbian bellflower
(Campanula poscharskyana).
*A pink 'New Dawn' rose,
which will eventually cover
the wall, climbs on the trellis
behind pink perennial bachelors'
buttons* (Centaurea cyanus).

Flowers grow right up, and are encouraged to grow over, the house to enhance the informal country look. Goldflame honeysuckle (Lonicera × heckrottii) has been trained over the back of the house. A windowbox filled with shade-loving annuals ~ blue browallia, New Guinea impatiens, and white lobelia ~ adds more color. The garden bed below contains white clematis (Clematis recta), an unusual form of non-vining clematis, and red valerian (Centranthus ruber).

Even in fall there is some color in the garden. By September, the flowers in this foundation planting of 'Nikko Blue' bigleaf hydrangeas (Hydrangea macrophylla 'Nikko Blue') have turned from bluish purple to salmon pink.

AN INSTANT COTTAGE GARDEN

Almost all gardeners dream of getting instant results in their gardens. But for most, that goal remains a dream; gardens evolve gradually over time, often looking woefully bare the first few seasons as plants mature. In the case of this yard, however, Linda Jones was able to work with Nancy DuBrule to create a charming cottage garden in a very short time. (Photographs on pages 28–32.) Nancy combined plants that quickly reached maturity with plants that spread rapidly like pink-and-yellow-flowered goldflame honeysuckle (*Lonicera × heckrottii*) and obedient plant (*Physostegia virginiana*). She filled gaps with annuals such as cosmos, spider flower (*Cleome hasslerana*),

cupflowers (*Nierembergia hippomanica* var. *violacea*), and snapdragons.

Four years ago the Jones's 50 by 80-foot property was a bare lawn; its only features were the house and a rental cottage. From the moment Linda and her husband bought the house, they visualized a country cottage with a lush garden, overflowing with flowers for cutting that would welcome them home from work each day; and they wanted it right away. Linda began by adding simple touches that would contribute character to the house, define the property, and set the tone for a cottage garden. She had gingerbread trim attached along the roofline and installed a trellis over the entryway, added window boxes, and a picket fence with a arched trellis over the front gate.

Linda drew a plan of her garden and had a specific list of plants that she wanted to

*F*ragrant roses, honeysuckle, and sweet peas
clamber over the trellis at the entrance to the garden.

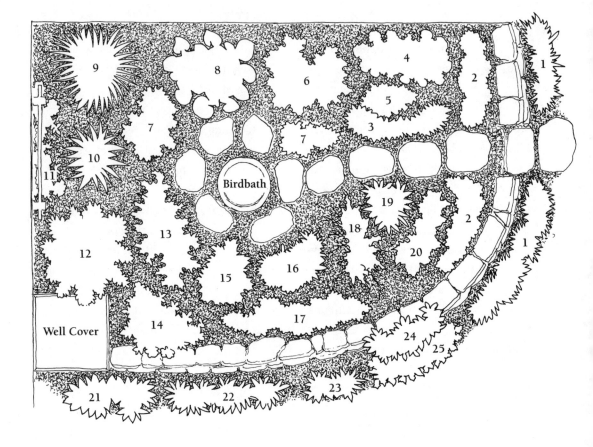

An Instant Cottage Garden

1. *Lavandula angustifolia* (lavender) **2.** *Saponaria officinalis* (bouncing bet) **3.** *Coreopsis rosea* (pink coreopsis) **4.** *Achillea* × 'Moonshine' (yarrow) **5.** *Chrysanthemum parthenium* (white feverfew) **6.** *Cleome hasslerana* (spider flower) **7.** *Antirrhinum majus* (snapdragon)

8. *Alcea rosa* (hollyhocks) **9.** *Miscanthus sinensis* 'Gracillimus' (maiden grass) **10.** *Lilium* (yellow lilies) **11.** *Rosa* 'New Dawn' (rose) **12.** *Cytisus scoparius* (pink scotch broom) **13.** *Aconitum napellus* (monkshood) **14.** *Rosa* 'The Fairy' (rose) **15.** *Echinops ritro* (globe thistle) **16.** *Chrysanthemum* × *superbum* (Shasta daisy) **17.** *Campanula poscharskyana* (Serbian bellflower) **18.** *Linum perenne*

(blue flax) **19.** *Phlox paniculata* (garden phlox) **20.** *Perovskia atriplicifolia* (Russian sage) **21.** *Centranthus ruber* var. *albus* (white valerian) **22.** *Salvia* × *superba* 'East Friesland' (salvia) **23.** *Lythrum salicaria* 'Robert' (pink loosestrife) **24.** *Euonymus fortunei* (wintercreeper) **25.** *Heuchera sanguinea* (coral bells)

include. She had always gardened in the shade, and, with a site in full sun, she wanted a garden with sun-loving flowers like roses and hollyhocks. She brought delphiniums and coralbells (*Heuchera sanguinea*) from a previous garden, and included hydrangeas because she associates them with a cottage by the sea.

Linda planned her garden in a carefully considered pastel color scheme of soft pink, white, blue, and lavender, with accents of darker purple and deeper pink. She placed blue 'East Friesland' sage (*Salvia* × *superba* 'East Friesland') in a grouping with magenta-purple 'Morden Pink' loosestrife (*Lythrum virgatum* 'Morden Pink'), and white valerian (*Centranthus ruber* var. *albus*). Pale pink 'The Fairy' roses and salmon pink 'Clara Curtis' chrysanthemums shared space with daylilies in other shades of pink, and blue cupflowers provided a contrasting accent. She included an occasional yellow only if it was a pale shade, but no oranges or reds.

Linda had to solve two major problems before she could begin planting. The first was the lack of privacy on the terrace on the east side of the house, which looked directly up at the rental cottage. Rather than wait for many years while shrubs reached maturity, Linda arranged for several yards of soil to be trucked in and installed a raised berm, approximately 15 feet long by 8 feet wide and 2 to 3 feet high. Linda brought soil in by wheelbarrow loads; she graded the pile to a gentle slope, and planted thickly to prevent erosion. To provide privacy for the terrace, Nancy planted this new bank with Russian sage (*Perovskia atriplicifolia*), 'The Fairy' roses, 'Clara Curtis' chrysanthemums, pink daylilies (*Hemerocallis* cvs.), and ornamental grasses. Each year she adds cupflowers and other low annuals such as Swan River daisy (*Brachychome iberidifolia*) and sweet alyssum (*Lobularia maritima*) to the edge of the perennial plantings. This handsome screen of foliage and flowers now gives their terrace complete privacy. To the west of the house, a hedge of rugosa roses (*Rosa rugosa*) provides privacy by closing off views of neighboring yards.

The second problem was the Jones's discovery of an old oil tank buried underground and surrounded by a barely visible stone wall, overgrown with euonymus and weeds, next to the rental cottage. Nancy cut out most of the weedy growth, and amended the soil above the oil tank with compost and organic fertilizer. Then she planted 'New Dawn' roses, clumps of pink Scotch broom (*Cytisus scoparius*), maiden grass (*Miscanthus sinensis* 'Gracillimus'), perennials, and self-sowing annuals. Blue-lilac Serbian bellflowers (*Campanula poscharskyana*) spill over the wall above 'Morden Pink' loosestrife, deep pink 'Appleblossom' yarrow (*Achillea* × 'Appleblossom'), and other perennials along the base of the wall.

Like most cottage gardens, this property does not have a formal foundation planting or a large grass lawn. Flower beds are planted on either side of the front entryway, and an informal, curving 3- to 5-foot-wide border runs along the inside of the picket fence. In order to create the best growing conditions for a wide range of fast-growing, closely spaced plants, Linda double dug each bed and enriched the soil by incorporating lots of compost and organic fertilizer.

Because Linda wanted her garden to look lush that first summer, she used a great many annuals to fill the empty spaces between perennials, especially those that would self-sow and "volunteer" the following year, like pink and white cosmos and cleome, blue fennel flower (*Nigella damascena*), larkspurs (*Consolida ambigua*), white flowering tobacco (*Nicotiana alata*), violet-blue cupflowers, and sweet alyssum. She also added spreading perennials like mallow (*Malva alcea*), gaura (*Gaura lindheimeri*), and Queen-Anne's-lace.

To fill in the space over the trellis while the roses matured, Nancy planted fast-growing white honeysuckle (*Lonicera halliana*) and beach peas (*Lathyrus littoralis*). In early spring and regularly during the season, she prunes back the honeysuckle to give the roses and beach peas room to spread.

As in all good cottage gardens, Linda allows plants to overflow their space, making sure the more aggressive ones don't take over. On the terrace, sedums, thymes, and pinks (*Dianthus* spp.) creep over the flagstones, and Linda plants pots each spring with geraniums, sweet alyssum, and cupflowers to add spots of color.

Now that the garden is becoming established, Linda rips out plants that are too aggressive, like pink bee balm (*Monarda didyma*). As the perennials expand, she uses fewer and fewer annuals. The cosmos, which overwhelmed the border garden the first two years, are now thinned each spring. The obedient plant, which outgrows its space every few years, is dug up and divided in early spring.

A COUNTRY OASIS

Although informal, Janie McCabe's flower garden is a carefully managed oasis in the middle of a sloping lawn and meadow. (Photographs on pages 49–53.) Its setting is a true country scene: a farmhouse and an orchard of old apple trees, a lawn with a woodland on one side, and on the other, a verdant hedgerow of native plants, including dogwood (*Cornus florida*), honeysuckle (*Lonicera sempervirens*), viburnums (*Viburnum* spp.), and bittersweet (*Celastrus scandens*), that obscures the road. Her flower garden, surrounded on three sides by a picket fence

A mix of lavender, campanulas, scabious, irises, coreopsis, and daphne creates an interesting combination of textures in one corner of the garden.

and framed by a 60-year-old apple tree and a Higan cherry (*Prunus subhirtella* var. *pendula*), is down the lawn from the house.

Janie designs landscapes and gardens professionally, but her own garden has taken 13 years to reach its present state. When Janie and her husband bought the property, there was already a flower garden in the open area left after some of the old apple trees died. For several years, Janie continued maintaining and adding to the original plantings, but the garden was frustrating. The planting lacked structure; it was difficult to maintain a steady succession of bloom; there were constant problems with drainage and runoff due to the sloping terrain and heavy red clay; and being unenclosed, the garden was under frequent attack from marauding woodchucks, as well as taking a beating from children's balls and frisbees.

Three years ago, Janie completely redesigned the garden. First, she thought not only about how to solve the design and maintenance problems she had, but also about what she wanted to accomplish with her garden. She wanted an inviting space ~ filled with exquisite flowers ~ which would offer tranquility in the midst of activity. Besides wanting a garden that would be beautiful to look at for as long as possible, she wanted a place where she could sit, relax, and draw inspiration from her plants. She also wanted to minimize the lawn, which had expanded as more apple trees died, but wanted to leave enough of it for her children's ball games and other outdoor activities.

The new garden is 24 by 36 feet ~ nearly triple the size of the old one. The enlarged garden offers considerably more room for plants, making it easier to have flowers in bloom all season long; plenty of room for a small terrace to sit on; and, of

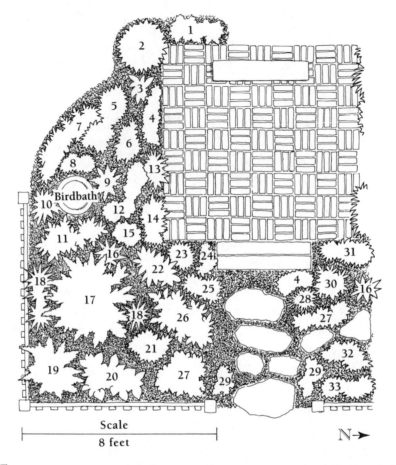

Scale
8 feet

N→

A Country Oasis

1. *Malva sylvestris* var. *mauritiana* (mallow) 2. *Helictotrichon sempervirens* (blue oat grass) 3. *Echinacea purpurea* (purple coneflower) 4. *Campanula poscharskyana* (Serbian bellflower) 5. *Echinops ritro* (globe thistle) 6. *Delphinium × elatum* (delphinium) 7. *Cimicifuga racemosa* (snakeroot) 8. *Aster novae-angliae* 'Hella Lacy' (aster) 9. *Artemisia ludoviciana* 'Silver King' (artemisia) 10. *Paeonia* 'Kansas' (peony) 11. *Anemone ×*

hybrida 'Margarete' (Japanese anemone) 12. *Veronica bonariensis* (speedwell) 13. *Euphorbia epithymoides* (cushion spurge) 14. *Lavandula angustifolia* 'Hidcote' (lavender) 15. *Coreopsis verticillata* 'Moonbeam' (coreopsis) 16. *Iris ensata* (Japanese iris) 17. *Buddleia alternifolia* (alternate-leaf butterfly bush) and *Buddleia alternifolia* 'Argentea' (silver alternate-leaf butterfly bush) 18. *Lilium* 19. *Artemisia lactiflora* (white mugwort) 20. *Brunnera macrophylla* (heartleaf brunnera) 21. *Doronicum caucasum* (leopard's

bane) 22. *Monarda didyma* (bee balm) 23. *Dianthus × allwoodii* 'Helen' (pink) 24. *Helianthemum nummularium* (common sun-rose) 25. *Rosa* 'Othello' (rose) 26. *Anemone × hybrida* (Japanese anemone) 27. *Heuchera micrantha* 'Palace Purple' (heuchera) 28. *Festuca cinerea* (blue fescue) 29. *Thymus serpyllum* (creeping thyme) 30. *Daphne* sp. (daphne) 31. *Scabiosa* 'Blue Butterflies' (pincushion flower) 32. *Geranium endressii* (geranium) 33. *Chrysanthemum* 'Clara Curtis' (chrysanthemum)

course, less lawn to care for.

Surrounding three sides of the garden with a 3-foot-tall picket fence was a simple solution to several of Janie's problems. The fence gives much-needed structure to the whole garden, and forms a backdrop to the many plants Janie grows for their attractive foliage. While her children are interested in the garden and enjoy bringing their friends there, they respect the enclosed area as off-limits for active games. And, surprisingly, the fence has made a big difference in the woodchuck problem. Janie surmises that the animals don't like being closed in, and so are reluctant to enter.

To provide a place to sit, Janie excavated a level 8-foot-square space, sited slightly off-center, for a terrace. She added steps leading down to the terrace, and surfaced both terrace and steps with brick.

The following spring, Janie began replanting with a few plants that she considered essential. These include climbing roses (for the structure they give to the garden), and some of the English roses developed by David Austin, which are resistant to blackspot and have fuller, more fragrant blooms than floribundas or hybrid teas. She planted butterfly bush (*Buddleia davidii*), because her daughter likes the butterflies that it attracts. Then she added a wide array of perennials for their attractive flowers and foliage.

Inside the garden, the colors are mostly limited to muted tones of blue, pink, and white, with accents of yellow and burgundy. In early fall, annual moonflowers (*Calonyction aculeatum*) bloom on the picket fence among the late-blooming clematis ~ wine-red 'Niobe' and mauve 'Comtesse de Bouchard'. 'The Fairy' rose, covered with small pink flowers, blooms in one corner, along with pink and white butterfly bushes mingled with Japanese anemones (*Anemone × hybrida*) in rosy pink, white, and pale mauve. Annual pink and white cosmos dance in the air next to blue spikes of mealy-cup sage (*Salvia farinacea*), pink 'Alma Potschke' asters (*Aster novae-angliae* 'Alma Potschke'), and the lingering flowers of both white and pink cultivars of purple coneflowers (*Echinacea purpurea*). With them are the bristly, gray-blue heads and distinctive light gray toothed leaves of globe thistle (*Echinops ritro*), black-eyed-Susans (*Rudbeckia hirta*), and a mauve verbena (*Verbena bonariensis*).

Anchoring the flowering plants are the gray foliage of lavender and artemisias, the dark purply brown leaves of 'Palace Purple' heuchera (*Heuchera micrantha* 'Palace Purple'), mahogany-colored perilla (*Perilla frutescens* 'Crispa'), a few carefully selected ornamental grasses, and variegated iris.

Today, the soil has good drainage and a nice dark color, and has gone from an acidic pH 5.6 to a nearly neutral pH 7.2, thanks to the use of organic fertilizers, composted yard debris, and manure from

Janie's two rabbits. (She composts the rabbit manure for about six months before she uses it.) To keep the soil in good condition, she top-dresses the entire garden with compost every spring.

Remaking the garden went very smoothly ~ a result of well-thought-out plans methodically executed. But as with any major project, there were plenty of lessons. Two things driven home to Janie were the importance of getting the big, "backbone" plants in first, and making careful plant choices. The first year after the fence went in she was impatient. One of the shrubs she put in, fountain buddleia (*Buddleia alternifolia*), has turned out to be much too big for the space, and so has a clump of Japanese silvergrass (*Miscanthus sinensis*). Her experiences with these plants remind her it's better not to be so eager. Now she's inclined to be very selective, especially in choosing the larger plants.

Although Janie says that her garden isn't finished, it already is achieving its goals. This informal, country perennial garden is a beautiful quiet space, one that can be separate from its surroundings, when the occasion warrants, without being isolated. When Janie walks out of her kitchen, she feels a pull toward the garden, and she notices that visitors feel the same attraction. Sitting as it does a good 25 feet from the house, the garden is clearly visible from upstairs windows.

Even in winter the garden is attractive, framed by the picket fence, the old apple tree, and the weeping cherry trees.

A WORKING HERB GARDEN

 When Martha and Richard Paul bought their house four years ago, Martha saw potential for pursuing her long-time interest in herbs. The 2-acre property offered plenty of space for a large and varied garden, and the house had room for giving classes and selling herbal products. (Photographs on pages 54–58.) Soon after moving in, she launched Martha's Herbary.

The 1830s house is set into a slope, with two stories visible from the front. The cellar is accessible from the lower rear of the house, and serves as a classroom, workroom, and cool place to keep potted herbs over the winter.

When the Pauls moved in, the existing garden ~ trees, shrubs, and perennials ~ was neglected and overgrown. In addition to tidying up and rejuvenating the existing plantings, Martha has added new garden areas. One is a charming little knot garden, roughly 15 by 10 feet. Martha's design for the knot garden is simple: a rectangle of neatly trimmed germander (*Teucrium chamaedrys*) surrounding two diamonds of gray and green lavender cot-

*Yarrow, bronze fennel, anise hyssop, and bee balm fill
one corner of the raised beds that surround the herb garden.*

tons (*Santolina chamaecyparissus* and *S.
virens*). Lavenders, thrift (*Armeria maritima*), creeping thyme, and pinks
(*Dianthus* spp.) fill some of the enclosed
areas. The knot garden is a dramatic and
unusual introduction to the front of the
house.

Behind the house are two very different
herb gardens. From the grassy terrace outside the cellar, stone steps bisect an
informal sloping border of herbs and
perennials leading to a formal herb garden
below. Randomly placed rocks along the
slope act as a natural-looking retaining
wall to hold the bank in place.

The informal garden on the bank was
part of the existing garden. Martha
thinned out the garden phlox, bellflowers
(*Campanula* spp.), and Siberian iris, then
improved the soil by adding leafmold,
sand, and manure to lighten its clay base,

and lime to raise the pH for the herbs she
would add.

The slope is bounded at either end by
tall plantings. At the northern end, a
rounded French lilac 10 feet in diameter
stands next to gray 'Silver King' artemisia,
deep blue baptisia (*Baptisia australis*), and
burgundy-flowered peonies. Peonies and
lovage (*Levisticum officinale*) grow at the
southern end, in partial shade. Lovage is
one of Martha's favorite herbs because of
its bold, architectural form and its beautiful celadon-green foliage. It is a good
substitute for celery in cooking.

Martha has introduced many herbs and
a variety of perennials to this part of the
garden. There's no overall pattern here;
just a mix of herbs and perennials that
flatter each other growing in loose abundance. Everywhere there are interesting
textural contrasts, such as the narrow,

pointed spears of Siberian iris foliage against softly rounded bloodroot (*Sanguinaria canadensis*) leaves and the pointed ones of St.-John's-wort (*Hypericum*); floppy purple cranesbills (*Geranium* spp.) next to stiff swirls of steel gray corkscrew allium (*Allium senescens* 'Glaucum').

At the foot of the steps, the ground levels out and opens onto a rectangular area bounded by an established 6-foot-high boxwood hedge. Martha decided the hedge created the perfect enclosure for a formal herb garden, as well as an effective barrier to deer and other plant-eating

wildlife, with its overall rectangular shape broken into symmetrical beds by grass paths. In fact, one of the happiest surprises for Martha was the way in which this garden, when viewed from above, looks like it has always been there, even though it is quite new.

Martha faced a challenge in installing this new herb garden ~ poor drainage. In general, herbs like soil with very good drainage. Not only was Martha's soil fairly heavy clay, but also the new garden would occupy level ground below a slope. To ensure that the plants would not sit in soil soggy with runoff from the perennial bor-

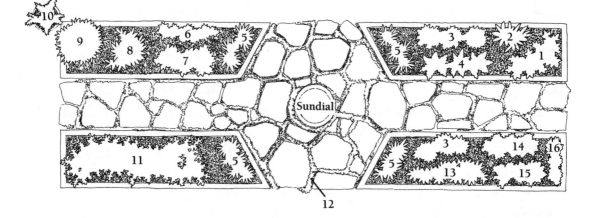

A Working Herb Garden

1. *Alchemilla mollis* (lady's-mantle) **2.** *Stachys byzantina* (lamb's-ears) **3.** *Chrysanthemum parthenium* (feverfew) **4.** *Chenopodium bonus-henricus* (good King Henry) **5.** *Calendula officinalis* (pot marigold) **6.** *Achillea millefolium* 'Rosea' (pink yarrow) **7.** *Heliotropium arborescens* 'Marine' (garden heliotrope) **8.** *Melissa officinalis* (lemon balm) **9.** *Perilla frutescens* (perilla) **10.** *Rosmarinus officinalis* (rosemary) **11.** *Pelargonium* cvs. (scented geraniums) **12.** *Thymus serpyllum* (creeping thyme) **13.** *Calamintha nepeta* (calamint) **14.** *Coriandrum sativum* (coriander) **15.** *Anethum graveolens* (dill) **16.** *Helichrysum italicum* (curry plant)

der above, Martha and Richard built raised beds about 6 inches high. They used rough-sawn pine to frame the beds rather than pressure-treated lumber, sacrificing longevity of the wood since they didn't want chemicals leaching into the soil. They filled the new beds with a custom mix of four parts loam, two parts each of sand and compost, and one part composted sheep manure.

Entrances on each side of the new formal garden divide the perimeter into four L-shaped beds. A sundial just opposite the stone steps forms the focal point of the garden. Bright yellow pot marigolds (*Calendula officinalis*), grown for their edible flowers, and fragrant purple heliotrope (*Heliotropium arborescens* 'Marine') border this area, giving it color and scent. Pots of scented geraniums (*Pelargonium* spp.) and lantana (*Lantana camara*) trained as standards add visual interest and height.

In the central area of the garden are six beds. Three are filled with a mix of herbs, but the remaining three are each devoted to many types of one herb: basils, sages, and scented geraniums.

Martha also grows several kinds of lavender. Lavender is very susceptible to fungal diseases, but Martha has found that a mulch of sand, extending from just beyond the branches to right up against the stem, discourages fungi by reflecting heat onto the plant and forming a barrier between the moist soil and plant stems.

At one end of the formal garden, a trellis of native cedar supports a golden hop vine (*Humulus lupulus* 'Aureus'). Traditionally, hops have been used in making beer, and Martha adds the flowers to a calming tea mixture she makes. But the golden form of this vine is more prized as an ornamental climber with its brilliant yellow leaves, greenish flowers, and decorative golden seedpods.

Early and late in the season, trees along the southern side of the property provide the right niche for herbs that enjoy shade, like sweet woodruff (*Galium odoratum*), Bethlehem sage, sweet cicely (*Myrrhis odorata*), and costmary (*Chrysanthemum balsamita*). The rest of the garden area is open and sunny throughout the day.

Another unexpected pleasure was finding a second well on the property, so that the garden has its own source of water. While the new garden was being dug, Martha installed a drip irrigation system for that area. She warns against falling for the popular myth that all herbs thrive in desert conditions. While many can get by with little water once established, herbs do need adequate and regular moisture, especially when newly planted.

Too much fertilizer, however, will result in lush growth and less-concentrated volatile oils, which give herbs their flavor or scent. A good shovelful of compost, worked in around each plant at the season's start, is all the enrichment herbs need. Because she doesn't have enough compost for her extensive plantings, Martha fertilizes long-established herb plantings and potted herbs twice a summer, early in the season and at midsummer, with fish emulsion or liquid seaweed, diluted according to package directions. Beds that are newly amended with composted manure, such as the ones in Martha's formal herb garden, won't need fertilizing for three or four years.

To discourage weeds and to keep the beds looking spruce, she mulches with cocoa or buckwheat hulls, depending on what's available. Some gardeners believe that a cocoa hull mulch promotes mold, but Martha hasn't had any such problems.

In the future there are plans for an herbal lawn and flagstone terrace just outside the cellar classroom, with pockets of thyme, Corsican mint (*Mentha requienii*), and other low-growing, fragrant herbs that can withstand some foot traffic, planted between the stones. Martha also plans to have compost bins beyond the boxwood hedge to demonstrate how to handle kitchen and garden wastes. She wants to have a children's garden with a sandpile in the center, surrounded by plants chosen for their smell, touch, or their appeal to a child's imagination: mints, honesty (*Lunaria annua*), lamb's-ears (*Stachys byzantina*), which were used as "band-aids" in earlier days, sunflowers (*Helianthus* spp.), and pansies (*Viola* spp.).

A BEAUTIFUL EDIBLE LANDSCAPE

 When my husband, Fred, and I bought our home 16 years ago, the plantings on our 1½-acre property were well-established and quite formal, appropriate to the English Tudor style of the house, with enclosed spaces and mature trees. (Photographs on pages 59–64.) There was a formal flower bed surrounded by a barberry hedge, with a flowering crabapple at its center. A pair of stunning kousa dogwoods (*Cornus kousa*) reaching well over 30 feet tall were banked against a dense stand of tall hemlocks.

The entire property was surrounded by established trees ~ American beech, white pine, hemlocks, red maples, Engelmann spruce (*Picea engelmannii*) ~ understoried with broadleaf evergreens and groundcovers of ivy, pachysandra, and ferns. The trees gave us complete privacy from our busy street and from a heavily traveled main thoroughfare just a quarter of a mile away. But the property required a lot of maintenance ~ keeping hedges trimmed, mowing lawns, raking leaves, and pruning dead tree limbs.

I was determined to feed my family with organically grown food from our own garden, and the landscaping was one of the projects we looked forward to. But since most vegetables need at least six hours of sun, the shade cast by some of our beautiful, tall trees was our biggest landscape problem.

Too much shade is a typical problem with established properties. As trees mature, they continually diminish the amount of sunlight that reaches the ground. To grow plants that require lots of sun, including vegetables, fruits, annuals, and many perennials, you have to find the courage to make some major changes. You may be able to achieve the desired goal by pruning lower branches and thinning the tree canopy, usually a job for a licensed arborist. Sometimes, though, it's necessary to remove healthy and beautiful trees. These decisions can be painful and often-times guilt-inducing, not only because

trees are beautiful, but also because they take such a long time to grow. When faced with these thoughts, it's helpful to remember that you're going to be replacing the tree with other beautiful plantings. And if you have major amounts of wood to clear, doing it in stages lessens the trauma. In the end, though, it boils down to this: If you have a shady property but you want to grow sun-loving plants, you're not going to be successful unless you make the difficult decision and get out the saw.

Over the years, we opened up the garden by taking down some trees and hedges and by not replacing others that became diseased. We took out the prickly barberry hedge, which was a chore to keep

This circular garden is divided into four sections, each containing different mesclun mixes.

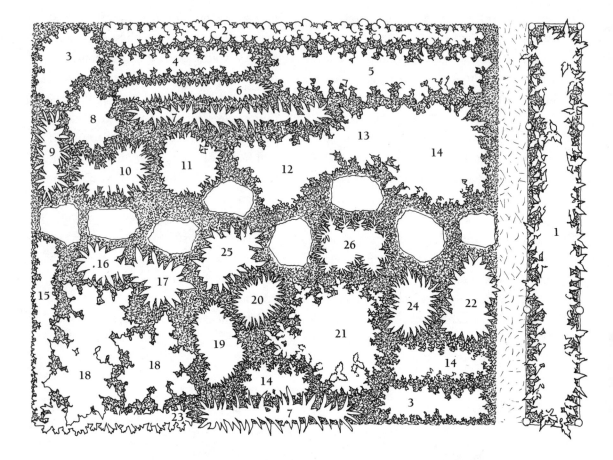

A Beautiful Edible Landscape

1. *Rubus* spp. (everbearing raspberries) **2.** *Tropaeolum* 'Empress of India' (nasturtiums) **3.** *Achillea millefolium* (yarrow) **4.** *Alchemilla mollis* (lady's-mantle) **5.** *Cucurbita pepo* (squash) **6.** *Allium schoenoprasum* (chives) **7.** *Allium sativum* (garlic) **8.** *Anethum graveolens* (dill) **9.** *Salvia officinalis* (sage) **10.** *Artemisia dracunculus* (tarragon) **11.** *Origanum vulgare* (oregano) **12.** *Papaver somniferum* (lettuce poppy) **13.** *Daucus carota* var. *carota* (Queen-Anne's-lace) **14.** *Chrysanthemum* spp. (chrysanthemums) **15.** *Thymus vulgaris* (thyme) **16.** *Myosotis sylvatica* (forget-me-nots) **17.** *Nicotiana alata* (flowering tobacco) **18.** *Rheum rhabarbarum* (rhubarb) **19.** *Malva alcea* (mallow) **20.** *Allium tuberosum* (garlic chives) **21.** *Fragaria* × *ananassa* (strawberries) **22.** *Rudbeckia fulgida* (orange coneflower) **23.** *Aquilegia caerulea* (Rocky Mountain columbine) **24.** *Helichrysum bracteatum* (strawflower) **25.** *Salvia elegans* (pineapple sage) **26.** *Tagetes* 'Lemon Gem' (Lemon Gem marigold)

clipped, and we gradually cleared trees and shrubs from the sunniest areas of the property to make room for vegetable gardens and a mixed garden of edibles and flowers, as well as a generous perennial bed around our patio.

We wanted plants to double as decorative features in our landscape and to bear food for the table, so we chose vegetables and fruit-bearing trees and shrubs carefully. We used blueberries in the foundation plantings on the south side of our house, so we have pretty, belllike blossoms in May and crimson fall foliage, as well as delicious smoky-blue berries in July. Blueberry bushes and raspberry canes also form the northern boundaries of the vegetable garden and the mixed garden. We try to keep an eye for beauty when planning the vegetable beds, too. There is a sea of blue forget-me-nots (*Myosotis alpestris*) around the red rhubarb stems, and the deep maroon foliage of cinnamon basil shares space with rose-pink chrysanthemums. Apple, pear, peach, and plum trees are beautiful in bloom but are messy when their fruit drops. We placed these trees at the edge of our property, where cleaning up fallen fruit is less important.

Some plants are just plain homely, and it takes imagination to fit them into a good-looking landscape. For instance, I like to surround tomatoes, not the most handsome plants, with blue-flowered borage, shiny-leaved basil, and bright yellow 'Lemon Gem' marigolds. I planted Jerusalem artichokes and sunflowers next to the toolshed across the lawn, so their bright color is seen at a distance instead of nearby where their gangly stems might detract from the stately yellow flowers.

We like to think of our entire yard as a beautiful edible landscape. For me, order is part of beauty, and I try to keep the gardens neat along the edges, where they are most visible, to create that sense of order. To that end, we laid out our vegetable gardens in raised beds to avoid competition and to make it easier to rotate crops from one year to the next, and separated them with pathways. To keep the weeds down in the paths, we put down a thick layer of newspaper and then covered it with wood chips. Whenever we make new beds, we always double dig and raise the bed by adding soil from adjacent pathways. We don't frame the beds with timbers, because this provides sowbugs and slugs with a good place to hide.

I try to organize the plantings to give us food from the garden every month of the year. Kale, Brussels sprouts, and Swiss chard last until late fall, and the kale can go even longer if protected with hay or leaves. Carrots and parsnips remain in the ground under bags of dry leaves to keep the soil from freezing, and I dig them all winter, or until they are gone. The spinach I plant in September overwinters as small plants, sheltered only by the protective blanket of leaves that blow against them. In March, the plants' major growth begins, and we eat luscious fresh spinach from mid-April through early June. We plant arugula and mesclun in early April for spring salads. Then we add all the typical summer crops: beans, carrots, tomatoes, onions, summer squash, eggplant, broccoli, peppers, zucchini, and cucumbers.

Because it's as important to have a feast for the eyes as it is to have food for the stomach, I surrounded our flagstone terrace just outside the kitchen with a curving flower garden. It's filled with a succession of blooms from bulbs, annuals, and perennials from earliest spring to late fall, beginning with tulips, daffodils, and bleeding heart (*Dicentra spectabilis*), and ending with annual blue-flowered mealy-cup sage (*Salvia farinacea*) and mauve Japanese anemone (*Anemone × hybrida*).

Today the backyard is a different place from the charming English-style garden we found. Formality has been replaced by a relaxed openness, which reflects the way we live ~ as opposed to the way the original owners of the house lived. The effect is abundant but controlled, with bounteous vegetables, herbs, and flowers contained within neatly edged beds. We look out through glass doors onto a yard that is full of color and food for our table.

Set in an open, grassy area, this enclosed country garden is deliberately set off from its surroundings. A shade garden is visually connected to it by an arbor covered with the fragrant red 'Lavender Lassie' rose, and overplanted with sweet autumn clematis (Clematis maximowicziana).

48

An enormous clump of
maiden grass (Miscanthus
sinensis 'Gracillimus')
provides a dramatic focal
point as you approach the
fenced area from the house.

↑

If you approach the garden
from the opposite direction, a
creamy white sweet autumn
clematis provide visual
accents.

An overall view of the sunken garden in September shows lots of colorful perennials and annuals linked visually with silver foliage plants such as 'Hidcote' lavender and artemisia.

A kaleidoscope of fall color includes deep pink Japanese anemones (Anemone × hybrida), white and purple coneflowers (Echinacea purpurea), lavender daisylike Frikart's aster (Aster × frikartii), tall white boltonia asters (Boltonia asteroides 'Snowbank'), annual blue mealycup sage, and a sea of silver 'Powis Castle' artemisia.

Martha Paul's garden contributes fragrance and seasonings to her home. A garland of dried herbs and spices adorns the kitchen window. The swag contains corn, okra pods, cinnamon sticks, bay leaves, walnuts, and dried fruit. Below is a braid of chili peppers.

Bottles of homemade herbal vinegar sit on her kitchen windowsill.

A mature boxwood hedge surrounds the formal herb garden, providing protection from wind and animals, and a perfect backdrop for a bench where vistors can enjoy the sight and smell of the herbs. Broad-leaved hostas, mountain bluets (Centaurea montana), and blue Siberian iris form a pleasing combination of perennials in the foreground.

In early summer, magnificent perennials on the slope above the main garden include single peonies, a yellow cinquefoil, silver lavender cotton (Santolina chamaecyparissus), blue Siberian iris, 'Crater Lake Blue' veronica, lady's-mantle (Alchemilla mollis), and blue hardy geranium.

The view from the house looks straight down the stone steps to the focal point of the garden: a flagstone pathway and stone birdbath. A heart-shaped stepping stone set into the grass adds a charming touch to the herb garden entrance.

↑

Mixed lavender cultivars enjoy the full sun and well-drained soil of the raised beds.

← In a shady corner, there is a granite bench from which the whole property can be seen. Just visible behind, an upturned clay pot provides a welcoming shelter for insect- and slug-eating toads.

An overall view of Marny Smith's garden in early summer shows four separate beds. To the left are vegetables newly planted with 'Finard' beans, peppers, broccoli, celery, lettuces, tomatoes, and 'Lemon Gem' marigolds. Running horizontally, behind, a mixed garden includes rhubarb, garlic, chives, poppies, pansies, and bellflowers. In the center is a circular garden of salad greens. To the right, a garden of perennial flowers adds a more formal touch. The kousa dogwood (Cornus kousa) in the background is nearly 40 feet tall and blooms throughout the month of June.

↑

Garlic (planted the previous August), yarrow, forget-me-not, blue columbine, and rhubarb are clearly visible. Sorrel, strawberries, and chrysanthemums are in the background. Self-sown poppies will bring color to the garden in July, after which summer squash, strawflowers, and zinnias will fill in the space.

← The mixed garden plantings change throughout the year to make maximum use of space. In June, they include lady's-mantle in the right foreground with purple chive flowers just behind.

There is always color during summer in the mixed
garden. Ornamental purple
'East Friesland' salvia and
purple and pink pansies provide color in late May and
early June. A circular wire
support holds balloon flowers. Sectional wire supports
peach-leaved bellflowers
(Campanula persicifolia) for
later summer color.

A perennial garden surrounds
the patio, providing color all
summer and enclosing this
area. In June, it is filled with
'Margot Koster' floribunda
rose, white peach-leaved bellflowers, 'Connecticut Yankee'
delphiniums, coneflowers (just
coming into bloom), and feverfew. Pansies and sweet alyssum
are along the front, with purple
heliotrope just in back of the
pansies.

This toolshed was made with wood from an old silo from a farm in Maine. The digging tools are over 15 years old and are cleaned after each use with oily sand from the bucket next to the shed door to prevent rust.

PART II

Creating a Country Garden

Practical information about sites, plants, and
incorporating the best into your backyard

Chapter One

Country Garden Basics

 Anywhere you walk in the country, there is life beneath your feet. A woodland or an overgrown meadow that has never felt a spade or seen a bag of fertilizer sustains an enormous variety of plant life. Likewise, a climax forest of tall trees is self-sustaining; the earth underfoot is a dark, rich humus, replenished by falling leaves, needles, and other plant detritus that form a new top layer of the forest carpet each year. Decomposition takes place continuously in nature, and the same nutrients are recycled in a never-ending process. The result is a thriving, diverse community.

A successful garden is one that works with this natural process. You will get nature on your side by encouraging the processes that duplicate what happens in the forest or meadow, and this begins with the soil.

Good soil is as important to plants as good health is to people. Soil consists of air, water, mineral fragments, and organic matter in varying stages of decomposition. If all of these ingredients are present and in the right proportions, plants will grow well. Because the soil around many homes is low in organic matter, you should enrich it regularly each year with compost (decomposed organic materials) or other organic materials like shredded leaves, mulch, or grass clippings. In this way, you can best create a medium for the slow release of nutrients necessary for healthy plant growth.

THE IMPORTANCE OF GOOD SOIL

Any soil can become good garden soil with the addition of organic matter, provided that it is aerated through cultivation and is watered sufficiently. After a year of adding organic matter in the form of compost or mulch to poor garden soil, the soil will come alive. For example, compost, added to sandy soils that normally drain quickly, absorbs and holds water, making it available to plants. Add organic matter to heavy clay soil that has been well loosened, and plants' roots will be able to reach out more easily in search of nutrients.

Organic gardeners ~ essentially gardeners who work with nature ~ feed the soil rather than the individual plant. Whether you are starting a new garden or rejuvenating an existing one, working with nature makes gardening easier in the long run, provided you are patient in the beginning and willing to be flexible as the garden evolves. This may mean having to eliminate a favorite flower or vegetable if it is not doing well in the ecological niche you have provided. For example, in parts of the Midwest where the soil is more alkaline, azaleas, rhododendrons, blueberries, and other acid-loving plants generally do not do well. Although alkaline soils can be amended to accommodate such plants, it's often easier to choose plants that are better suited to existing soil conditions.

HOW TO PREPARE THE SOIL

If you are starting your garden in a grassy location, you must remove the sod completely. If sod is just tilled or turned under, bits of grass will continue to sprout throughout the garden, and your plants will become the underdogs, competing with the decomposing sod for nitrogen.

Skim the sod off with a sod cutter or a sharpened flat digging spade, so you can cultivate the soil beneath with a digging fork and spade or a tiller. For large areas, renting a sod cutter saves time and yields neat rolls of sod that you can use elsewhere. If you don't need the sod to patch bare spots or make a new lawn, start a compost pile. (Be aware that unless there is sufficient heat in your compost pile, rhizomatous weeds will not be killed off.)

Another way to rid the garden area of sod is to smother it underneath black plastic, landscape fabric, or thick layers of newspaper, well-anchored with stones, wood chips, or shredded bark. Do this in the fall, since it will take several months for the sod and its roots to decompose. (To speed decomposition, spread dried manure and organic fertilizer over the area before laying down the cover.) In the following spring, till or dig the soil and plant immediately; newspaper can be dug in, but be sure to remove the plastic or fabric covering before tilling.

If your chosen place for the garden is an overgrown weed patch, cut the weeds down as close to the ground as possible with a mower, clippers, or a string trimmer. Then smother it as above. If you want to plant sooner, use a grub axe to remove the weeds. This can be hard work, and the plot will need plenty of compost to replace the organic matter you remove, but it is the most effective way to control woody weeds. Killing the weeds by smothering, but leaving their remains, supplies much needed organic matter to the soil and gives it a good start on its way to fertility.

Finally, once you have removed the weeds or grass, double dig the ground (see "How to Double Dig a Garden" on page 69). Double digging cultivates the area deeply while maintaining the original order of the soil layers. It may be hard work, but it is the best preparation for garden soil and is well worth the effort.

THE VALUE OF COMPOST

Compost is decomposed organic matter. In a country garden, it is the main soil food, and building compost is an ongoing and essential process.

Making compost is an accelerated version of nature's way of building soil, except you gather the materials together in one place instead of letting the leaves fall where they may.

Making compost from organic waste can become a habit, perhaps even a passion for a while. There is compost potential in a wide range of materials, from chopped-up cattails to Canada goose guano; kitchen wastes, too, are reliable compost materials. Other commonly found materials, such as grass clippings, leaves, garden weeds, wood ashes, and twigs, may be added to the compost pile as they accumulate.

You can even grow certain plants specifically for compost. I grow comfrey (*Symphytum officinale*), because its long taproots draw minerals from deep in the soil. Three times during a growing season I cut the leaves and add them to the compost to boost the trace mineral content. I also grow lots of yarrows (*Achillea* spp.), because their flowers and foliage add calcium and potassium to the compost.

Use finished compost for vegetable and flower gardens, as a mulch around shrubs and trees, or screened as a topdressing for lawns. Since it takes time to produce the first batch and you can never have too much, you may wish to look for other sources of compost. Your community, for instance, might have a leaf composting program, or a local farm or riding stable may have composted manure. More and more food-processing plants are concerned with environmentally clean waste disposal, and are producing composting mixtures that may be available. Of course, there are also many commercial composts now available at most garden centers.

How to Build a Compost Pile

Garden catalogs are full of composting equipment, from aerators to turning forks to compost starters. All you really need is an enclosure and a fork to turn the material. If space is limited or you need compost fast, try a compost tumbler. It promises finished compost in as little as three to four weeks.

How to Double Dig a Garden

Double digging requires two good tools: a spade with a flat, uncurved blade that is straight across the bottom, and a digging fork with squared (not flat) tines. The spade is used for edging and skimming sod as well as for digging, so it should have a good sharp edge, easily achieved with a file. Squared fork tines are stronger than flat ones, which can bend out of shape in heavy digging. The working end and the neck of these tools should be one piece of tempered steel, and the hardwood handle should fit tightly into the neck so there is no weak spot where wood and metal meet.

1. Mark off a garden bed, between 3 and 4 feet wide and 12 feet long, and edge all around it with a sharpened flat spade. Skim the sod or other vegetation from its surface, piling it to one side.

2. Spread a thin layer, 3 to 4 inches thick, of compost or aged manure over the surface of the skimmed bed.

3. Dig a trench across the narrow end of the bed, about 1 foot wide and 10 to 12 inches deep. Pile the soil at the opposite, narrow end of the bed.

4. Plunge the fork tines into the subsoil along the bottom of the trench, wiggling the fork around to get the tines in all the way. The object is to aerate the compacted subsoil by rocking the fork to loosen it. Remove any large stones, using a pickax, grub axe, or crowbar.

5. Break up the sod skimmed from the surface into smaller pieces, and scatter some of it across the loosened subsoil. If dry leaves, chopped stalks, and manure are available, add them to the bottom of the trench as well.

6. Facing the first trench, dig a second parallel trench, throwing the topsoil from the second trench into the first, on top of the skimmings and other materials. Loosen the subsoil with the fork and scatter skimmings as before.

7. Dig a third trench next to the second and repeat the process described above to the end of the bed. The last trench will be filled with the pile of topsoil removed from the first.

8. Shape the bed with the fork, leveling the top, but leaving it rough to allow air and rain to permeate the soil for a week or more. When ready to plant, add compost and any mineral amendments indicated by a soil test, and mix them into the topsoil. Because air and organic matter have been added to the original volume of soil, the completed bed will have an unevenly raised surface. The soil has been loosened and fluffed up, making it easier for seedlings to send their roots downward.

Compostable Materials

HIGH-CARBON	HIGH-NITROGEN	OTHER
Bark	Bloodmeal	Rock phosphate
Corn cobs	Bonemeal	Seaweed
Dry leaves	Coffee grounds	Soil
Dry weeds	Cottonseed meal	Wood ashes
Hay	Fruit wastes	
Pits	Nut shells	
Sawdust	Green weeds	
Shredded newsprint	Hair	
Stalks	Manure	
Straw	Tea bags	
Wood chips	Vegetable wastes	

You can construct a bin for a compost pile in various ways:

- Assemble wooden stakes and 1-inch wire mesh into a simple bin 4 feet square and 4 feet high. Build a second and third as they become necessary.

- Build a 4-foot-high, 4-foot-square bin of rot-resistant wood. Paint or otherwise seal the wood to reduce decay caused by moisture and hungry microorganisms. Avoid treated woods that might release toxic compounds into your compost and, subsequently, into your garden.

- Make holes in the sides and bottom of a large garbage can and use it as a bin. Dump compost out into a pile when the bin is full and start refilling the can.

- Use no enclosure at all. Simply layer materials in a pile that is roughly 5 to 7 feet square at the bottom and no more than 5 feet high.

Before starting a compost pile, loosen the earth beneath it so there will be interaction between the composting material and the soil microbes below. Then build the pile in layers, starting with a layer of brush, sunflower, or corn stalks so there will be air at the bottom. As you build, alternate carbon and nitrogen by adding an armful of leaves or wood chips after each layer of grass clippings, garden weeds, or kitchen waste (see "Compostable Materials" above). Keep a leaf pile or some hay nearby and grab an armful to cover vegetable or fruit scraps to prevent odors. Every couple of feet, add a 1- to 2-inch layer of soil. This will introduce more

Five Steps to Successful Compost

1. Build your compost in layers, like a cake, with the cake made of slow-decaying high-carbon materials and the filling made with fast-decaying materials high in nitrogen. There should be a much larger volume of high-carbon material than high-nitrogen, but both are essential. A compost pile of nothing but corncobs, husks, and stalks will not decompose without some form of nitrogen, and a pile of kitchen waste will become a putrid mess without some dry leaves, sawdust, or straw ~ all high in carbon ~ to balance it.

2. Make sure the pile doesn't dry out completely. Microorganisms, earthworms, sowbugs, and other decomposers cannot live without moisture, and decomposition will come to a standstill. To prevent this, locate the compost pile in the shade, or in semi-shade with a cover; or use an enclosed compost tumbler that is opened and turned daily for aeration.

3. Use only appropriate materials ~ no diseased plants, oily kitchen wastes, bones or meat, dog or cat feces ~ to prevent the spread of disease and to make the pile less appealing to rodents. Don't locate the pile near an invasive plant such as ivy, mint, bittersweet, or weedy vine that will quickly take up residence in rich compost.

4. Break or cut large items into smaller pieces so they will decompose more quickly. An entire watermelon rind will take far longer to decompose than one that is cut into smaller cubes. Break large sticks or tough stalks into smaller pieces for the same reason.

5. For best results, use three compost bins side by side. When compost is built gradually rather than all at once, you must turn it from time to time to reactivate the decomposing process. If you have three bins, when the first bin is filled, turn the material into the second and start building a new batch in the first. When the first is filled again, turn the second into the third, first into the second, and start building again in the first. One month after two turnings, the compost in the third bin should be ready for use.

microorganisms and speed up the process. Whenever available, add seaweed, wood ashes, or rock phosphate. Seaweed is extremely high in trace minerals and potassium, and the salt is no problem in compost. Wood ashes also add potassium or potash, but they should be sprinkled over the compost periodically rather than added all at once in a big dose.

Shredded newspaper can be used as a carbon substitute for leaves or hay. It should not be the only carbon source, however, because the chemicals used in the paper-making process will concentrate as the newspapers decompose and could harm plants.

When your compost bin is full, turn the mixture into another bin to rest, and cover it with a tarp, boards, or black plastic to keep the moisture in. Start filling the first bin in the same order as above. After two months in summer, turn the compost again into another bin or a pile and cover. If the turning is completed in the fall, cover the pile and let it rest for the winter, or until you are ready to add it to the garden in spring.

USING MANURE

Manure is readily available to country gardeners and is often free for the taking. Riding stables and horse, dairy, or cattle farms are good sources, and neighbors who keep horses, rabbits, or poultry may be happy to let you come and haul it away.

Do not apply fresh manure directly to your garden; its high nitrogen content can damage plants. Pile it up and let it rot for half a year, or add it to your compost pile. A great way to use manure is to mix it with sawdust or wood shavings, which you may also obtain free from a wood shop or mill. Again, give the mixture plenty of

time to age before using. Because wood products use nitrogen as they decay, they can rob the soil of this important plant nutrient if used fresh. But mixed together, the manure provides the nitrogen the wood needs, so that by the time the sawdust or shavings have decayed, the manure has mellowed. You end up with a soil amendment to use as a mulch for trees, shrubs or perennials, or as a side-dressing in the vegetable bed.

TESTING YOUR SOIL

Your eyes and hands can tell you whether your soil has good tilth and adequate drainage, but they won't reveal much about the available nutrients or whether your soil is acid or alkaline (see "Adjusting the pH of Your Soil" on page 175). For

---

Manure Tea

You can also make a liquid fertilizer ~ "manure tea" ~ from rotted manure. Put 1 quart of dry, well-rotted horse, sheep, or cow manure in a burlap bag and suspend it in 3 to 4 gallons of water. Stir the mixture daily. After a week, you should have a dark-colored "tea" that you can use to water plants. Don't use manure tea on plants more than once every two to four weeks, and be careful to keep the liquid off the leaves or they will burn.

that, you'll need a soil test.

Sometime during the first year, preferably right after tilling or digging, take a sample of your soil according to directions from a soil lab or the Cooperative Extension Service. Send it off to be analyzed (your local Cooperative Extension agent will be able to tell you where) for pH and the major plant nutrients and ask for recommended amounts of organic amendments. Based on the results, the testing laboratory or your extension agent may recommend applications of materials such as chicken feather or cottonseed meal, rock phosphate or bonemeal, greensand, or granite dust. Incorporate most soil amendments in fall, in preparation for spring planting, but withhold additions of nitrogen sources, such as manures, bloodmeal, alfalfa meal, and cottonseed meal until just prior to planting; otherwise, the nitrogen may leach away before planting.

Once established, microorganisms will keep the soil chemistry in balance, so that the necessary nutrients are availible to your plants. Soil testing may not be needed after the first year or two, especially since the presence of composted organic matter tends to move soil pH gradually toward the neutral range.

If the soil pH in your region tends toward extremes of acidity (low pH) or alkalinity (high pH), check with your local Cooperative Extension office or land-grant university for the best ways to moderate this effect.

LOW-MAINTENANCE TECHNIQUES

Whether your goal is to create a beautiful flower border or a bounteous food garden, to improve the general appearance of your landscape or merely to derive pleasure in the act of gardening, make low-maintenance techniques part of your plan.

If you minimize high-maintenance features such as large lawns, messy trees, clipped hedges, and invasive groundcovers in your garden, you will eliminate a great deal of work. If you mulch at the proper time and establish a good watering system before planting, you will also reduce maintenance. Finally, if you choose the right trees and shrubs with appropriate growth habits to fill a given space and perennials, annuals, and vegetables that are suited to your soil and climate, you will reduce the amount of work and increase your chances of success.

MULCHING

One of the secrets to keeping plants happy is mulch. After you have prepared the soil properly and taken steps to assure its ongoing fertility, mulching the planted garden will maintain the benefits of your hard work. Most important, it will keep the amount of time you spend in watering and weeding to a minimum.

Most organic mulches will enrich the soil as they become food for the microorganisms and earthworms. On the surface the mulch looks neat and pleasing; underneath, earthworms, sowbugs, and centipedes eat, digest, and excrete castings that are far richer than the mulch material. (Earthworm castings contain 5 times the nitrogen, 7 times the phosphorus, and 11 times the potassium found in whatever the worm has eaten.)

Mulch also moderates temperature changes, acting as a buffer between the soil and any extreme variations in air temperature. During hot, dry spells, it shades the soil, keeping it cool and moist; during a heavy rainfall it prevents soil from running off or splattering on plant leaves. A mulch covering acts as a barrier against weeds because sunlight fails to reach their seeds, reducing germination. The few weeds that do sprout through the mulch can be pulled easily from the soft, crumbly soil below.

Mulch materials are everywhere in the home landscape: Leaves, grass clippings, plant trimmings, and tree prunings all make good mulch. You can use year-old wood chips as a mulch for landscape plantings or to form weed-free pathways. If you use fresh wood chips, add nitrogen to the soil first because wood chips will temporarily deprive the soil of nitrogen as they begin to decompose.

In my garden, we even throw weeds to dry out on top of the wood-chip pathways, or put them back onto the hay- or fern-mulched beds from which they were pulled to add to the thickness of the mulch cover. We use leaves from comfrey plants to mulch raspberries, and put dry grass clippings around flowers in the cutting garden. In rock gardens you can use stones as mulch; pine needles make a soft pathway covering and can be used to mulch blueberries and other acid-loving shrubs.

Shred just about any organic material that is free from disease into uniformly sized pieces to make your own mulch. We shred oak, maple, and beech leaves directly onto garden beds as a winter mulch. In spring, the shredded leaves make an attractive covering beneath strawberries and perennial flowers. In the vegetable garden, we cover shredded leaves with hay or grass clippings to help retain moisture, and plant vegetable seedlings right into the mulched bed. Unshredded leaves are not a good mulch for perennial plants because, once wet, they tend to mat and can cause crown rot.

If you are especially concerned about the appearance of your garden, you can find more aesthetically pleasing mulches than leaves or grass clippings at garden centers. Buckwheat hulls are a favorite for specimen flower or herb gardens, and although they cost a little more, a 2-inch layer will last a season. Bark chips and shredded bark mulches are excellent for trees and shrubs, but, like fresh wood chips, they must be sprinkled with some bloodmeal or another nitrogen source to avoid depleting the soil nitrogen. Cottonseed and peanut hulls, cocoa bean hulls, bagasse from sugarcane, dark licorice root bark, and coconut fiber are all attractive and long-lasting mulches.

Other mulches may be free. These include bedding from riding stables or wood chips from tree crews working for the power company. No matter which mulch you choose, the purpose is the same: to cut down on the hours spent on garden maintenance by reducing the need for watering and weeding, and to add organic matter to the soil.

MINIMIZING YOUR LAWN

A perfect example of a high-maintenance landscape is a large lawn. It must be mowed, fed, trimmed, watered, and raked free of leaves each fall. A small lawn in a landscaped yard can be an important aesthetic feature, but a large one makes demands on both your energy and petrochemical resources.

Wherever possible, reduce the amount of space given over to your lawn and plant it instead with groundcovers. Groundcovers add color and texture to the landscape, making it more interesting and much easier to maintain. During the first year, new groundcovers need to be mulched, watered, and weeded, but once established, most require little care.

Shrubs and trees growing in a sea of groundcover are usually healthier than those growing on a lawn, because the cover acts as a living mulch and the woody plants are less likely to be injured by careless mowing. In problem areas, where there is too much shade or not enough moisture for most plants, use durable groundcovers such as ajuga (*Ajuga reptans*) or wintercreeper (*Euonymus fortunei*).

Instead of planting a lawn on a slope or beneath a tree that has protruding, surface-feeding roots, make the slope into terraced beds for flowers or low-growing shrubs, and underplant the tree with a groundcover.

Even after you have reduced the area of lawn in your garden, you can further reduce the maintenance it requires by designing the grassy areas in continuous, easily mowable swaths. Similarly, minimize mowing time by installing strips of brick, slate, or flagstone flush with the lawn's surface for the wheels of the lawnmower to ride around the periphery of a small lawn. You can then cut right up to the edge of the mowing strip, eliminating the need for hand trimming.

WATERING WISELY

Without water, neither soil nor plant can live. Mature plants that do not have enough water are easily stressed; when under stress, they become prey for insect pests and diseases. It is important to water properly, however. Avoid watering with an overhead sprinkler between 9 AM and 4 PM during the hot summer months, for instance. Such watering is both inefficient and wasteful because a relatively large percentage of water evaporates before it hits the ground. Also, an overhead sprinkler can actually add to plant stress by soaking the leaves, so that they aren't able to dry out quickly enough to avoid being burned by midday sun or invaded by mildew at night. Water sprinkled overhead is caught by the leaves, so not enough moisture reaches the soil. The roots reach up to the surface for what moisture there is, and then dry out when the sprinkler isn't used regularly.

An overhead sprinkler for a garden and lawn is appropriate in spring, when beds are newly planted with seeds and seedlings, or in late summer when grass seed has been spread. A hand-held watering wand will provide thirsty plants a drink in the late afternoon during a hot and very dry period, but it should not be the main source of water.

If you are a low-tech gardener, you may prefer to rely on mulch applied right after a heavy rainfall to keep moisture in garden soil. A nearby rain barrel (see "How to Make a Rain Barrel" on page 78) makes spot watering easy. I give my garden a seri-

ous watering only in the first week after planting or after a spell of intense heat and drought in midsummer. That is because my watering "system" is a slow process. It takes an afternoon, using a bubbler attachment at the end of the hose and laying it section by section around the garden for 10- to 15-minute intervals to allow deep penetration. The bubbler disperses the water gradually, adding moisture to an area 2 to 3 feet in diameter. I fill this valuable time with all sorts of garden chores such as staking, deadheading, weeding, and learning which insects and other creatures are in residence in the garden.

Drip irrigation is perhaps the most efficient method of delivering water to the plant's root zone without losing any moisture to the air. There are several types of systems: drip tape, plastic tubing with built-in microsprinklers, emitters, and soaker hoses. Which type to use depends on the size and shape of your garden, the plants you want to grow, how much you want to spend, and to some extent, the type of water you have (a high calcium content can clog some emitters). To get the best results, you may need to combine two or more methods of drip irrigation ~ drip tape and microsprinklers, for example.

A soaker hose is perhaps the simplest type of drip irrigation. A network of soaker hoses is installed on the soil surface and covered with mulch or buried a few inches underground, where the hoses ooze

Drought- and Disease- Resistant Grasses

A little foresight before planting turf grasses will allow you prevent your lawn's turning brown from drought or disease. Choosing the proper grasses and planting them the right way are simple ways to avoid many lawn problems.

In order to lessen drought effects and weak growth, which encourage pests and diseases, the grasses you choose must be appropriate to the local climate. Kentucky bluegrass (*Poa pratensis*) is the most common turf grass in northern states. It is one of many grasses that grows better in cooler climates, since hot weather induces dormancy and faded coloration. It does not grow well in the South because of the consistently high temperatures.

Grasses such as Bermuda grass (*Cynodon dactylon*) and zoysia grass (*Zoysia* spp.) grow well in the heat of southern summers, but will not work well in cooler areas, which lack an adequate hot-weather growing season. Bermuda grass, zoysia grass, and other grasses with high-temperature growing seasons tend to be more drought-resistant.

Mixing species of grass when seeding will encourage a healthier, more robust lawn: Each grass will provide specialized disease-resistance to protect the other grasses, and the plants will be able to take advantage of differing soil and shade conditions as well as yearly climate variations. For example, mixing bentgrass (*Agrostis stolonifera*), which enjoys full exposure to the sun, with fine-leaved fescue (*Festuca rubra*), which grows well in shady areas, ensures a more consistently healthy lawn.

Another consideration when selecting grasses is how endophytic they are. Endophytic grasses contain endophytes, which are fungi repellent to plant pests such as cutworms, aphids, and weevils. Among the endophytic grasses availible are several types of ryegrass (*Lolium* spp.) and fescue (*Festuca* spp.), sold by seed companies and garden centers.

Before seeding or sodding your lawn, consult the local Cooperative Extension Service to find out the recommended mix for your area and the best mowing height for the grasses you select. To minimize drought effects, let the grass grow taller, which will result in a stronger, deeper root structure.

water from their pores. Water seeps into the soil, moistening an area 12 to 18 inches on either side of the hose. A well-laid-out drip irrigation system, properly timed, will keep the moisture level in the garden constant and the plants free from stress, even during the worst droughts. Automatic timers can be attached to most systems to turn on the water at a certain time of day.

How to Make a Rain Barrel

Rain barrels used to be an important part of the irrigation system for traditional country gardens. Today, with water supplies endangered by chemical runoff and water rationing caused by drought and population pressure, rain barrels make good environmental as well as economic sense.

Plastic rain barrels are available from garden supply catalogs. These are easy to install, don't leak, and provide everything you need in one large package. Or you can make your own authentic rain barrel.

You'll need a 50-gallon oak barrel with a lid, available second-hand from wineries or distilleries or by special order from some garden centers; an 8-inch length of 1-inch-diameter PVC pipe, for runoff; a tapered wooden spigot, available at wine-making supply stores; and a tube of silicone sealant to seal the holes for the spigot and runoff pipe.

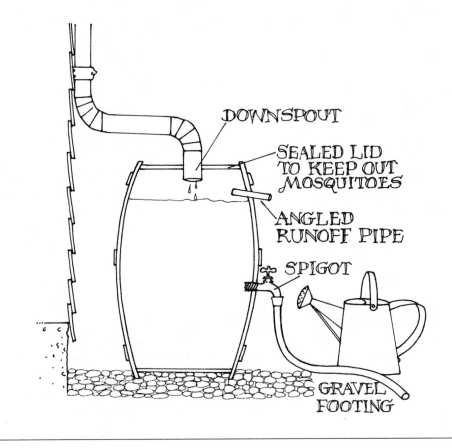

DOWNSPOUT

SEALED LID TO KEEP OUT MOSQUITOES

ANGLED RUNOFF PIPE

SPIGOT

GRAVEL FOOTING

A drip system can make a beautiful garden possible, even if you have very sandy soil or thin soil over rock ledge. Many garden catalogs offer all of the components of a drip system ~ soaker hoses, connectors, timers ~ and some even offer free help with designing a layout if given a sketch of your property.

LOCATING AND CHOOSING PLANTS

Choosing the right location for a plant is also key to keeping your garden work manageable. In your enthusiasm to achieve a full or complete look in a bed or border, it is easy to overcrowd the plants, resulting in needless pruning. When you plan your garden, take into account the size of each shrub, tree, or perennial at maturity and resist the temptation to fill every empty space. Trees and shrubs will fill those spaces as they mature, and cosmetic pruning will be minimized.

Also try to select a hedge that will not need constant clipping. Unlike boxwood, barberry, or privet, a hedge of azaleas or forsythia needs no trimming and provides an added bonus of color when it blooms.

Choosing the right plant for the right place is one of the great challenges and is essential to low-maintenance gardening. If a particular plant is not suited to its conditions, it will need extra care and attention just to survive. Unless such a plant is an absolute must, it is far wiser and more practical to replace it.

Within your country garden, however, there are many different ecological niches that offer homes to a wide variety of plants. It may take you a while to learn which plant will thrive next to the warmth of a stone wall in springtime, by the heat of a blacktop driveway in summer, or in deep shade beneath a group of evergreens, but once the plant is matched to its proper niche in the landscape (and assuming that the soil has been tended to), it will mostly take care of itself, requiring only water and deadheading or trimming as necessary.

CONTROLLING DISEASES AND PESTS

In a healthy garden, there are insects and other animals above as well as in the soil. A garden empty of these creatures ~ spiders, bees, butterflies, beetles, and earthworms ~ would be a dead space. The gardener's job is to learn which ones are helpful and encourage them. Quiet observation in the garden at different hours of the day and seasons of the year helps in this understanding by revealing who is eating whom or what.

The natural world is a complex system of relationships that keep things in balance. In a garden, most creatures are either pests that eat the plants or predators that eat the pests. The survival of each predator depends on a good supply of its favorite food, while the plant-eating pest must have its chosen plant or plants close at hand to exist at all.

Most flowers have a particular insect pollinator that is attracted to the flower by its color or odor. The flower's reproduction depends on the pollinator's ability to find and fertilize it so there will be seed to start a new generation.

In an organically tended country garden ~ one that is maintained without synthetic chemicals, well-watered, and enriched only with compost, mulch, and minerals in their organic form ~ in which the plants are in their ideal ecological niches, there should be an equilibrium between predators and pests. There will be few insect infestations that are serious enough to require special treatments, and those are more likely to occur in the early stages of such a garden. If pesticides have been used in the past, however, it may take longer for you to restore the balance. But once achieved, a balanced ecosystem should eliminate any need for battling tiny enemies via a spray tank full of some poisonous potion.

Generally, insects attack plants that are in trouble or under stress because the plants are thirsty or starving. The first rule of insect control, therefore, is to provide good conditions so that plants will be healthy enough to survive whatever threatens them. This means planting in the right location and keeping the plants well-fed.

To begin controlling pests or diseases, there is no substitute for spending time in the garden each day. You can see a new white moth, for instance, fluttering about the cabbage plants, or some holes in the rose leaves that weren't there the day before. Watching where the moth lands will give you a clue as to what it is after and where it will lay its eggs, and a closer inspection of the rose will usually reveal the culprit responsible for the holes. A quick pinch between thumb and forefinger ends the life of both eggs and insects. (And a good pair of garden gloves makes it less disgusting!)

The successful organic gardener often becomes an amateur entomologist, whether or not she or he intends to. Understanding an insect's life cycle is helpful in knowing when to start looking for damage. A squash vine borer, for example, doesn't start out that way. An innocuous-looking brown moth lays a few equally harmless-looking eggs on the stem of the squash plant near the soil. When the eggs hatch into larvae, they immediately burrow into the plant stem and do their feeding invisibly, until one day the big, healthy host plant starts to droop. If you know what time of year to look for the moth's eggs, you can stop the damage before it is too late. (The squash vine borer moth lays eggs over a six- to eight-week period beginning in early summer.) Knowing when to look for eggs comes with experience and with the help of a good encyclopedia of insect controls (see

Ten Plants for Arid Climates

Where summers are hot and dry ~ conditions that prevail in the landlocked mid-western and southwestern United States ~ matching the plant to the location can be difficult. The following ten plants are star performers under very dry conditions.

Eschscholzia californica (California poppy)
Gazania spp. (gazanias)
Hypericum spp. (St.-John's-worts)
Iris hybrids (bearded iris)
Phlox subulata (moss pink)

Salvia officinalis (garden sage)
Santolina chamaecyparissus (lavender cotton)
Sedum spp. (sedums)
Stachys byzantina (lamb's-ears)
Thymus serpyllum (creeping thyme)

"Recommended Reading" on page 251).

The life of an insect is divided into three or four stages: egg, nymph, and adult, or egg, pupa, larva, and adult. The nymphal and larval are usually the hungriest stages, and they are what you should to be on the lookout for. (There are exceptions, however, such as Japanese beetles, which do their worst damage as adults.) Seeing the insect in its adult stage warns you that eggs will soon be laid and will be followed by the arrival of ravenous larvae whose mission is to eat themselves into pupation. One way to minimize insect infestations is to turn the soil over in the fall so that frost can kill insects overwintering in your garden as eggs or pupae.

Planting to Minimize Diseases and Pests

The traditional practice of companion planting to ward off pests has some scientific support. However, many of the combinations are unproven and are still a matter of experimentation. But there are some plants that I have found helpful in confusing, starving, and foiling pests and in warding off the diseases they carry.

I have tried interspersing strong-smelling herbs and flowers throughout the garden to confuse the moths, whose sole daily chore is to find their offspring's favorite food plant and to lay their eggs on its leaves or stem. I scatter dill plants in the vegetable garden, for example, and grow chives here and there not only to confuse potential insect pests, but also to have attractive flowers. In my vegetable garden I use lemon balm and mint to repel cabbage moths, although they must be kept pruned during the growing season and weeded out; otherwise, they will take over all available space. White geraniums planted next to roses confuse rose-eating insects.

Crop rotation is another means of foiling pests. Rotating plants in the garden each year will help to starve out the insect pests that may have overwintered in the soil. Bean beetles, for example, that have overwintered in the soil as eggs or adults have a harder time finding their favorite food if it is growing somewhere else in the garden.

Keep a record of your garden layout each year to make rotation easier to plan. Without rotation, a deficiency of a particular trace element can develop, making plants susceptible to disease. Since each plant family has different nutrient requirements, divide your vegetable garden into beds rather than rows and make sure that plants of a particular family are not grown in the same bed for two consecutive years.

Rotation is a technique used primarily for annual vegetables and flowers, but you may also want to divide and move perennials if diseases become a problem. Disease-causing fungi and bacteria also tend to congregate and build up when one species is grown in the same place year after year. Although it is generally not good practice to move peonies, for example, it may be necessary if botrytis blight becomes a serious problem. Iris borers, which overwinter as eggs in the foliage or in debris on the soil surface, however, can be devilishly persistent, and are best avoided by starting with fresh, new rhizomes in another place.

When the damage to annuals from insects such as flea beetles or leafminers passes the tolerable point, try changing the planting time, as well as the location, to foil the insect's timetable the next year.

Garden Sanitation

Good garden sanitation is essential in minimizing pests and diseases. Keeping the garden free of weeds and trimmed around the edges gives a neat, cared-for appearance, and it also removes potential habitats for insect pests. Clipping away dead stems and leaves and deadheading flowers opens up new space for air to move freely among plants and reduces the potential for mildew and other fungal diseases. Roses and phlox particularly benefit from this treatment. Mildew on phlox can often be avoided by thinning plants to no more than seven strong stems each spring. Pruning out any stems heading inward on roses similarly improves air circulation around the plants.

Destroy diseased plant material. Seal the diseased material inside a black plastic bag to "bake" in the sun for several days (this will kill disease-causing organisms). Don't add diseased material to the compost pile, even after baking. Instead, throw it out with the garbage or into an out-of-the-way spot designated for just such things.

Your garden tools can carry diseases too, and they should be cleaned after each

The Value of Seaweed

The beneficial effects of applying seaweed to plants is grounded in scientific research, and its use, in practical terms, is best described as a way to help plants help themselves. Foliar feeding allows plants to quickly absorb food. Use seaweed fertilizers in foliar sprays to enhance growth and to give plants the strength to withstand disease.

Add 2 teaspoons of liquid seaweed to a mixture of 3 tablespoons baking soda per gallon of water to give plants a boost in repairing diseased or damaged tissue. The trace elements found in seaweed ~ iron, zinc, boron, calcium, sulfur, manganese, and magnesium ~ stimulate the plants to produce more enzymes and hormones for their own healthy growth.

use. After pruning away diseased stems or foliage, dip the blades of shears or clippers in a 10 percent bleach solution to destroy any pathogens.

At the end of the garden season, after a few hard frosts, clean up your garden for the winter and remove debris to the compost pile.

You can add compost to the top of the vegetable garden in spring, but adding it in fall and turning it into the topsoil means the garden will be ready for planting in the next growing season. In either case, mulch each bed with salt hay or shredded leaves to keep soil temperatures even and prevent any loss of soil nitrogen to the air. Evergreen boughs cut from the Christmas tree make good covers for perennials, once the beds are frozen. Boughs keep the plants and the soil around them frozen during warm spells, when many perennials are lost to rapidly changing temperatures.

Beneficial Insects

Many insect pests have specific enemies that prey upon or parasitize them, so to protect your plants you should attract those enemies to the garden. Plants of the parsley or carrot family (Umbelliferae), for example, whose flowers are borne in slightly curved or flat-topped clusters, attract beneficial insects to a garden. The flowers of carrots, celery, parsley, dill, caraway, fennel, and Queen-Anne's-lace, all umbels, attract tiny braconid, chalcid, and ichneumon wasps and tachinid flies. These are beneficial insects that lay their eggs in the bodies of caterpillars and, when the eggs hatch into larvae, proceed to eat their hapless hosts from the inside out.

Plants of the daisy family (Compositae) attract lady beetles, commonly known as ladybugs. Their value to the garden has always been well known, even though we

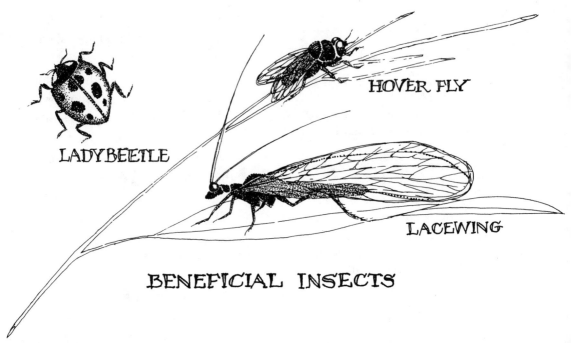

HOVER FLY

LADYBEETLE

LACEWING

BENEFICIAL INSECTS

may not easily recognize their useful off-spring. Lady beetle larvae are small, long, and dark gray, with contrasting patches and spines, and can eat their weight in common garden pests like aphids, spider mites, whiteflies, and scale every day. Ladybugs like to lay their eggs on tansy and yarrow leaves.

Composite flowers, such as coreopsis, black-eyed Susans, asters, yarrow, golden-rods, and mountain bluets, also attract syrphid flies and lacewings. Syrphids, such as hover flies, resemble large, slender houseflies that hover and dart in the garden as they feed on pollen and nectar. They lay their eggs among aphids and other insect pests, so that when the eggs hatch, the long, greenish gray larvae will have food immediately.

Bright green lacewings also prey voraciously on aphids. Their larvae look like homely little dragons, yellowish gray with brown markings and scimitar-shaped mandibles. You can recognize lacewing eggs because each sits on its own slender stalk, commonly in groups. You should also leave alone white, parchmentlike cocoons attached to leaves or hidden in protected places in the garden, since they may contain pupating lacewings.

Fennel (*Foeniculum vulgare*) holds a particular attraction for beneficials. But because many plants will not grow near it, plant it somewhere out on the periphery of your yard.

You can order most of the beneficials mentioned above through catalogs. But to include some of the composite and umbellate flowers they are attracted to is a less troublesome way to bring beneficials to your garden. Several other insect predators are available through mail-order catalogs. These include parasitic nematodes ~ which you can introduce into garden soil to infest cutworms, Japanese beetle grubs, and other beetle larvae ~ and praying mantis egg cases. Left to hatch out in the garden, the mantids will at first have a free-for-all eating each other, leaving a few survivors that will have a voracious appetite for most garden pests.

When a particular pest population seems to have exploded in your garden, bear in mind that sprays that are toxic to the pests will kill off the beneficial insects as well. In the long term, a large population of pests almost guarantees that their predators will find them, and usually these beneficials stay in your garden the next year to keep things in balance. If a heavily infested plant is expendable ~ an annual or an easily-replaced perennial ~ you're probably better off yanking it out and sending it to the dump, pests and all, in a tightly closed bag.

Sprays, Traps, and Barriers

For centuries, oil sprays were used on fruit trees to suffocate the egg cases of insect pests before they hatched. The viscosity of these oils was so heavy that they had to be used when trees were dormant, so the sprays wouldn't kill the trees as well as the pests. Today, there are much lighter, superior horticultural oils that pose little danger to either plants or applicators. You can use these superior oils on roses and in vegetable gardens, as well as on fruit trees and grapes, to control mealybugs, aphids, whiteflies, scale, and some caterpillars. Since they will also kill beneficial insects, use oil sprays very selectively and beware of spray oils that are mixed with toxic insecticides.

Insecticidal soap sprays, made of the fatty acids from animals and plants, are among the safest insect controls on the commercial market. They break down within a day or two of use, and thus do not build up in the food chain like DDT and many of the other older pesticides. You can even use them on food crops right up to harvest time. Insecticidal soap sprays control soft-bodied insects that come in contact with the spray, but bees, wasps, and adult beetles with harder shells are not harmed. Add 1 tablespoon of isopropyl alcohol to each pint of insecticidal soap spray to make it even more effective.

A seaweed spray used early in the season is a wonderful growth enhancer (see "The Value of Seaweed" on page 83), and as such is a guard against many of the most common insect pests. If used at regular intervals throughout the season, seaweed sprays nourish the plants, making them less susceptible to sucking and chewing insects.

There are several plant-derived materials, known as botanical insecticides, that are used in spray or dust form. These are toxic to bees, birds, fish, and humans, but for a much shorter time than synthetic chemicals; they are quickly broken down by sunlight and microorganisms. Rotenone, a heavily used insect control before DDT became available, is made from the resin of Malaysian derris roots (*Derris elliptica*) and from the South American lonchocarpus. Pyrethrum, a fast-acting botanical, is actually the dried flowers of two chrysanthemum species (*Chrysanthemum cinerariifolium* and *C. coccineum*). Sabadilla, derived from the tropical lily *Schoenocaulon officinale* from Central and South America, and ryania, from the stems of a woody South American shrub, are both used in commercial farming. Despite their plant origins, these botanicals pose danger to harmless and beneficial creatures as well as to pests. Use them only as a last resort.

Bacterial insecticides are far less dangerous and are today considered the safest and most effective defense against many of the most common insect pests. *Bacillus thuringiensis* (BT) is used against caterpillars and leaf-eating larvae. BTI (*B.t.* var. *israelensis*) kills mosquito and blackfly larvae without affecting other underwater life. *Bacillus popilliae*, also known as milky spore disease, is applied to the grass and makes its way into the soil where it infects Japanese beetle grubs. There are still other *Bacillus* strains aimed at specific pests, and more are being developed each year.

Recipes abound for homemade sprays to repel insects. Garlic, hot pepper, liquid Ivory soap, horsetail (*Equisetum* spp.), and stinging nettles (*Urtica* spp.) are just a few of the ingredients that you can liquefy in an old blender, dilute with water, and spray on your plants. Hardier souls have even made sprays out of the bodies of insects of the species they are trying to eliminate. Carefully apply any spray in early morning or late afternoon, to avoid damaging plants, and repeat the applications after every rain or artificial sprinkling. Wear protective clothing when applying any pest control material, and follow the appropriate precautions when storing or disposing of leftovers. While anything is worth trying once, homemade sprays have always seemed more trouble than they're worth, and I prefer to attract beneficial predators and parasites to combat insect pests.

Before the advent of insecticides in spray cans, old-fashioned flypapers were a familiar sight in kitchens, especially during the jam- and jelly-making season. They trapped the ubiquitous flies before they got into the jam (or the cook's hair). Today the same principle is applied to various traps sold through garden catalogs. There are red balls that look like apples, for example, which are impregnated with a scented lure and coated with a sticky substance to trap the apple maggot. When apple maggot flies emerge from their pupal cases in early summer, they head for the "apple" with the strongest scent to lay their eggs and promptly become trapped on the sticky surface.

Yellow boards coated with a greasy or sticky material will trap whiteflies and aphids in the garden. Better still, white flowering tobacco (*Nicotiana alata*) has a naturally sticky surface that traps whiteflies and aphids. Because it self-sows readily from year to year and also adds lovely flowers and a strong, sweet fragrance late in the day, flowering tobacco earns its place in any country garden plan.

Pheromones (which imitate the odor of the insect's mate) and floral scents lure insects to a sticky death before they can damage trees or plants. Japanese beetle traps use both methods to lure the insects. Locate these beetle traps well away from the garden unless you want to lure the neighbors' beetles as well as your own to just where you don't want them!

The best slug barrier is a 3-inch-wide copper strip. Attach copper strips around the sides of pots, tree trunks, or the frames of raised beds, and fold the top 1 inch down and out to form a flange at a 90-degree angle. When slugs and snails try to cross the barrier, the copper gives their wet bodies enough of an electric shock to

deter them. Alternatively, eliminate the slugs and sowbugs before they reach your plants. Since they both like dark, moist places, put a board on the ground near the area where plants are being eaten. If you lift the board during the daytime, you can remove the slugs and sowbugs that have congregated there.

For vegetable crops, floating row covers of translucent polypropylene fabric or other lightweight material will cover vegetable crops lightly, admitting light and moisture while acting as a barrier against moths looking for plants on which to lay their eggs.

WILDLIFE PESTS

Nothing is more discouraging to a country gardener than watching the leaves of newly emerged spring flower bulbs disappear overnight, or seeing a late fall crop of chard, arugula, or spinach nibbled to nubs in a few short hours. Nothing short of a special deer fence will keep out the culprit, that graceful leaper, the white-tailed deer. As their natural habitats disappear at an ever-increasing rate, deer and other pests like raccoons, skunks, woodchucks, and squirrels search for garden delicacies to their liking. Red squirrels fatten up on rows of ripe unstaked peas, beds of strawberries, or crocus and tulip bulbs. Skunks mess up a lawn in no time looking for grubs (although they help to keep down next year's Japanese beetle population).

A pair of ducks visit my garden regularly. They used to pull up succulent vegetable and weed seedlings alike, leaving their guano as calling cards. Even though our entire acre is contained within fences and a stone wall, we use invisible black netting over anything that is being eaten to keep visiting animals from taking it all. If the netting is cut into pieces just big enough to cover small sections of the garden, it can be removed easily when there are things to be picked. The netting does not detract from the aesthetics of the garden because it can't be seen, even close at hand. Nancy DuBrule has had good luck keeping rabbits away by sprinkling dried blood around asters and other favorite rabbit food plants. They think there is a dead animal nearby and stay away; however, inquisitive dogs are sometimes attracted by the smell.

Ultimately, a country garden should not cause stress. Insects and wildlife vastly outnumber us, and it is far better to accept their presence; having a sort of laissez-faire policy toward their activities will go a long way toward nipping frustration in the bud. Once logical steps are taken to identify who is doing what damage and the barriers or traps are put in place, then you would do well to become philosophical about what happens in the garden. You are bound to have more successes than failures, more beauty and bounty than failed attempts. As long as humans, plants, and wildlife inhabit this planet together, it will be to everyone's benefit to share its space with grace ~ within reason, of course!

An Effective Deer Fence

If your garden is regularly being eaten by deer, you may want to enclose the area within a special deer-proof fence. The key is in understanding that although deer can jump high and wide, they can't do both at the same time. An effective deer barrier is essentially two fences in one: a sturdy 5- by 6-foot vertical fence, and on the outside, a 6- or 7-strand wire fence attached to the vertical fence at the top and sloping down to the ground at a 45-degree angle. This outside wire fence prevents the deer from getting close enough to the vertical fence to jump it. Your local Cooperative Extension office can supply you with detailed instructions about how to build such a fence.

Chapter Two
Country Meadows &
Woodland Walks

I first saw the possibilities for "intentional" meadows in urban landscape design some years ago, when my husband came across a beautiful garden in a new development. On a gentle slope adjacent to a glass-faced office building, there was a meadow of nodding flowers: pink, blue, white, and some scarlet. In an effort to be a good corporate neighbor, the owner of the new building had created a temporary meadow on the exposed earth by sowing annual seeds of cosmos, mountain bluet (*Centaurea montana*), scarlet flax (*Linum grandiflorum* 'Rubrum'), and various pinks (*Dianthus* spp.). Seen from the street, the slope was a delightful pastel tapestry that caught everyone completely by surprise.

In many respects, a meadow can be seen as the most basic country garden and the most natural country look. Interest in meadow gardening reflects a move away from traditional foundation plantings and lawn and toward a less formal arrangement of native plants, naturalized bulbs, perennials, and ornamental and wild grasses.

A garden of native plants ~ a meadow, perhaps, or a woodland walk ~ can reflect the unique character of the region in which you live. Properly designed, it will be harmonious with the surrounding natural ecosystem, providing a sanctuary that invites reflection and relaxation.

First off, it is necessary to understand that a meadow is not maintenance-free. In nature, specific groups of plants succeed one another over time. Meadows naturally move toward woodland as woody plants ~ trees and shrubs ~ grow up among the herbaceous flowering plants and grasses. Meadows persist in nature only if the woody plants are somehow prevented from taking over, usually by fire or human intervention. To maintain a meadow as the climax vegetation, you must arrest its natural development toward becoming a woodland by mowing it in the fall. This will cut back shrub or tree seedlings that appear every growing season. But to get the meadow started in the first place, you must prepare the soil to receive the wildflower and grass seeds.

PREPARING THE SOIL

There is more than one school of thought on how to start a meadow garden. Commercial landscapers recommend using an herbicide before tilling the soil to eliminate weeds. Herbicides are not an option for organic gardeners, however, and a better alternative is to cut vegetation as low as possible in the fall and smother the stubble with black plastic, old cardboard, or layers of newspaper 6 to 8 sheets thick. After the vegetative covering is dead, till the entire area and water. There will be a second crop of weeds from seeds exposed during the tilling. A second shallow tilling, just before the weeds go to seed, will eliminate a great many more weeds.

How to Use a Scythe

A scythe is a traditional tool for cutting long grass or weeds and is especially valuable where a normal mower is impractical ~ in a meadow garden, on steep slopes, or in stony areas.

Although the effort is reduced if it is used properly, working with a scythe still requires some stamina. Grasp the scythe by both of its handles, the top handle in your left hand (knuckles facing up), and the lower handle in your right with knuckles facing down. (If you are left-handed, reverse the positions of your hands.) The handles can be adjusted to fit your arms. Swing the scythe blade forward, reaching out in front of you as you would with a rake, and then pull the blade straight back along the same line, keeping the blade parallel to the ground throughout the swinging motion. Do not swing the blade from side to side. The blade should be roughly the same distance from the ground throughout the swing.

Scything can be tiring, and you will probably want to rest every 10 minutes or so. Try to take short swings instead of long ones and let your body move with the motion, so that a rhythm develops and your body and the scythe work as one unit.

Sharpening the blade regularly, about every half-hour, is absolutely essential. Carry a flat honing stone, about 10 inches long, in your pocket for this purpose. Sweep the stone with short thrusts all along the top or cutting edge of the blade to give it a good edge. Do not sharpen the side of the blade that is next to the ground.

Is a Meadow Right for You?

Meadows aren't for everyone. There are several things to consider before planning a meadow garden. Depending on what grasses and forbs (flowering plants) are included, an unmown meadow can reach knee-high or waist-high. Will this style of planting fit your property? Your lifestyle? Your neighborhood? If you live within city or town limits, there may be local ordinances against allowing lawns to grow above a certain height. In that case, you may need to get a variance.

If you decide that a meadow is right for you, follow these steps to ensure that your future garden is not going to become a sore point in the community. Start by obtaining a copy of local weed ordinances, which will provide you with a list of plants that are illegal to grow because they are noxious weeds. Informed by this list, decide which plants you are going to grow. Talk to your neighbors or send them letters, telling what you plan to do, and explain the positive reasons for doing it. Then, fully prepared because you've done your homework, approach city officials, tell them what you want to do, and inform them that your neighbors are aware of it.

Rodale Research Center tests show that after smothering the vegetation with black plastic for several months, casting wildflower seeds directly over the dead vegetation results in even better germination and less competition from weeds. If, however, you decide to till the meadow area, level the newly plowed earth, scatter the wildflower seeds, and cover with a dusting of soil.

For small meadows of up to 1,000 square feet, the smothering technique ~ without tilling ~ is a practical way to kill off competing vegetation while maintaining a high level of organic matter in the soil from the dead turf and roots. Scatter seed over this area in late summer or fall to simulate the natural course of events in a meadow at the end of the growing season, when dry seedpods are bent over by rain and snow, and their seeds fall onto the dormant meadow surface.

If your meadow is to be large ~ a quarter acre or more ~ use the traditional organic farming practice of plowing or tilling the area and planting buckwheat, which grows thick and lush in a very short time. Its strong, branching roots loosen hard-packed soil and will overwhelm any undesirable plants. As soon as the buckwheat begins to flower, plow it under and replant with more buckwheat. (If you wait until the buckwheat sets seed, you'll have it coming up everywhere, fighting the

Sunflowers

To gardeners in the central midwestern states, the word "meadow" conjures up images of bright, golden sunflowers. Along roadsides and at field edges, these natives lift cheery faces to the sun, following it from east to west as it rises and sets.

The genus *Helianthus* is diverse, including both annual and perennial species. The common sunflower (*H. annuus*) grows to 12 feet, and its seed is eaten by birds, animals, and humans and is pressed to make a popular cooking oil.

The hybrid perennial sunflower (*H. × multiflorus*) grows to only 5 feet and is a good plant for the perennial border. This easily cultivated perennial is good for cutting.

The Jerusalem artichoke (*H. tuberosus*), which grows to 12 feet, has edible knobby tuberous roots that can be enjoyed either raw or cooked. (This member of the sunflower genus can become weedy in good garden loam.)

wildflowers.) Plow the second crop of buckwheat under and plant winter rye. Once the winter rye has grown thick and lush, plow it under as well. These three plantings will eliminate all competition from weeds, and the soil will be very rich in organic matter, ready to nourish meadow seeds.

PLANTING A MEADOW

For a small country meadow, use commercially grown seedlings of certain wildflowers, such as butterfly weed (*Asclepias tuberosa*), daisies, yarrow, sunflowers (*Helianthus* spp.), black-eyed Susan (*Rudbeckia hirta*), coneflowers (*Echinacea* spp.), and goldenrods (*Solidago* spp.) from a garden center; or collect the seeds and grow them yourself. Some meadow wildflowers, like Queen-Anne's-lace (*Daucus carota* var. *carota*) and chicories (*Cichorium* spp.), are difficult to transplant because they have long taproots, and you will have better luck starting them from seed in specially designed containers (see "How to Start Wildflowers with Taproots" on page 93). Then leave your lawn grasses to grow high, as in a meadow. Or you can plant the seedlings in a bed prepared by smothering or tilling and then overseed them with flowering tobacco (*Nicotiana alata*), cosmos, poppies (*Papaver* spp.), sweet rocket (*Hesperis matronalis*), or any other self-sowing annual or herb.

If you buy a meadow mix in a can or by the pound, choose the right one for your region and make sure the mix contains a high proportion of perennial wildflowers and native grasses. As with packaged foods, so too with packaged wildflower mixes:

Read the label! Research the species to learn just what they are and what their habits are. Give preference to mixes with a moderate number of species; you'll get more visual impact because you'll have more flowers of the same kinds.

Different plants have seeds of varying sizes, shapes, and weights. Mixing the seed with sand will help you cast it more

How to Start Wildflowers with Taproots

Many gardeners prefer to start plants indoors, where it's easier to control moisture and other conditions. Wildflowers with taproots can be started indoors if you can devise a way to keep the long taproot from being disturbed during transplanting. One way to do this is to use cardboard tubes from paper towels, bathroom tissue, and gift wrap for planting containers.

Bathroom tissue tubes are the right length for most germination projects; longer tubes can be cut to this length with a knife or scissors. Cover one end of each tube with a bit of newspaper held on with a rubber band. Stand the tubes on end (covered end down) in a watertight tray and fill them with moist, sterile seed-starting mix. If the tubes don't completely fill the tray, you may need to tie a string around the whole batch, firmly but not too tightly, to keep the individual tubes from falling over. Sow seeds at their proper depth. Keep the medium moist by watering from the top.

At planting-out time, roll or cut the rubber band away, handling each tube gently so it doesn't fall apart. Plant the whole thing ~ seedling, tube, and all.

One final precaution: Don't start seeds too early, or the taproot may outgrow the tube. Check plant references to learn the typical germination time for the seeds you're growing. If you want to start seed in the spring, count back from your average last frost date the number of weeks or days required to germinate the particular seed you're planting. Then sow your seed at the appropriate time.

Plants for a Western Prairie Garden

If your average annual rainfall is 30 inches or less, think about having a prairie instead of a meadow. Besides many of the species listed for meadows, there are many beautiful native prairie plants to choose from. What follows is just a sample.

FLOWERS

Allium cernuum (nodding onion): 1–2 feet tall, rose or white flowers in summer.

Anemone patens (pasque flower): 8 inches tall, blue-violet flowers in spring.

Eryngium yuccifolium (rattlesnake-master): 3–4 feet tall, white flowers in summer.

Gentiana andrewsii (closed gentian): 1–2 feet tall, blue flowers in fall.

Liatris aspera (rough gayfeather): 2–4 feet tall, purple flowers in late summer.

Lobelia spicata (pale-spike): To 4 feet tall, blue-violet or white flowers in summer.

Sisyrinchium campestre (blue-eyed grass): To 1½ feet tall, blue flowers in late spring.

Thalictrum dasycarpum (meadow rue): To 6 feet tall, purple flowers in early summer.

GRASSES

Andropogon gerardii (big bluestem): 4–6 feet tall, turns auburn after frost.

Bouteloua curtipendula (side-oats gramma grass): 1–3 feet tall, attractive scythe-shaped flower and seed heads; turns tan in winter.

Sporobolus heterolepis (prairie dropseed): 2–3 feet tall, ornamental seeds in fall.

Stipa spartea (needle grass): 2–4 feet tall, ornamental seeds in summer and fall.

evenly. Mix 1 cup of seed with 5 cups of sand for every 1,000 square feet and cast it by hand. Once the seed is spread, cover it lightly with soil, or roll it to be sure the seeds are in contact with the earth. Water well.

Like any newly planted seedbed, keep the soil moist by misting with a sprinkler until the seeds have germinated and seedlings become established. This is easier if planting takes place in the fall, as it does in nature. Fewer weed seeds germinate late in the season, meaning less competition for your seedlings.

How to Plant an Easy-Care Meadow

Using a mix of non-native or hybrid perennials and annuals, Nancy DuBrule has created an easy-care meadow. She calls it a new American meadow ~ one that is geared to the busy person who loves flowers, but whose working days are too long to permit much time for gardening.

Originally, Nancy's meadow began as an orderly 25 by 15-foot rectangle, with carefully prepared soil, enriched with compost and organic soil amendments, and planted with perennials. By the garden's third year, her business took so much time that she could only give the garden a quick spring cleanup and rearrange a few plants. That year she noticed many volunteer seedlings: globe thistles (*Echinops* spp.), coneflowers (*Echinacea* spp.), cosmos, sweet rockets (*Hesperis* spp.), catnip, oregano, bronze fennel (*Foeniculum vulgare* var. *purpureum*), and pansies (*Viola* spp.). Eventually she began to think of the garden as more of a wild meadow than a garden and stopped trying to impose a pattern of rows and beds on this free-spirited plot of ground. Instead, she actually added more plants, such as foxglove (*Digitalis* spp.), flowering tobacco (*Nicotiana alata* 'Grandiflora'), bee balm,

Six Easy Natives to Grow from Seed

If growing wildflowers is new to you, the following are good plants to start with. Some of these plants need to be stratified, or exposed to cold for a period of time, before they germinate. Stratification imitates the dormancy that the seeds experience when they overwinter; it is a simple procedure. Put some barely damp sand, sowing mix, or vermiculite in a plastic bag, mix the seeds in (one kind to a bag), and close tightly. Label the bag and store it in the refrigerator for the required time.

Aquilegia canadensis (wild columbine): 1½–2 feet tall, red-and-yellow spurred flowers, spring-blooming. Stratify for one month; don't cover seed. Full sun to light shade. P

Asclepias tuberosa (butterfly weed): 2½–3 feet tall, orange flower heads in summer. Butterflies love it. If seed isn't absolutely fresh, stratify for two months. Full sun, dry soil. P

Echinacea purpurea (purple coneflower): 3–4 feet tall, large pink daisy flower with bold, bristly center cone, summer-blooming. Attracts butterflies and bumblebees. Stratify for one month. Needs light to germinate; don't cover seeds. Full sun. P

Helianthus spp. (sunflowers): The common sunflower *H. annuus* grows to a whopping 12 feet. *H. debilis* is better suited to gardens, reaching a modest 4 feet, and makes a good cut flower; summer-blooming. Full sun, moist, rich soil. P and A

Lobelia cardinalis (cardinal flower): 2–3 feet tall, bright red flowers in late summer. Needs woodland conditions: shade, moist soil. Attracts hummingbirds. Stratify for two months. P

Rudbeckia hirta (black-eyed Susan): 1–3 feet tall, large yellow daisylike flower with dark center. Summer-blooming. Sow in spring. Full sun. A or B

Key: A: Annual   B: Biennial   P: Perennial

Echinacea

Purple cone-flower (*Echinacea purpurea*) is native to the eastern Great Plains. This beautiful prairie plant is a good choice for a dry meadow planting and makes a stunning border plant, too.

The genus name comes from the Greek word for hedgehog, because the dried seed heads look like a bristly brown hedgehog.

tansy, and white valerian, that would self-sow and insert themselves into the already crowded space. To give the meadow some late-season color, she planted late-blooming 'Alma Potschke' asters, white mugwort (*Artemisia lactiflora*), and zebra grass (*Miscanthus sinensis* 'Zebrinus'), plus 'Stargazer' lilies for fragrance. Hardy daisy-like 'Sheffield' and 'Mary Stoker' chrysanthemums, which were part of the original garden, self-sowed and even crossed. By the fourth summer the garden was truly a meadow. For more easy-care meadow plants, see page 107–108.

Since then, Nancy has let the perennials and self-sowing annuals follow their own course. All of the plants in her meadow are strong spreaders that stand up to competition. Their needs are minimal: In late fall she cuts all of the dead plant stalks down to the ground and spreads wood ashes (about 2 quarts, or 2 pounds for this 375-square-foot rectangle) over the bed. In the spring, the only time when the garden is bare, she adds a topdressing of 2 to 3 inches of compost and a balanced organic fertilizer (the balance is determined by a soil test every three to four years). When she adds new plants, Nancy mixes bonemeal and rock phosphate with the soil in the planting holes.

WEEDS AND WILDLIFE IN A MEADOW

The so-called weeds that grow in a meadow often turn into meadow grasses, but you should learn to recognize the few weeds that will choke out and kill other vegetation. For example, multiflora rose (*Rosa multiflora*), kudzu vine (*Pueraria lobata*), brambles or wild blackberries (*Rubus* spp.), and bindweed or wild morning glory (*Calystegia sepium*) all become pernicious weeds when left to grow at will. In your region there may be other local field weeds that will need to be kept under control. Call your local Cooperative Extension agent to find out which plants you should guard against.

A meadow will attract wildlife: Mice, rabbits, snakes, hornets, and birds all make their homes in meadows, and deer

Plants That Attract Butterflies

In a more formal flower border, plant zinnias, lantanas, single cultivars of marigolds, *Phlox* and *Scabiosa* spp., rose verbena (*Verbena canadensis*), and gayfeathers or blazing-stars (*Liatris* spp.), as well as common lilac (*Syringa vulgaris*) and blueberry (*Vaccinium* spp.) bushes to bring butterflies into the garden.

In a meadow garden, the following plants will attract butterflies:

YELLOWS AND ORANGES
Asclepias tuberosa (butterfly weed)
Coreopsis spp. (coreopsis)
Rudbeckia hirta (black-eyed Susan)
Solidago spp. (goldenrods)

WHITES
Buddleia davidii cultivar (orange-eye
    butterfly bush)
Cephalanthus occidentalis (buttonbush)
Chrysanthemum leucanthemum (oxeye daisy)
Eupatorium perfoliatum (boneset)

PINKS AND PURPLES
Asclepias purpurascens (purple milkweed)
Aster novae-angliae (New England aster)
Buddleia davidii cultivar (orange-eye
    butterfly bush)
Echinacea purpurea (purple coneflower)
Eupatorium purpureum, E. fistulosum, and
    E. maculatum (Joe-Pye weed, bonesets)
Monarda fistulosa (wild bergamot)

BLUE
Eupatorium coelestinum (mist flower)

PAINTED LADY
Vanessa cardui

PIPEVINE
SWALLOWTAIL
Battus philenor

like to visit. Tall grass and wildlife may not suit everyone's taste, so it would be wise to check local ordinances to see if meadows are permitted in your town.

How to Attract Butterflies

Butterflies are dividends that come with gardening organically. Pesticides used on trees, lawns, and gardens are as fatal to butterflies (and many other beneficial insects) as they are to pests. But in a garden where no toxic synthetic chemicals are used to control pests, butterflies will abound.

On a sunny day, the citron yellows of the sulphur butterflies, the orange, black, and white of the monarchs, viceroys, and painted ladies, the sky blue of the early azures, and the white cabbage butterflies all contribute their own delicate touches of color to a country garden. Cold air immobilizes butterflies, and it is not until the sun raises their body temperatures that they become active. Until then, they can be seen basking in the sun on a stone wall or a fieldstone pathway, absorbing the warmth radiating from the stone beneath them. Appropriately, their favorite nectar plants grow best in full sunlight, in meadows or other open places.

A meadow-style garden is probably the most inviting to butterflies. To attract and sustain butterflies, your garden should have some wild plants that are more than likely on most gardeners' list of "weeds."

Butterflies have antennae that detect odors, and their feet, curiously, are sensitive to taste. When a butterfly lands on a leaf, its feet tell whether this is the right place to lay its eggs. The larvae of the familiar monarch, for example, feed only on milkweed and butterfly weed (*Asclepias* spp.). Viceroys, which closely resemble monarchs but are smaller, lay their eggs in cherry and plum trees because their larvae prefer the leaves of these fruit trees. The fritillary butterfly's larvae feed mainly on violets (*Viola* spp.). Black swallowtail larvae (magnificent iridescent green-, yellow-, and black-striped caterpillars commonly known as parsleyworms) eat only parsley and other members of the carrot family. Painted ladies and red admirals feed on cornflowers (*Centaurea cyanus*), thistles (*Cirsium* spp.), and nettles (*Urtica* spp.).

CREATING A WOODLAND GARDEN

If you have many mature trees on your property, a natural and practical means of creating a country look is to plant a woodland garden. Little will grow in the darkness of a pine and hemlock forest, but the seasonal and intermittent light beneath tall, deciduous trees permits an understory of smaller trees and shrubs as well as a wealth of unexpected wildflowers and groundcovers.

Just as buildings have different stories or floors, forests, too, have layers: a canopy of the tallest, climax trees, an understory of lower-growing trees and shrubs, and a floor covered with a carpet of detritus that is renewed each year. The degree of shade cast by the canopy of tallest trees sets the limits for what you can grow beneath. The dim light, almost darkness, of evergreen forests permits only ferns, lichens, and mosses to survive; often there is just a floor covered with pine needles. But trees that lose their leaves seasonally create a moderately shaded setting, where many more plants can grow in the understory. Then, by limbing up the lower branches of trees and opening up the top canopy, you can create a habitat of dappled light suitable for partial-shade-loving as well as shade-loving plants (see "Improving the Light in a Woodland Garden" on page 100).

To enhance your woodland setting, look at the landscapes of local parks and open spaces for indigenous trees and plants adapted to the region. Form and texture are important qualities to note. Study the shapes of understory trees, the color and texture of their bark, their leaf color in spring and fall, and their growth habits.

Some trees and plants have an upright growth habit, good for creating a vertical accent in the landscape. Examples are the red vein enkianthus (*Enkianthus campanulatus*), an unusual flowering shrub reaching 12 to 15 feet tall with a vertical branching habit and bell-shaped flowers, and the fastigiate yew (*Taxus baccata* 'Fastigiata'), a dark evergreen with a striking narrow upright habit. Others, such as Japanese maple (*Acer palmatum*) and flowering dogwood (*Cornus florida*), spread horizontally, giving a freer, more spacious feeling.

The texture of the leaves, especially in the lower-growing plants, either adds weight or gives a feathery, light feeling to a planting. Silver or yellow-green leaves, as well as small-leaved plants, give a sense of lightness, while plants with dark or blue-green leaves and large-leaved plants seem heavier. For example, think about the light-textured, fine foliage of the glossy abelia (*Abelia grandiflora*) as compared to that of some of the large-leaved hostas (*Hosta* spp.). Glossy leaves, like those of hollies (*Ilex* spp.), seem weighty and anchored, while leaves with dull or velvety surfaces, such as the leatherleaf viburnum (*Viburnum rhytidophyllum*) appear much coarser and more subdued.

THREE GOOD CHOICES FOR A LOW-MAINTENANCE WOODLAND WALK

Three favorites for ease of care and season-

Improving the Light in a Woodland Garden

If your woods are dark and deep and the shade is too dense to grow the plants you want, there are three ways you can increase the light. You can thin the woods by removing those trees and shrubs that are undesirable or too numerous, you can limb up trees by removing low or drooping branches, or you can open up the canopy of trees by selectively removing upper branches. A combination of these three techniques can bring significantly more light into the area.

Thinning isn't always necessary, but if it is, it should be done first. Limbing up can mean removing all of the branches from the lower 10 feet of trunk or the lower 40 feet, depending on the tree and how it grows. Opening up the canopy can let in a considerable amount of light without changing the shape of the tree very much. Opening up large trees requires skill, experience, and special equipment; to do this, you should call in an arborist.

long beauty are hostas, ferns, and rhododendrons. It is possible to create a woodland garden that ~ once established ~ is nearly care-free. No matter where you live, the rules for creating an almost care-free woodland garden are the same: Keep the plant list simple, rely heavily on shrubs and trees, and choose native or adapted perennials or wildflowers.

When planting a woodland garden, chances are you will have to amend the soil and get rid of unwanted plants. By planning ahead, you can accomplish both tasks simultaneously with almost no work. Simply pile leaves knee-high or deeper on the area you want to plant. That's it. Eighteen months later, you'll have a weed-free area of lovely leaf mold ~ just the right kind of soil for woodland plants. Shredding the leaves and layering them with manure or some organic fertilizer will cut the waiting time to a year.

Hostas

Hostas, also known as plantain lilies, are herbaceous perennials that like shady places and are so undemanding that once in place, they can remain there for decades. Late each summer, without any encouragement, fragrant hosta (*Hosta plantaginea* var. *grandiflora*) sends up its tuberose-like flowers in the shade of my 40-foot hemlocks, a remnant from our enclosed English garden of 30 years ago.

Although this hosta has incredibly fragrant and elegant flowers, most hosta flowers are less distinctive than the leaves. There is a broad range of leaf colors, from chartreuse to dark green, blue-green, and variegated with white and gold; any of these colors may have contrasting edging colors.

Some hosta leaves have a powdery look, and some have clearly defined veins. The leaves form a basal rosette that grows slowly but can reach up to 5 feet in diameter after many years in one place. They are useful in combination with plants that like to have their feet shaded, like clematis, or with the late-blooming magic lily (*Lycoris squamigera*). Like ferns, hostas prefer shade and soil that is rich in humus, and they are perfect plants for a woodland walk. Here are some of my favorite hostas:

H. fortunei: Dark green ribbed leaves; lilac flowers.

H. plantaginea var. *grandiflora*: Fragrant white flowers late in summer; large, light green leaves.

H. plantaginea 'Honeybells': Bright green leaves; pale lavender flowers on spikes in midsummer.

H. sieboldiana 'Frances Williams': Large, puckered blue-green leaves with gold margins; pale lilac flowers.

H. tardiflora: Narrow, dark green leaves; pale purple flowers that last well into fall.

H. undulata: Wavy green leaves striped with white, lavender flowers, deeper color in shade; late spring to early summer.

H. ventricosa: Dark green leaves and

Violets

Violets are blue ~ and white, pink, purple, and yellow. They are also great plants for naturalizing in woodlands. Most of them are hardy and easy to grow, and they carpet the ground with color in spring. Some violets are real spreaders and, once established, can quickly colonize an area. Plant violets close by a walk or bench, where you can enjoy their charming and pretty blossoms up close. Here are some to try:

Viola labradorica (Labrador violet): 3 inches tall, bluish purple flowers.

V. odorata (sweet violet): 4–8 inches tall, flowers white, rose, deep purple, pink, all shades of blue.

V. pedata (bird-foot violet): 3–10 inches tall, white or purple flowers.

V. pubescens (downy yellow violet): 16 inches tall, yellow flowers.

V. sororia (woolly blue violet): Low-growing and stemless, flower shades of blue, purple, or white.

---

deep purple flowers; one of the best hostas for flower color.

Ferns

Wherever a woodland already exists, ferns will likely have staked out spaces and

---

Fall-Blooming Bulbs

Spring bulbs are familiar in woodland settings. But these late-summer and fall-blooming bulbs will provide colorful accents in woodland shade at other times of the year.

Colchicum autumnale (autumn crocus): 6–8 inches tall, rosy purple and white flowers. Zone 4.

Cyclamen hederifolium, syn. *C. neapolitanum* (cyclamen): 4 inches tall, small red, pink, or white flowers appear before leaves in late summer; plant in July. Zone 5.

Lycoris squamigera (magic lily): 1½–2 feet tall, foliage appears in spring and dies down; rose-pink flowers appear in late summer; very fragrant, naturalizes and multiplies well. Zone 4.

Narcissus cyclamineus: 4–8 inches tall, yellow flowers in winter to early spring. Zone 6.

Sternbergia lutea (winter daffodil): 1 foot tall, bright yellow flowers, straplike leaves; biblical lily-of-the-field; naturalizes well. Zone 7.

---

established themselves. They are native to shady woodlands, where the soil is a rich, moist humus, well-suited to their rather complicated propagation process.

There are several genera of ferns that are suitable to the moist, acidic soil of woodlands. Maidenhair ferns (*Adiantum pedatum*) have delicate, airy foliage borne in whorls on wiry black stems. Cinnamon ferns (*Osmunda cinnamomea*) have tall fronds, either brown, fuzzy, and fertile, or green and sterile, that add interest to the clump of waxy fronds. Because they grow up to 3 feet tall, cinnamon ferns are best used as background plants. Another member of the genus *Osmunda,* the interrupted fern (*O. claytoniana*), has edible fiddleheads. The evergreen Christmas fern (*Polystichum acrostichoides*) adds a nice spot

of green to the winter landscape, and the impressive ostrich fern (*Matteuccia pensylvanica*) grows 4 to 5 feet tall.

The widespread availability of commercially grown ferns makes them suitable for use in every woodland garden.

Rhododendrons

Rhododendrons love cool, moist, acid soil, and the rich humus of a woodland is nicely suited to these handsome, broadleaved evergreens and deciduous native azaleas. They do not like wet feet, however, so good drainage is essential. While growers argue that rhododendrons do best in sun, provided the soil is rich and moist, there are native species that do well enough in the dappled light of a woodland to make them worth the extra effort of regular watering in the first year. In fact, it is difficult to imagine a woodland walk without azaleas, the most colorful members of the *Rhododendron* genus.

There are literally hundreds of rhododendrons and azaleas, and the best cultivars for a particular locale are usually available at reputable local nurseries. Here are some of my favorites.

R. calendulaceum (flame azalea): 9 to 15 feet tall; yellowish orange-scarlet flowers in early June after leafing out; very showy! Zone 5.

R. canadense (rhodora): 3 feet tall; rosy purple flowers in May before leafing out; takes more moisture than other azaleas. Zone 2.

R. maximum (rosebay rhododendron): 12 to 36 feet tall; open, loose; pale pink flowers in June and July; evergreen; excellent backdrop plant. Zone 3.

R. mucronulatum (Korean spice rhododendron): 6 feet tall; Easter-egg-pink flowers in early April before leafing out, cheerful harbingers of spring on the edge of a woodland, striking yellow to bronze-red foliage in fall. Zone 4.

R. periclymenoides (pinxterbloom azalea): 6 feet tall; white to light pink flowers in May before leafing out. Zone 3.

R. prinophyllum (roseshell azalea): 9 feet tall; like pinxterbloom, but flowers are larger, pinker, more fragrant. Zone 3.

R. vaseyi (pinkshell azalea): 6 to 9 feet; tall, light rose flowers in May before leaf-ing out; tolerates more moisture than other May-blooming azaleas. Zone 4.

WOODLAND BULBS

Bulbs are wonderful additions to a woodland garden in spring. The earliest ones add cheerful, bright colors to the bleak spring landscape. Snowdrops (*Galanthus spp.*) and glory-of-the-snow (*Chionodoxa luciliae*) are the earliest of all bulbs to flower, even with snow still on the ground. Squills (*Scilla spp.*) come a little later and, if left undisturbed, will multiply and form a carpet of blue starlike flowers after a few years.

In a woodland garden, naturalize bulbs by allowing them to establish themselves and increase on their own.

Naturalizing mixes of crocuses, snowdrops, grape hyacinths (*Muscari* spp.), and daffodils are available at most garden centers at the appropriate time for planting in the fall. Such mixes, which must be checked for substandard bulbs, are less expensive than new specimen bulbs and consist of prolific cultivars of which the grower usually has a surplus.

Not all bulbs can be naturalized. While daffodils, squills, and crocuses multiply rapidly in a naturalized planting, tulips seldom bloom more than two years before losing their strength.

All bulbs must be allowed to grow after their flowers fade in order to manufacture and store food for the following year's bloom. For this reason if you plant large bulbs in a lawn, do not cut the grass for several weeks after flowering, until the foliage has yellowed and died.

The ideal place for naturalizing bulbs is where the grass can be allowed to grow high, as in a meadow. There is nothing fresher and more uplifting to a winter-dampened spirit than a sea of daffodils in varying shades of yellow, orange, cream, and white nodding above the greening grasses, or a naturalized clump of snow-drops blooming against a stone wall or tree trunk in the woodland in late February.

If you are interested in naturalizing bulbs over a large area, you can do this by digging a series of holes roughly 15 inches in diameter, to the depth required by the bulbs you are planting (8 inches deep for the larger bulbs of tulips, hyacinths, and daffodils, and 5 inches deep for the smaller bulbs of crocuses, grape hyacinths, squills, and snowdrops). The holes should be widely spaced, 1 foot or more apart, to form drifts over the area you want to naturalize.

Mix a generous cup of rock phosphate and plenty of compost into the soil in each planting hole. Plant five to nine bulbs in each hole, spacing the large bulbs at least 4 inches apart and the smaller bulbs 2 inches apart. Cover with soil, and water well to get the bulbs' root growth started.

If properly planted, the bulbs can be left where they are for many years. Bulbs form new offsets, or small bulbs, at their base each year. If, after a few years, plants are producing fewer flowers, lift and separate these offsets from the bulbs.

Lift the clumps of bulbs after they have finished blooming and the foliage has begun to yellow, shake off the soil, and leave them in the open air in a shady place for a day or two to dry out. Separate the bulbs, and replant the larger ones with more rock phosphate and compost mixed into the planting holes.

Using Moss as a Woodland Groundcover

Don't overlook the value of moss in a woodland garden. Moss will grow in deep shade or in very moist or acidic ground, where other plants may not flourish; it makes an excellent groundcover for diminutive woodland bulbs and flowers; and many mosses are evergreen, providing brilliant green color even during winter.

If moss already grows in your woodland and you'd like more, try this unorthodox method for increasing your plants. Gather the kind of moss you'd like to propagate, shake soil loose from it and put it in a blender, along with a cup of watery beer and a spoonful of sugar. Blend until the moss is broken up and the mixture is fairly homogeneous ~ rather like a moss daiquiri. Spread it where you want the moss to grow. Tiny moss plants should appear in five to six weeks. Meanwhile, keep the area moist.

❃ M E A D O W   P L A N T S ❃

PLANTS FOR SUNNY, DRY MEADOWS

Name FLOWERS	Height	Color	Bloom Time	Zone	Key	Comments
Achillea millefolium (common yarrow)	1–2'	white	June–Aug.	3–9	P	feathery leaves, flat heads of rich flowers in summer
Anaphalis margaritacea (pearly everlasting)	to 20"	white	July–Aug.	3–8	P	clusters of small, cottony flowers good for drying
Apocynum androsaemifolium (common dogbane)	to 2'	pink	midsummer	3–10		
Asclepias tuberosa (butterfly weed)	1–3'	orange	summer	4–9	P	umbelliferous, attracts butterflies, prefers dry sandy soil
Aster ericoides, A. laevis, A. novae-angliae, A. sericeus (asters)	1–4'	blue-violet to deep purple and white	late summer to fall	4–9	P	
Baptisia leucantha (prairie wild indigo)	1–4'	white	early summer	3–9	P	
Chrysanthemum leucanthemum (oxeye daisy)	to 2'	white	May–June	3–10	P	often weedy in fields, reseeds easily
*Cichorium intybus (chicory)	3–6'	sky blue	all summer	3–10	P	light foliage, daisylike flower
Cirsium vulgare (bull thistle)	to 5'	lavender	all summer	4–10	P	very prickly
*Daucus carota var. *carota* (Queen-Anne's-lace)	to 3'	white	all summer	3–9	A B	lacy foliage
Echinacea purpurea (coneflower)	2–4'	purple, white	all summer	3–8	P	daisylike flowers with prominent central cone
Eupatorium purpureum (Joe-Pye weed)	4–6'	purple	Aug.–Sept.	4–9	P	clusters of flowers
Gentianopsis crinita (fringed gentian)	1–3'	blue	fall.	3–10	B	
Helianthus spp. (sunflowers)	4–5'	yellow	July–Sept.	4–9	P	
Heliopsis helianthoides (oxeye daisy)	2–5'	orange-yellow	midsummer to fall	3–8	P	
Hieracium spp. (hawkweeds)	6"–5'	orange to red	late summer	3–9	P	flower clusters on a hairy stem, can become weedy
Lespedeza capitata (bush clover)	2–4'	cream	late summer	2–10	P	

continued

PLANTS FOR SUNNY, DRY MEADOWS—CONTINUED

Name	Height	Color	Bloom Time	Zone	Key	Comments
Linaria vulgaris (butter-and-eggs)	12–15"	yellow and orange	all summer	3–10	P	flower spikes resemble small snapdragons
Lupinus perennis (wild lupine)	2'	blue	summer	3–10	P	
Monarda fistulosa (wild bergamot)	to 4'	pinkish lavender	summer	3–9	P	composite flowers; separate, pointed petals
Oenothera biennis (evening primrose)	3–5'	yellow	June–Oct.	4–9	B	flowers resemble large buttercups
Penstemon digitalis (beardtongue)	3–5'	white to pinkish	summer	4–9	P	
Petalostemon purpureum (purple prairie clover)	1–3'	violet to crimson	summer	4–9	P	
Phlox pilosa (prairie phlox)	1–2'	red-purple	early summer	3–6	P	
Potentilla fruticosa (shrubby cinquefoil)	3'	yellow	midsummer to fall	3–8	P	saucer-shaped flowers
Prunella vulgaris (self-heal)	to 2'	purple	summer	4–10	P	low-growing plant, upright stems
Ratibida pinnata (prairie coneflower)	1–3'	yellow	summer	3–6	P	
Rosa blanda (prairie rose)	to 6'	purple to pink or white	summer	2	P	shrub
Rudbeckia hirta (black-eyed Susan)	1–3'	yellow	summer	4–9	A	daisylike flowers, lance-shaped foliage
Solidago spp. (goldenrods)	3–5'	yellow or white	late summer and fall	3–8	P	coarse-looking prairie meadow plant
Trifolium spp. (clovers)	8"–2'	pink or white	May–Sept.	3–10	P	needs sun and well-drained soil
Verbena hastata (blue vervain)	4–5'	purple, pink, or white	all summer	3–10	P	slender flower spikes
Vicia cracca (bird vetch)	5'	violet blue		4–9	P	trailing plant, finely cut leaves
GRASSES						
Andropogon scoparius (little bluestem)	2–4'	stems orange in fall	fall	6–9	P	
Panicum virgatum (switch grass)	3–5'	auburn foliage in fall	July–Sept.	5–9	P	clusters of flowers
Sorghastrum nutans (Indian grass)	3–5'	purple, bronze fall color	July to frost	6–10	P	

Key
A: Annual
B: Biennial
P: Perennial
* must be grown from seed

PERENNIALS, ANNUALS, AND BIENNIALS FOR EASY-CARE MEADOW GARDENS

Name	Height	Color	Bloom Time	Zone	Key	Comments
***Anemone vitifolia* 'Robustissima' (Japanese anemone)	2'	mauve-pink	late summer and fall	3–8	P	large-toothed, densely woolly underneath
Anthemis tinctoria (golden marguerite)	to 3'	golden yellow	midsummer	3–7	S P	daisylike flowers
****Aquilegia* spp. (columbines)	1–2'	all colors	late spring	3–8	P	long spurs, delicate foliage
Aster spp. (asters)	3–5'	white, pink, or blue	fall	4–9	P	clusters of small daisylike flowers
****Campanula glomerata* (clustered bellflower)	2'	deep purple	summer	3–8	P	clusters of upright flowers, invasive
Centaurea cyanus (cornflower, bachelors' buttons)	1–3'	bright blue, pink, or mauve	summer		S A	will not bloom in extreme heat
Centaurea montana (mountain bluet)	18–24"	blue	spring	3–10	P	thistle-shaped flowers
Cleome hasslerana (spider plant)	3–5'	pink or white	all summer		S A	large, striking plants
Coreopsis spp. (coreopsis)	1–3'	bright yellow	summer	3–8	S P	daisylike flowers, finely cut foliage
Cosmos bipinnatus (cosmos)	3–5'	pink, white, or magenta	summer to frost		S A	lacy foliage
Chrysanthemum parthenium (feverfew)	1–3'	white	late summer	6–8	S P	little daisies with pungent foliage
Consolida ambigua (rocket larkspur)	1–2'	violet, pink, rose, or blue	summer	3–10	S B	spikes of flowers
Digitalis purpurea (foxglove)	2–4'	white, pink, or lavender	early summer	4–9	S B	spikes of flowers
Echinops spp. (globe thistles)	1–4'	blue	summer	3–8	S P	round prickly flowers, good for drying
****Eupatorium coelestinum* (hardy ageratum)	2–3'	blue	fall	6–10	P	fringed flowers
Gaura lindheimeri (gaura)	3–4'	white	summer	5–9	P	thin, spikelike flowers
Helenium autumnale (common sneezeweed)	2–6'	yellow, red, or orange	summer	3–8	S P	daisylike flowers with raised centers
Helianthus spp. (sunflowers)	4–5'	yellow	late summer	4–10	P	sunflowers with daisylike flower
Heliopsis helianthoides (oxeye daisy)	2–5'	yellow	late summer	3–9	P	single or double flower, also known as false sunflower

continued

PERENNIALS, ANNUALS, AND BIENNIALS FOR EASY-CARE MEADOW GARDENS—CONTINUED

Name	Height	Color	Bloom Time	Zone	Key	Comments
***_Hemerocallis fulva_ (tawny daylily)	2'	orange-red	summer to early fall	3–9	P	flowers last for a day
***_Hesperis matronalis_ (sweet rocket)	3–4'	white, pink, or lavender	spring and early summer	3–8	S P B	fragrant phloxlike flowers
***_Lilium tigrinum_ (tiger lily)	3–4'	orange	midsummer	3–9	S P	bulb; trumpet flowers flecked with black spots; reproduces by black bulblets in leaf axils
Lupinus perennis (wild lupine)	2'	vivid purple, rose, white, blue, or yellow	late spring	4–9	S P	spikes of flowers
***_Macleaya cordata_ (plume poppy)	to 7'	creamy pink	summer	3–8	S P	pest-free, dramatic plant with flower spikes, lobed leaves
Malva spp. (mallows)	2'	pink	all summer	3–8	S P B	hibiscus-like flowers
***_Monarda didyma_, _M. fistulosa_ (bee balm, wild bergamot)	2–3'	red, lavender, pink, or white	midsummer	4–9	S P	attractive to bees
***_Muscari_ spp. (grape hyacinths)	8"	blue	spring	4–8	P	bulbs
***_Narcissus_ spp. (daffodils)	4–18"	yellow, orange, and white	spring	4–9	P	bulbs
***_Nicotiana alata_ 'Grandiflora' (nicotiana, flowering tobacco)	1–4'	white	all summer until hard frost in late fall		S P A	tubular flowers, very fragrant at night
***_Phlox paniculata_ (garden phlox)	2–4'	magenta, pink, or white	late summer	4–8	S P	panicles, fragrant; self-sows but not true to cultivar
Salvia farinacea (mealycup sage)	2–3'	purple or blue	early summer	8–10	S P A	annual in North, perennial in South; spike flowers
Tanacetum vulgare (common tansy)	3'	golden yellow	summer	3–9	S P	button flowers in clusters, fragrant fringed foliage
Valerian officinalis (valerian)	3–5'	white	spring to early summer	5–10	S P	fragrant panicles
Verbena bonariensis (verbena)	18"	purple	all summer	7–10	S P	flowers on long rough stems; treat as an annual in the North

Key

A: Annual   P: Perennial

B: Biennial   S: Self-sowing

***will tolerate partial shade

PLANTS FOR A WOODLAND GARDEN

FLOWERING PLANTS FOR WOODLAND GARDENS

Name	Height	Color	Bloom Time	Zone	Key	Comments
Anemone quinquifolia (wood anemone)	3–5"	white	spring	3–8	P	solitary flowers, protected shade only
Aquilegia canadensis (wild columbine)	to 2'	yellow and red	spring to midsummer	3–8	P	dainty flowers; likes dry soil, needs some sun
Arisaema triphyllum (Jack-in-the-pulpit)	to 9"	green and purple	summer	4–9	P	erect flower produces red berry cluster in fall
Aruncus dioicus (goat's beard)	5–7'	white	summer	3–7	P	showy flowers; needs partial shade
Cimicifuga racemosa (snakeroot)	4–7'	white	summer	3–8	P	showy flowers; spikes; distinctive scent
Cimicifuga simplex (Kamchatka bugbane)	3–5'	white	late summer and fall	3–8	P	flowers, spikes ; distinctive scent
Hosta spp. (hostas, plantain lilies)	to 2–3'	white to purple or violet-blue	midsummer	3–9	P	belllike flowers, some fragrant; handsome foliage
Mertensia virginica (Virginia bluebells)	to 2'	pink fading to lavender-blue	early summer	3	P	likes moist soil
Phlox divaricata (wild blue phlox)	8–12"	lavender-blue	spring	3–9	P	narrow green leaves, slightly fragrant flower
Polemonium caeruleum (Jacob's ladder)	15"	blue	late spring to early summer	2–7	P	complements spring bulbs; ferny foliage
Polygonatum odoratum (fragrant Solomon's seal)	18–24"	white	spring or early summer	3–9	P	bell-shaped flowers, arching stems, blue to black berries
Primula spp. (primroses)	4"–3'	broad range of colors	early summer	5–7	P	good for mass plantings, needs sun and moist soil
Pulmonaria saccharata (Bethlehem sage)	12"	white, pink to blue	spring	2–3	P	white-spotted leaves
Smilacina racemosa (Solomon's plume)	2–3'	white	spring to midsummer	3–7	P	tall, arching branches, flowers in terminal cluster form red berries in fall
Tricyrtis formosana syn. *T. stolonifera* (toad lily)	2–3'	pale mauve	early fall	4–9	P	arching stems; funnel-shaped flowers
Viola spp. (violets)	4–16"	white, violet, blue, lilac, rose	summer	4–8	P	lovely heart-shaped foliage; some species fragrant

Key

A: Annual

B: Biennial

P: Perennial

S: Self–sowing

GROUNDCOVERS FOR WOODLAND GARDENS

Name	Height	Color	Bloom Time	Zone	Key	Comments
Ajuga reptans (carpet bugleweed)	3–6"	white, blue, purple	spring and early summer	3–9	P	invasive in lawns; deep green or bronze foliage
Asarum europaeum (European wild ginger)	to 3"	green	spring	4–7	P	glossy evergreen leaves, very handsome groundcover
Bergenia spp. (bergenia)	12–18"	pink or purple	early spring	3–8	P	leathery, glossy, semi-evergreen leaves
Brunnera macrophylla (Siberian bugloss)	to 18"	blue	spring	3–7	P	cluster of showy, small flowers, similar to forget-me-nots
Convallaria majalis (lily-of-the-valley)	to 8"	white	late spring	2–7	P	fragrant, bell-shaped flowers on racemes
Epimedium spp. (bishop's hat)	to 12"	red, violet, white, pink, or yellow	spring	4–8	P	heart-shaped green leaves turn bronze in fall
Galium odoratum (sweet woodruff)	to 12"	white	spring	4–8	P	bright green leaves in whorls, delicate flowers; good groundcover near rhododendrons
Lamium maculatum (spotted lamium)	to 12"	lavender	all summer	3–8	P	variegated dark green and silvery white leaves, small flowers
Liriope spicata (creeping lilyturf)	to 10"	white to lilac	summer to fall	4–9	P	flower spikes like grape hyacinths
Myosotis scorpioides var. *semperflorens* (forget-me-not)	to 18"	blue	spring	3–8	P	low-growing variety
Phlox stolonifera (creeping phlox)	12–18"	violet, lavender	spring	2–8	P	can form solid mat in woods
Tiarella cordifolia (Allegheny foamflower)	to 12"	white	late spring or early summer	3–8	P	stems with terminal racemes, downy basal leaves
Vaccinium angustifolium (lowbush blueberry)	to 12"	white	early summer	2–6	P	woodland groundcover, vivid red foliage in fall
Vinca minor (periwinkle)	to 10"	blue, white, or purple	spring to early summer	4–9	P	some cultivars have variegated leaves

Key
P: Perennial

UNDERSTORY TREES AND SHRUBS

TREES

Name	Height	Flower Color	Zone	Comments
Acer palmatum (Japanese maple)	20'	red	5–8	'Osakazuki' best red color in fall; finely cut leaves
Amelanchier arborea (downy serviceberry)	15–25'	white	5–9	good fall color; gray streaked with red bark
Amelanchier canadensis and *A. laevis* (serviceberry and Allegheny serviceberry)	35–40'	white	4–8	clusters of white delicate flowers, pinkish gray bark; edible red-purple berries in fall; susceptible to fireblight
Carpinus caroliniana (American hornbeam)	30'	green	3–9	slow-growing; orange to red leaves in the fall; smooth bark
Cercis canadensis (Eastern redbud)	25'	reddish purple or white	4–8	low-branching; yellow fall foliage
Chionanthus virginicus (white fringetree)	30'	white	5–9	6" panicles of white fringelike flowers, blue clusters of berries, yellow leaves in fall
Cornus florida (flowering dogwood)	20–25'	white, pink, or red	4–7	showy flowers; scarlet berries; wine red foliage in fall
Halesia carolina (Carolina silverbell)	30'	white	5–8	clusters of bell-shaped flowers; yellow foliage in fall; striped bark on mature trees; also known as wild olive
Oxydendrum arboreum (sourwood)	20–25'	white	5–9	spectacular flowering tree with drooping racemes, attractive seedpods, and crimson foliage in fall; needs some sun
Styrax japonica (Japanese snowbell)	30'	white	5–9	small, bell-shaped flowers on undersides of branches, clefted bark; no serious insect pests or disease

SHRUBS

Name	Height	Flower Color	Zone	Comments
Abelia × grandiflora (glossy abelia)	5'	white	6–9	multi-stemmed, dense shrub, foliage turns maroon after frost
Cornus alba 'Sibirica' (Siberian dogwood)	7'	creamy white	2–8	red bark colorful in winter, small flowers; white berries in summer
Cornus sericea 'Flaviramea' (yellow-twig dogwood)	7'	white	2–7	chartreuse yellow bark showy in winter; white berries

continued

UNDERSTORY SHRUBS—CONTINUED

Name	Height	Flower Color	Zone	Comments
Euonymus alata 'Compactus' (winged euonymus, burning bush)	9'	greenish white	3–8	dark green elliptical leaves on corklike branches and twigs; attractive pink to wine red fruit
Fothergilla spp. (fothergillas)	6–9'	white	5–9	native shrub, bottlebrush flowers, excellent fall color
Hamamelis virginiana (common witch hazel)	15'	yellow	4–9	ribbonlike flowers in fall; autumn leaves are golden yellow
Hydrangea quercifolia (oakleaf hydrangea)	4–6'	white	5–9	erect flower heads, large leaves resembling giant oak leaves turn deep maroon in fall
Kalmia latifolia (mountain laurel)	7'	white and pink	4–9	leathery evergreen leaves, variegated flowers
Kerria japonica (Japanese kerria)	4–6'	gold	4–9	bright single or double flowers; stems remain green in winter
Leucothoe fontanesiana (dog-hobble)	3–5'	white	5–9	delicate flowers in axils of leaves; greenish bronze new leaves, turning dark green for most of the summer and fall, purplish in winter
Mahonia aquifolium (Oregon grape)	3–6'	yellow	6–9	dark, evergreen hollylike leaves, fragrant flowers, clusters of grapelike blue fruit in early summer
Pieris japonica (Japanese pieris)	9'	white	6–8	handsome broadleaved evergreen, drooping sprays of flowers, spring foliage often bronze, turning to deep green; many good cultivars
Rhododendron spp. (azaleas and rhododendrons)	1–20'	white, yellow, orange, pink, red, lilac, magenta, purple	5–9	many attractive species and cultivars; some species evergreen, some deciduous (see "Rhododendron" on page 102)
Vaccinium corymbosum (highbush blueberry)	6–12'	white	3–8	belllike flowers and edible dark blue fruit, gorgeous red fall color
Viburnum trilobum (American cranberry bush)	12'	white	3–7	edible red fruit, attractive through winter

Opening clearings selectively to let in light and rain creates the right conditions for woodland plants. This mix of azaleas and rhododendrons is planted with Alberta spruce, blue spruce, bleeding heart, and other woodland plants.

↑

This tiny garden along a wooded driveway shows how simple woodland effects can be created in a relatively small area. Groundcovers like blue-flowering ajuga (Ajuga reptans) *and Bishop's weed* (Aegopodium podagraria), *both aggressive spreaders, create a tapestry effect mixed with wild phlox (Phlox divaricata), violets, the ornamental grass blue fescue in the foreground, and self-sown gray-leaved mullein against the rocks.*

114

↑

'Nora Barlow' and 'Raspberry Treat,' both double-flowered columbines, mark a dainty contrast to the dark background of a Norway spruce.

Bring light to the woodland shade with variegated plants like this Japanese painted fern (Athyrium goeringianum 'Pictum'), growing here with Jack-in-the-pulpit (Arisaema triphyllum). The water in this rustic birdbath also reflects the light. →

Rather than trying to keep
this slope cut, the owners
leave the grass unmowed.
Oxeye daisy (Chrysanthemum
leucanthemum) is a wonderful
perennial for a meadow.
It enjoys full sun and will
tolerate almost any soil.

As *a visual transition from a lawn to neighboring woods, this owner let the grass grow up and planted it thickly with black-eyed Susans* (Rudbeckia hirta). *This native prairie annual blooms through July and self-sows freely.*

Cornflowers (Centaurea cyanus) *and* Thelesperma burridgeanum, *a hardy annual very similar to coreopsis, naturalize and spread freely in the sunny, well-drained soil of an open meadow.*

In a shady meadow garden, flowering tobacco (Nicotiana alata *'Grandiflora'*), *cosmos, and columbines are among the many plants that will readily self-sow. Dried columbine seedpods add to the mix of textures.*

The essence of cottage garden design is a kind of ordered chaos where flowers grow in an exuberant mix. Several traditional cottage garden favorites flourish around this simple picket fence ~ hollyhocks in the background, with white flowering tobacco, orange coneflowers, and cleome in front of the fence.

One of the charms (and challenges) of a cottage garden is its casual appearance; it should look almost as if it were unplanned. Daylilies, oxeye daisies, catmint (Nepeta mussinii), lemon verbena, roses, achillea, borage, and other herbs, flowers, and vegetables are planted thickly and allowed to spread and spill over the fences, gates, and paths in this garden.

↑

Even in a formal yard, you can create a distinct area for an informal cottage garden. A circular bed bisected by a casual brick access path is filled with cottage garden favorites and adds color to this suburban lawn. Ornamental onions (Allium spp.), sedums, thymes, and tansy fill the outer ring. The center circle is highlighted by yellow coreopsis and mauve gayfeather (Liatris spicata).

Try to position borders so that they are most often viewed along their length. This perspective shows their lush combinations of colors, textures, and forms to best advantage. Here, a pair of borders enhances a back-yard, directing the eye beyond a sundial to the distant mountains. →

Dooryard gardens are close cousins of the traditional cottage garden. Both tend to be informal collections of flowers and herbs, some-times with vegetables and fruit chosen because they are useful or simply favorite plants. At this farmhouse, hollyhocks, mullein, and sneezewort (Achillea 'The Pearl') fill the beds.

Because of the lively mix of flowers and plants in the cottage garden, it is often safer to limit your range of colors. Sometimes, however, it is hard to resist introducing a vibrant contrast like this mix of purple-blue lavender with annual orange-yellow California poppies (Eschscholzia californica).

Yarrow is a perennial herb that has a long history in cottage and herb gardens. It was well-known to American Indians as a treatment for various ailments. The yellow flowers of 'Coronation Gold' yarrow are useful cut for fresh or dried arrangements.

One of the great pleasures
of planning a cottage garden
is that there are few rules.
Although there are some
traditional favorites, you can
plant almost anything that
pleases you. Annuals can
mix with perennials, bulbs,
shrubs, herbs, and vegetables.
In this late June border,
common white yarrow and
delphiniums mingle with
lilies, roses, and buttercups.

Chapter Three
Cottage Gardens and Country Borders

Ask anyone their definition of a cottage garden and most will describe a Cape Cod cottage surrounded by a rose-covered picket fence, with lots of old-fashioned flowers such as hollyhocks (*Alcea* spp.) and violets (*Viola* spp.). While this description is accurate, the cottage garden ~ with its humble origins ~ has become a style that can be created almost anywhere, regardless of property and climate, and, for many, it is the essence of a country garden.

Nancy DuBrule planted an eclectic mix to bring color to this late summer border. The somber dark purples of butterfly bush (Buddleia davidii) and New England asters (Aster novae-angliae) are brightened by clumps of white chrysanthemums and boltonias and by orange accents of annual Mexican sunflowers (Tithonia rotundifolia).

HISTORY OF THE COTTAGE GARDEN

The term "cottage garden" originated with the English farm laborer, or "cottager," who was provided with a small cottage to live in by his employer, the owner of the farm. Cottagers used their front yards ~ between the cottage and the lane on which it fronted ~ to grow food and medicinal plants for their families.

It was a poor man's garden, and its contents were vital to the survival of his family. Most of the plants in it were either brought from the wild or were gifts from the landlord, neighbors, or monks and nuns who shared slips, cuttings, and seeds of the medicinal herbs that they grew in their monastery gardens for treating the sick.

The basics of these early cottage gardens were homely vegetables like cabbages, broad beans, leeks, and onions, and usually an apple tree, or possibly a pear tree. No cottage garden would be without some seasoning herbs, such as parsley, chives, dill, and thyme, and some aromatic herbs to strew about the house to dispel odors: southernwood (*Artemisia abrotanum*), hyssop (*Hyssopus officinalis*), rue (*Ruta graveolens*), lavenders (*Lavandula* spp.), and sage (*Salvia officinalis*).

Plants gathered in the wild, which cost the cottager nothing, such as mulleins (*Verbascum* spp.), mallows (*Malva* spp.), self-heals (*Prunella* spp.), St.-John's-worts (*Hypericum* spp.), herb Robert (*Geranium robertianum*), and columbines (*Aquilegia* spp.), were introduced into the garden for their medicinal value and for use as dyes.

Early cottage gardens were often planted more or less at random. While the pleasing effect was accidental, other gardeners liked the concept enough to copy and then personalize it. Drawing inspiration from the cottage gardens of English farmhouses and villages, English garden designer Gertrude Jekyll planned highly sophisticated "cottage-style" gardens in the late nineteenth century. With an intuitive sense of proportion and an artist's eye, she designed herbaceous borders with carefully planned drifts of color to give the effect of a cottage garden on an enlarged scale.

In the sense that the cottage garden was a living larder and pharmacy for the family, similar gardens, just outside the door, have been common in all cultures from the time when humans first discovered they didn't have to wander from place to place gathering food, but could plant it intentionally. No matter what they were called ~ cottage garden, kitchen garden, or *potager* ~ these gardens met needs that were universal.

In colonial America, the front dooryard gardens contained not only necessities for the home, but also the best-loved plants that were brought to the New World by the early settlers to remind them of their former home. It was said that the most important things these brave people brought with them were their Bibles and their seeds: The familiar flowers, blooming among the more essential plants of the colonial dooryard garden, must have given comfort during those first years of living in a strange land.

Because of their continuity, some cottage gardens are seed banks for many of the old-fashioned varieties of plants that have become hard to find today. Ipswich pinks, a strain of *Dianthus* developed by the Thompson and Morgan Seed Company in England that were thought to have been lost during World War II, were found in an Ipswich garden a few years ago, where they'd been lovingly grown for nearly 50 years.

HOW TO DESIGN A COTTAGE GARDEN

In her book *America's Cottage Gardens*, Patricia Thorpe suggests that cottage garden design "develops from the landscape, the flowers, and the spirit of the garden." Design in the usual sense of the word has never been an important feature of cottage gardens. The plants make the garden, and whatever flowers are there give the whole its distinct charm (although you should plan successions of flowers to provide color and interest throughout the seasons).

Before you plan your cottage garden, first find out if your property gets enough sun. Most traditional cottage garden plants must have at least eight hours of sun daily to be able to thrive; all day is best. Check the sun over a period of several weeks to see if there are places in your garden that are in shade, and for how long. If the shady areas are few, you can plant accordingly. If the entire area you intend to plant gets only six hours of sun each day, limit your choices to shade-tolerant plants, such as foxgloves (*Digitalis* spp.), bleeding heart (*Dicentra spectabilis*), woodland geranium (*Geranium maculatum*), and astilbes.

Make a list of your favorite flowers and herbs, and organize your garden plan around them. If you have not grown them, research their general size and growth habits, as well as their period of bloom. This will help you avoid planting 6-inch plants among 2- and 3-footers (except for early spring bulbs, primroses, and pansies, which bloom before the larger plants mature).

Make a scale drawing of existing and proposed beds in your garden on graph paper. For a new garden, this will help you plan your color scheme, figure out the number of plants you will need, and generally help you organize your space. At this stage, decide how you want to use color: scattered at random throughout the garden, in drifts or in special combinations, or each color in its own section. It is all a matter of personal taste.

Plan your blooming season by making a chart showing which flowers bloom in which months (see "Seasons of Bloom" on page 148). If you have a very tiny space for a garden, limit your choice of plants to those that bloom for a long time (see "Long-Blooming Perennials" on page 137), such as the long-blooming bleeding heart (*Dicentra* × 'Luxuriant'), which flowers all summer, and garden phlox (*Phlox paniculata*), which blooms from midsummer on, or choose plants with striking foliage like hostas. If you know that you will be there to enjoy your garden only during June, July, and August, plan your garden to bloom for those months.

Planning on paper up to this point will help you get started and will assure you of having the plants you really want. Don't plan the garden down to the last plant. Let it evolve. You will be making changes over the years, moving, eliminating, or adding plants to give the effect you want.

Selecting Larger Plants

Start your garden with basic, permanent

plants that will form the "plant bones" or skeleton of the garden. Typically, these are trees, shrubs, and woody vines. There are two reasons for planting these first: they generally take longer to reach their mature form than herbaceous plants and they will form the structure on or against which you'll be adding smaller plants. All of the following trees and shrubs are appropriate for cottage garden "bones" (see "Vines" on page 154 for information on climbing plants).

Old Roses

Old roses ~ also called historic, antique, or old-fashioned roses ~ are important plants in cottage-style gardens. Four good ones are 'Tuscany Superb', a French gallica rose with deep wine-red, velvety flowers in early summer; 'Reine des Violettes', a hybrid perpetual Bourbon rose growing to 6 feet with very fragrant lilac purple flowers; 'Souvenir de la Malmaison', a Bourbon rose that produces loads of pale pink flowers in early summer and blooms intermittently thereafter; and 'Old Blush', a pink-flowered China rose, hardy to Zone 6.

Roses: Roses are important plants in a cottage garden. Hybrid tea roses, which need a lot of air space around them and are very prone to diseases, are not recommended in a cottage design. Instead, use shrub roses, which are much more vigorous and can stand being crowded. Allow 3 square feet per shrub rose. These plants are very robust, often growing to 5 feet tall. They can be pruned in early spring and again in mid-July after their first flush of bloom to control their size.

Climbing roses, which will occupy mostly vertical space, are a key feature in achieving a crowded, abundant look. They can be given as little as 1½ to 2 square feet in the garden, as the canes will grow upward. Be sure to find out whether your climbing rose blooms on new wood each year or on shoots that come from 1-year-old wood. If the latter is the case, you must develop a woody framework and not prune the rose back hard in fall or spring or you will sacrifice blossoms the second year.

Lilacs: The common lilac (*Syringa vulgaris*) is a traditional cottage garden favorite. It can grow to 20 feet tall and take up 5 to 6 square feet in the garden. Often, it is allowed to grow upward, then is topped each year to keep its height within bounds and the flowers within easy picking range. Control the horizontal spread of the common lilac by regular removal of suckers.

Fifteen Plants for Western Cottage Gardens

You can have a cottage garden no matter where you live simply by using plants that will thrive in your conditions, and that give a profusion of foliage and flowers. Here's a list of cottage-style plants that grow well in the western United States, where rainfall is scant and the alkaline soils range from sandy to heavy clay.

Asclepias tuberosa (butterfly weed): 1–2 feet. Orange flat-topped flowers in midsummer. Zones 3–10. P

Consolida ambigua (rocket larkspur): 2–5 feet. Spikes of pink, purple, blue, or white all summer. A

Crocus spp. (crocuses): 3–6 inches. Grown from bulbs (corms) planted in the fall. Blooms in very early spring. For best effect, plant in large drifts of 10–25 bulbs. Zones 3–8. P

Dyssodia tenuiloba (Dahlberg daisy): 8–12 inches. Lacy green foliage, tiny golden yellow daisy flowers. A

Eustoma grandiflorum (prairie gentian): 2–3 feet. Cup-shaped purple, pink, or white bellflowers on top of long stems. Sow seed outdoors in very early spring. B but usually treated as A

Iris spp. (irises): 6 inches–5 feet depending on species. Purple, pink, white, yellow, or orange flowers in late spring or early summer. Zones 4–9. P

Lavandula angustifolia (lavender): 12–24 inches. Spikes of lavender-purple flowers all summer. Zones 5–9. P

Narcissus spp. (daffodils): 6–18 inches. Yellow, white, and orange flowers in early spring from bulbs planted in fall. Zones 3–10. P

Nepeta × *faassenii* (catmint): 1–2 feet. Lavender-blue flowers and blue-green foliage from late spring through summer. Zones 3–10. P

Penstemon spp. (penstemons): 1½–3 feet. Flowers on thin spikes with tubular pink, blue, or purple blossoms in midsummer. Zones 3–10 depending on species. P

Perovskia atriplicifolia (Russian sage): To 3 feet. Thin lavender-blue spikelike flowers and silvery gray foliage. Blooms midsummer to early fall. Zones 5–10. P

Salvia spp. (sages): Annuals, biennials, perennials, and evergreen shrubs. Heights vary with species. Culinary sages have gray, purple, or variegated foliage all season. Ornamental sages include plants with purple, blue, or pink spikelike flowers. Most bloom in late spring and early summer. A B P

Tulipa spp. (tulips): 6 inches–4 feet depending on species. Flowers of every color bloom in the spring after fall bulb planting. Zones 5–7. P

Verbascum spp. (mulleins): 2–5 feet. White, yellow, or pink flowers on tall spikes. Midsummer blooming. Zones 5–10 depending on species. P

Zauschneria californica (California fuchsia): 1–3 feet. Red funnel-shaped flowers bloom all summer on semi-evergreen shrub. Zones 8–10. P

Key

A: Annual   B: Biennial   P: Perennial

To renew overgrown lilacs, remove one-quarter to one-third of the oldest stems down to the ground after blooming, and thin out the suckers. This will open up the plant and allow more light and air into the center. For smaller gardens, consider less aggressive lilac species and cultivars that only reach 5 to 6 feet in height, such as Korean lilac (*S. meyeri*) and Manchurian lilac (*S. patula* 'Miss Kim'). Both bring prolific, fragrant flowers to the cottage garden without the pruning requirements of the common lilac. Lilacs are susceptible to powdery mildew. Dwarf forms, although they will have some mildew in wet years, are much more disease-resistant.

Buddleia: The butterfly bush (*Buddleia davidii*) is a welcome addition to the cottage garden. It provides fragrant panicles of flowers in late summer and fall and attracts hundreds of butterflies to the garden. Butterfly bushes are vigorous shrubs that put on 5 to 6 feet of vertical growth per year. In Zone 5, they normally die back to ground level each winter. In Zones 6 to 9, they often do not die back at all. In these areas, unless you want your butterfly bush to grow to 12 to 15 feet or more, cut it back to ground level each year to maintain its height at 5 to 6 feet in the garden. For continuous bloom into the fall, deadhead the butterfly bush on a regular basis.

To incorporate a butterfly bush into your cottage garden, place it at the back of the garden for height, or in the middle, removing lower branches and side shoots as it grows to create a fountain effect. Prune anytime until the end of June, when the current year's flower buds will be forming. Allow about 3 square feet for a mature bush.

Hydrangea: These plants provide excellent color in the cottage garden in midsummer. Hydrangeas have enormous rounded or conical flower heads. Their height and spread depends upon the species and cultivars. Among the most popular are:

•Bigleaf hydrangea (*Hydrangea macrophylla*): The bigleaf hydrangea grows 35 feet tall and 3 to 4 feet wide, with rounded terminal flower clusters. There are two flower forms of the bigleaf hydrangea. Lacecap hydrangeas (*H. macrophylla* 'Caerulea', for example) have fertile inner flowers and showy sterile outer flowers, creating an illusion of a ring of lace around a flat interior.

Other bigleaf hydrangeas have no fertile flowers and the flower heads are enormous rounded balls. An example of this type is *H. macrophylla* 'Nikko Blue'. The color of the hydrangeas in this species depends upon the pH of the soil. Shrubs growing in acid soil with a high level of available aluminum will have blue flowers, while those growing in an alkaline or neutral soil will have pink flowers. Flowers are formed from buds produced on 1-year-old wood, so these hydrangeas should be pruned only by removing the oldest stems (2 to 3 years old) down to the base. They are marginally hardy in Zone 5, where a cold winter will kill the first-year stems. In these areas, wrap the hydrangeas to provide winter protection.

•Smooth hydrangea (*H. arborescens* 'Grandiflora'): This is the old-fashioned hills-of-snow often found on old farms. It has white rounded flower clusters on 3- to 4-foot shrubs. Flowers are formed on the current year's growth, making it hardier in northern climates. This plant is very vigorous and spreads by suckers. Old stands of hills-of-snow can cover 20 square feet or more, but they can be easily divided if they begin to spread out of control or cut back down to the ground each spring to manage their size.

•Peegee Hydrangea, tree hydrangea (*H. paniculata* 'Grandiflora'): This becomes a large shrub or a small tree up to 20 feet tall in the cottage garden, with creamy white conical flowers that turn pinkish white in the fall. Young plants have multiple trunks, so if your goal is to establish a hydrangea tree, select three to five of the straightest, strongest stems and remove all lower side shoots until you have reached the desired height of the trunk. Continue to remove all suckers that arise from the base.

This plant blooms on new growth formed in the current season, so it is easy to control its height or shape by pruning in the early spring. This hydrangea provides excellent dried flowers. Harvest only when the white flowers have begun to fade to pink, and air-dry them.

Evergreens: If winter interest is important in your garden, include some evergreens. Use hollies (*Ilex* spp.) as background plantings for spring-blooming shrubs. 'Blue Princess' has glossy blue-green foliage and abundant red berries, and 'Golden Girl' has satiny foliage and yellow berries in early fall. Use needle-bearing evergreens such as the slow-growing Swiss stone pine (*Pinus cembra*) for winter interest and as a support for a climbing vine in summer. Rose daphne (*Daphne cneorum*) is a good evergreen goundcover for a cottage garden; it has sweet-smelling, rosy pink flowers in May.

Choosing Perennials and Smaller Plants

With the major plantings in place, position the large perennials and biennials next, such as hollyhocks (*Alcea* spp.), globe thistles (*Echinops ritro*), fall asters, sunflowers (*Helianthus* spp.), Russian sages (*Perovskia atriplicifolia*), peonies, and Joe-Pye weed (*Eupatorium purpureum*). Follow these with the mid-sized perennials you want to have in the garden. These should include foxgloves (*Digitalis* spp.), tansy (*Tanacetum vulgare*), lupines (*Lupinus* spp.), delphiniums, balloon flowers (*Platycodon grandiflorus*), and asters; and

Bulbs for Southern Gardens

In Southern gardens, tender or semi-hardy bulbs make good accents, especially in a cottage setting. Gardeners from Texas to Florida can have permanent plantings of amaryllis (*Hippeastrum* hybrids), which bloom in spring, late summer, or fall in shades of red, red-orange, pink, or white; magic lilies and red spider lilies (*Lycoris squamigera* and *L. radiata*), which bloom in July or September, in pink, white, or red, depending on species; crinum lilies (*Crinum* spp.), which flower in late spring to late fall in shades of pink and white; and paperwhite narcissus (*Narcissus tazetta*), whose white or yellow flowers open in midwinter.

ums create a cottage garden atmosphere. But there are particular plants that give an untamed cottage garden effect and fill the garden with a cloud-like softness. Baby's-breath (*Gypsophila* spp.), the white-flowered wands of gaura (*Gaura lindheimeri*), blue flax (*Linum perenne*), and the white or violet-pink flowers of boltonia (*Boltonia asteroides*) all give a soft, naturalistic effect.

Plant the lowest-growing border plants last. A common element of most cottage gardens is an edging or low hedge at the front, like a symbolic corset that holds in all the abundance. For the edging, consider perennial violets or pinks, annual pansies, ageratums, or garden nasturtiums (*Tropaeolum majus*), or a hedge of lavenders (*Lavandula* spp.) or thymes (*Thymus* spp.). In front of this, place a few plants to spill out over the path. You can easily experiment with different border combinations from year to year.

Once you have put your basic perennial plantings in place, embellish with annuals, especially in the first year, before the perennials have filled out. Cosmos, snapdragons, flowering tobacco (*Nicotiana alata* 'Grandiflora'), heliotropes (*Heliotropium arborescens*), and cleomes (*Cleome hasslerana*), for example, will give the lush effect you want during the first season. Now you can buy many annuals in 4-inch pots; these will quickly fill in any empty spots. But remember: They, too, can grow very large. Plant them singly or in pairs so

smaller plants such as bellflowers (*Campanula* spp.), astilbes, columbines (*Aquilegia* spp.), phlox (*Phlox* spp.), sweet rocket (*Hesperis matronalis*), common valerian (*Valeriana officinalis*), and lilies (*Lilium* spp.). Consider the height and color of each, always keeping in mind the succession of bloom so that you will have color throughout the growing season.

Old-fashioned flowers such as roses, pinks (*Dianthus* spp.), hollyhocks (*Alcea* spp.), violets (*Viola* spp.), and delphini-

they don't smother the newly planted perennials.

Use annual vines such as morning glories (*Ipomoea* spp.), moonflowers (*Ipomoea alba*), sweet peas (*Lathyrus odoratus*), or nasturtiums to fill in while roses and clematis are getting established. Alternately, plant vines to climb over shrubbery after it finishes flowering or before it starts, to give more continuous color. A perennial sweet autumn clematis (*Clematis maximowicziana*), for example, climbs over a forsythia and through a butterfly bush in Lucie Carlin's garden, illustrated on page 12, and a curly clematis (*Clematis crispa*) flowers in June on the glossy abelia (*Abelia* × *grandiflora*) near our front door, before the abelia begins its own flowering period.

In the fall, plant spring-flowering bulbs between the perennials. It is almost essential to have a graph-paper plan to refer to when you do this, as some perennials die back out of sight. In the following spring, to add a final touch, find space for some Oriental poppies (*Papaver orientale*), autumn crocuses (*Colchicum autumnale*), and bulbs of tuberose (*Polianthes tuberosa*), all of which bloom later in the season.

Long-Blooming Perennials

Besides annuals, there are few plants that can be counted on to give bloom all season. Many perennials bloom for only ten days to two weeks. There are exceptions; the following perennials have an outstandingly long season of bloom. Removing spent flowers regularly encourages any plant to keep blooming.

Achillea filipendulina (fernleaf yarrow): 2–4 feet. Large yellow flower heads during June and July. Zones 3–8.

Achillea millefolium (common yarrow): 18–24 inches. Pink, peach, red, and lilac flowers during June and July. Zones 3–8.

Aster × *frikartii* (Frikart's aster): 18–24 inches. Lilac or blue daisy flowers bloom from midsummer until frost. Zones 4–9.

Campanula carpatica (Carpathian bellflower): 8 inches. Blue or white flowers from midsummer to fall. Zones 3–8.

Dicentra × 'Luxuriant' (bleeding heart): 18–20 inches. Pink flowers from spring until fall. Zones 3–9.

Heuchera sanguinea (coral bells): 1–2 feet. Red, pink, or white flowers on wiry wands from late spring to early summer. Zones 3–9.

Phlox paniculata (garden phlox): 1½–4 feet. Large cone-shaped flower heads of white, lilac, all shades of pink, or deep rose, from mid- to late summer. Zones 3–8.

Scabiosa caucasica (pincushion flower): 2 feet. Lavender-blue or white ruffled flowers from early summer to late autumn. Zones 3–9.

MAINTAINING A CROWDED LOOK

In many respects, a cottage garden is a gardener's garden. It looks casual and abundant, but that doesn't mean that it is unplanned or completely care-free. Cottage gardens are for people who like spending time in a garden and who enjoy doing the work that a lush, beautiful garden entails. Throughout the growing season, it is important to look for space for additional plants, in order to replace those that have finished blooming. This will ensure continual color.

Cut back plants that tend to become invasive, like orange daylilies (*Hemerocallis fulva*) and Siberian iris (*Iris sibirica*), and partially remove them to make room for self-sowing annuals such as cosmos and cleome, or perennials like garden phlox or Joe-Pye weed (*Eupatorium purpureum*), which share the same space but bloom later than lilies and irises. Remove yellowed or rotting foliage of bulbs to make additional space for new plants. As you plant, amend each new planting hole with compost and organic fertilizer to keep the soil rich, and water well before and after the plant goes in.

As conditions become more crowded, prop up or stake plants that stretch out for more light. Use staking to help create a fluid composition, tilting the plant in this or that direction; flowers can be where you want them, blending into clusters of other flowers if you enjoy that look. Tie up vines like wild sweet pea (*Lathyrus latifolius*), honeysuckles (*Lonicera* spp.), clematis (*Clematis* spp.), and climbing roses to trellises, arbors, poles, or trees. For smaller plants, use ordinary garden stakes of bamboo, painted an unobtrusive green. For larger plants and vines, use round plant supports, single-stem supports, linking L-shaped stakes, or tepee-shaped supports, all made of plastic-coated steel. Use green twine or plastic-covered (not paper-covered) wire "twist-ems" to tie plants loosely to the supports.

To keep the garden looking pretty during summer, deadhead such plants as coreopsis (*Coreopsis* spp.), columbines (*Aquilegia* spp.), lupines (*Lupinus* spp.), delphiniums (*Delphinium* spp.), and hollyhocks (*Alcea* spp.). Promptly deadhead

---

Hardy Bulbs

Three hardy bulbs authentic to cottage gardens are the crown imperial (*Fritillaria imperialis*), with crowns of yellow or orange blossoms in spring; poet's daffodil (*Narcissus poeticus*), with white petals surrounding a red-rimmed yellow cup in late spring; and the Madonna lily (*Lilium candidum*), with white flowers in midsummer.

Dividing Perennials

To prolong the life, health, and vigor of your perennials, you must divide them at the proper time. Some perennials, such as bearded iris, must be divided every four to five years to keep the clump producing flowers and to help prevent borers from infesting the rhizomes.

It is easy to tell whether a perennial needs dividing. Here are some signs to look for:

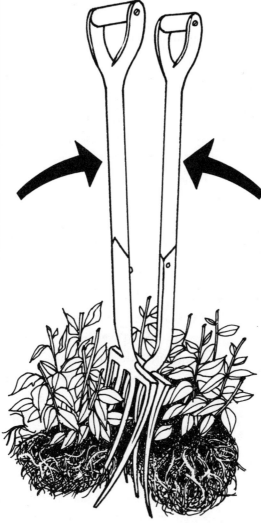

•The inside of the plant clump is dying out, while the plant looks healthy on the outside edges.

•The plant produces few flowers, or the flowers are smaller.

•The plant has outgrown its space or is encroaching on a neighboring plant's territory. Some perennials, such as evening primroses (*Oenothera* spp.) and bee balms (*Monarda* spp.), are vigorous to the point of being invasive. Keep them in check by dividing them on a regular basis.

When dividing perennials, always look for the growing points, called crowns, of the plant you are working on. The crown is where new leaves and stems emerge. Pull the foliage aside to reveal the individual crowns. When dividing a multi-crowned plant, make sure any cuts you make are between the crowns and that each division has at least one healthy, new growing point.

Some perennials require a sharpened spade to properly divide them. Daylilies (*Hemerocallis* spp.) and Siberian iris (*Iris sibirica*) that have been left in the ground for five years or more are examples of this type of plant.

repeat bloomers such as roses and balloon flowers (*Platycodon grandiflorus*). Be careful not to remove the spent flowers and seedpods of self-sowing plants that you always want to have in your garden ~ like cosmos, larkspurs, cleome, love-in-a-mist (*Nigella damascena*), and fennel (*Foeniculum* spp.) ~ or they won't return. I selectively deadhead feverfew (*Chrysanthemum parthenium*), black-eyed Susans (*Rudbeckia hirta*), and coneflowers (*Echinacea purpurea*) in my garden, leaving only a few seed heads to give me a small number of new plants each year. You can do this with any self-sowers if you don't want to be overrun with their seedlings. Pull out annual plants like cornflower (*Centaurea cyanus*) when they have finished blooming, and shake their seeds out into the garden for next year's bloom.

Self-Sowing Plants

Volunteer plants ~ those that are self-sowing ~ are a boon to the cottage gardener. Not only do they save you work and money by sowing themselves, but they contribute to the garden's informal look.

Because of these self-sowers, you should never weed out a plant you can't recognize. Wait until it reaches a size where you can identify it. If in doubt, leave it be. Eventually you will know whether it is a seedling of a garden flower or just a weedy lookalike. If it is a flower,

you don't have to leave it where it came up. For example, larkspur (*Consolida ambigua*), which closely resembles perennial delphinium but is a much smaller plant, may come up next to a delphinium and be overshadowed by the larger, more statuesque plant. Move the larkspur to another location where it is not competing with a larger version of itself.

Sometimes you may have to thin a very dense clump of self-sown seedlings or none of them will produce flowers. Poppy seeds often germinate in a clump in my garden, and if I don't thin them out to one or two plants, I can expect nothing more than a few scraggly, marble-sized blossoms.

To make room for self-sown seedlings, thin out existing foliage whenever you can. Deadhead selectively if you want plants to self-sow, and be sure to leave enough seed pods.

Biennials

Biennials are plants that grow foliage the first year of their lives, die back and go dormant during the winter, then reappear and bloom, set seeds, and finally die the second year. Many favorite old-fashioned cottage garden flowers such as hollyhocks, foxgloves, sweet William (*Dianthus barbatus*), larkspur, and Canterbury bells (*Campanula medium*) are biennials.

Growing biennials is not difficult once you understand their life cycle. Start them from seed in midsummer (June to July), and pot up the seedlings. If they have grown to be good-sized, established plants by fall, transplant the seedlings into their proper places in the garden and mulch well over the winter. If your garden beds are not ready in the fall, or if the biennial seedlings are not established enough to withstand planting out, put them in a cold frame over winter and plant them in the early spring. Plants started in the summer, grown as foliage plants through to fall, and properly overwintered will grow vigorously and bloom the following year in your garden.

Many biennials are vigorous self-sowers. Generally, this is the most common way that they propagate themselves. If self-sown plants are your goal, do not deadhead all of the spent flower stalks on your biennials. Let the seeds ripen and drop to the ground. Weed carefully in that area so as not to disturb the seedlings of your biennials that will sprout up everywhere.

EVENING GARDENS

If you include flowers in your cottage garden that come into their own after dusk, you will gain extra hours of pleasure. Light colors of cream, ivory, and pale yellow, which serve as foils for brighter hues during the day, begin to glow after dusk and are essential to an evening garden.

Better still are the vespertine, or evening, flowers, which withhold their fragrance during the day and release it when the sun goes down, perfuming the air. Plant evening-scented vines to climb a trellis or arbor where you sit, so that they will perfume the night air around you. Honeysuckle, for example, which can look tangled in the daytime, has a breathtaking scent at night; moonflower (*Ipomoea alba*) has pure white morning glory-like blossoms and a spicy, lily-like fragrance.

Some botanical names suggest that flowers are night-scented. *Hesperis matronalis*, commonly called sweet or dame's rocket, is derived from Hesperus, the evening star. *Linnaea borealis*, or twinflower, reminds us of the *Aurora borealis*, the spectacular northern lights.

But there are other familiar flowers which give no clue to their nighttime distinction. Many of the best-known lilies, for example, should always have a place in an evening garden. The Madonna lily (*Lilium candidum*) and the Easter lily (*L. longiflorum* var. *eximium*) both decorate June nights with their glowing whiteness and their strong fragrance. The goldband lily (*L. auratum*) and the regal lily (*L. regale*) give off a spicy scent in July. Formosa lilies (*L. formosanum*) fill the nighttime air with their special perfume in September and October. Some of the daylilies, too, show best at night. Mostly pale yellow and creamy white, they seem misnamed; they should be "nightlilies."

Flowers for Evening Gardens

Night-scented flowers are pollinated by night-flying moths. Often unspectacular in color, such flowers attract the moths after dark with their fragrance, adding to the pleasure to be had in a garden. Here are some fragrant choices for a night garden:

Abronia latifolia (yellow sand verbena): Trailing habit to 10 inches; pale yellow flowers smell of honey; *A. fragrans*, 2 feet; smells of vanilla. Zones 8–10. P/A

Heliotropium arborescens (common heliotrope): 4–6 feet; blue to white flowers, May to September, vanilla fragrance. An annual in the North. Zones 8–10. P/A

Hesperis matronalis (sweet or dame's rocket): 3–4 feet; white to lilac, highly fragrant flowers. Zones 3–8. P S

Ipomoea alba (moonflower): 5 foot climber; pure white flowers; nick seed with a file and soak overnight to encourage germination. Zones 9–10. A S

Lonicera × heckrotti (goldflame honeysuckle): Vigorous vine; heavily perfumed, especially after sunset. Zones 5–9. P

Matthiola longipetala (evening stock): 1–2½ feet; has a cabbagy smell during the day which turns pleasant at night; pale, lilac pink flowers. A S

Mirabilis jalapa (four-o'clock): 2–3 feet; white or yellow flowers open at 4 PM and remain open until daylight the following morning; orange-blossom scent; August to September. Zones 8–10. P/A S

Nicotiana alata (flowering tobacco): 1½–4 feet; white flowers literally shine at dusk, very fragrant; sun or shade. A S

Oenothera biennis, O. caespitosa, and *O. odorata* (evening primroses): 4 feet; yellow, white, or pink flowers open in late afternoon; lemony jasmine fragrance. Zones 4–8. P

Polianthes tuberosa (tuberose): 2–3½ ft.; waxy white flowers with a scent like orange blossoms or hyacinths; start indoors in pots in April and plant out in June, for August to September bloom. Zones 9–10. P/A

Key
A: Annual
P: Perennial
S: Self-sowing
P/A: Tender perennial usually grown as annual

ENCLOSURES, STRUCTURES, AND PATHWAYS

When designing your cottage garden, remember to include the non-plant features on your drawing. Consider the following traditional cottage garden elements to be the "structural bones" of the garden throughout the year, and ideally build or install them before you start to plant.

Hedges, stone walls, lattices, and fences give a feeling of intimacy, keep animals out, and provide supports for plants to climb. Picket fences are most commonly used to create a "cottage" effect. Use arbors, trellises, benches, swings, or statu-

Three Trellis Designs

Attached to a wall or fence or freestanding at the back of a border, a simple wood trellis contributes added height to a cottage garden design. Plant climbers such as white field roses (*Rosa arvensis*), honeysuckles (*Lonicera caprifolium* and *L. periclymenum*), white summer-flowering clematis (*Clematis vitalba*), or one of the vines listed in "Vines" on page 154 to clamber over them.

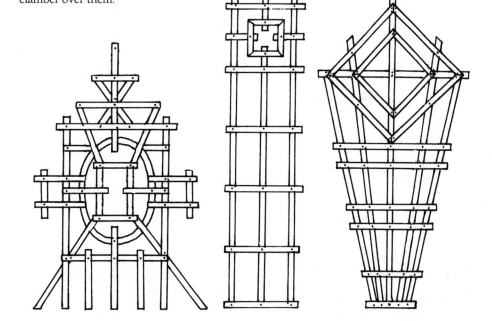

ary as focal points or destinations; these may also serve as homes for vines.

Make paths meander, leading from flowerbed to flowerbed or to a seat, a bird bath, or some other special focal point. A path can take you around the corner to a surprise, or deep into a lushly planted area of tall plants, so that you feel secluded or completely alone.

Because a cottage garden is informal by nature, pathways should be made of infor-mal, natural materials like stone or brick rather than concrete, asphalt, or railroad ties. The main path could be gravel over landscape fabric, edged with brick, flag-stone, or wood to keep the gravel from traveling; or it could be patterned brick or flagstones placed in stone dust, with spaces left between for "pathway" plants like mother-of-thyme (*Thymus serpyllum*), maiden pink (*Dianthus deltoides*), dwarf yarrow (*Achillea millefolium* 'Rosea'), or

Corsican mint (*Mentha requienii*). These low-growing plants will spill out onto the pathway in places, softening the overall look and giving off pleasant fragrances when they are stepped on.

If you want plants to come through the path here and there, set a few stones in sand or set flat fieldstones right into the grass. Bear in mind that plants growing in a pathway or grass growing around stepping stones have to be trimmed from time to time, since the most important role of a path is to give access. Equally informal is a path of stepping "stones," such as decorative wooden rounds placed on gravel or randomly-shaped concrete paving blocks, textured to look like wood or stone.

Once the structures are in place, prepare the soil by double digging (see "How to Double Dig a Garden" on page 69). Because cottage garden plants tend to be crowded, provide them with a deeply cultivated bed in which their roots can reach down easily for nutrients and moisture. After the digging is completed, let the soil rest while you have a soil test done. Add the recommended amounts of organic soil amendments, such as rock phosphate, greensand, granite dust, dehydrated manure, or fish meal, and plenty of compost. Then install the plants you've chosen, according to your garden plan. Once your garden is established, each time you add a new plant, put some compost in the planting hole and water thoroughly.

COTTAGE GARDEN POTPOURRI

In days of old, baths were few and cleaning agents rare. The Magi brought gifts of frankincense and myrrh, sweet incense derived from trees that grow even today in

---

Three Scented Favorites

A ROSE BOWL

1 cup each of rosebuds and patchouli leaves
1 teaspoon orris root
2 drops rose oil

Toss gently to mix the ingredients.

ROSE WATER

Fill a saucepan with red rose petals and cover with water.

Bring to a boil; lower heat and simmer for 15 minutes.

Let cool with lid on pan. Strain into glass jars.

WOODSTOVE-TOP AIR FRESHENER

Mix one pint rose water and a pinch of powdered cloves in a pan on top of a hot woodstove to fill the air with the fragrance of fresh garden roses. Feel free to adjust these proportions to achieve the fragrance you want.

India, Somalia, and Ethiopia, because incense was as valuable as gold, and its sweet smell an appropriate gift for a newborn king. With the availability of flowers and herbs from cottage gardens, strewing these throughout the house was a less expensive way to offset bad smells than to purchase incense from distant lands. When the fresh supply was out of season, bowls of potpourri could dull the nastiness of stale, household smells.

Potpourri is a French word meaning "fragrant pot" or "rotted pot." The latter refers to moist potpourri, where the petals and leaves are preserved with salt and take on a brown, unappealing "rotten" look. Although moist potpourri smells more flowery and lasts longer, its homely appearance is usually concealed in opaque jars with perforated covers. Dry potpourri mixes are muted versions of flower garden color and fragrance. They are pretty enough to keep in open bowls around the house.

The flowers typically found in cottage gardens are perfectly suited to potpourris: old-fashioned roses, hollyhocks (*Alcea* spp.), lavenders (*Lavandula* spp.), carna-

---

How to Make Potpourri

On a bright morning, after the dew has dried but before the sun is too hot, cut flowers just after they open; remove any bruised or brown petals.

If your flowers are very small, dry them whole; otherwise separate the petals. Lay them in a dimly lit room in a single layer on a window screen propped up on bricks or the backs of two chairs, or on any drying rack that permits good air circulation. It will take from two days to two weeks for the flowers to dry.

If the humidity is high, you may have to finish the drying process in the oven, set at its lowest temperature. Leave the oven door ajar so moisture can escape during drying, and turn the flowers gently with a spatula.

The faster the flowers dry, the more color they will retain. The best way to preserve the color of whole flowers picked just at their prime is to dry them in powdered silica gel, which can be found at florists and garden centers.

When they are dry, store the petals of different flowers in separate jars, clearly labeled. (Dried flowers all tend to look alike.)

When you are ready to make potpourri, mix the dried flowers and petals gently in a glass or ceramic bowl with fixative, oils, and spices, using your hands or a wooden spoon. The proportions of a potpourri are a matter of taste, but a good general rule of thumb is to use 1 cup of dried flower petals to 1 teaspoon each of fixative and spices, and 1 or 2 drops of fragrant oil.

tions (*Dianthus caryophyllus*), jasmines (*Jasminum* spp.), peonies (*Paeonia* spp.), and the leaves of some scented geraniums (*Pelargonium* spp.).

Of all the flowers used in potpourris, roses and lavenders retain their fragrance and color best. Shrub or heritage roses, including the moss rose (*Rosa centifolia* 'Muscosa'), the damask rose (*R. damascena*), and the tea rose (*R. odorata*), are the most fragrant.

A bowl of these flowers or their dried petals still needs the help of a fixative, some spices, and fragrant oils to bring out the scent; these are available at many garden centers. Fixatives, derived from plants and animals, seal in the flower oils and prevent their evaporation. The most common of the plant-derived fixatives is orris root, which comes from orris (*Iris × germanica* var. *florentina*) rhizomes and has a light violet scent.

You can use the strong, pleasant odors of familiar spices ~ cloves, nutmeg, cinnamon, and ginger ~ and those of sweet flag (*Acorus calamus*) and allspice berries (*Pimenta dioica*), or dried lemon, orange, and lime rinds to enhance the less pungent flower fragrances in potpourri mixtures. A few drops of fragrant oils pressed from fresh roses, violets, carnations, and jasmine will replace the fragrance lost in the drying process.

COUNTRY BORDERS

 Country borders bring to mind many gardens I have seen, and many more that I have imagined: two straight beds overflowing with color, bordering a grass pathway, and leading the eye to a view of distant hills, a water view, or a gazebo.

Because it is contained within a defined linear space, there is more organization to a border than to a cottage garden. A border is often the best solution if you want a country look but don't have a lot of room. You can space plants according to size and color, and keep them staked and trimmed as necessary to always look their best. Borders are considered more formal than cottage gardens, but formality is not an end in itself. In fact, there is no hard-and-fast rule that says you must conform to previous concepts when it comes to creating any kind of a garden, particularly a border. The parameters are wide and your taste dictates the form, function, and plant materials used.

Plants earn a place in a border because of how they look and behave, rather than how useful they are to the household. Place them for their color impact, so that their shape or height will enhance an overall pattern, repeating drifts of the same plant at intervals, to give a sense of continuity and order. Leave sufficient space between clumps or drifts of flowers to let them to spread to their full size. As the plants fill out, patches of color will blend into one another in the manner of an Impressionist painting.

In the borders she designed, Gertrude Jekyll worked to create a tapestry effect with color. In midsummer she would "drop in" potted plants in full bloom, which she had in reserve for just this purpose, to add color where she felt it was needed. Weeds and "volunteer" seedlings were quickly banished because the space had already been earmarked for intentional plants and not for uninvited upstarts. The effect was full but not crowded. The color scheme was a choice rather than chance juxtapositions of color as in a cottage garden *mélange*.

If you will be viewing the border year-round, include evergreen shrubs or shrubs whose branches are colorful or otherwise distinctive in a winter landscape, and fill it out with perennial and annual flowers for the warmer months. If you want to hide a work area or busy driveway next door, or provide privacy without building an unfriendly or costly wall or fence, use taller shrubs and dramatic ornamental grasses in the border. Some shrubs that grow 9 feet or taller include the bottle-brush buckeye (*Aesculus parviflora*), doublefile viburnum (*Viburnum plicatum* var. *tomentosum*), forsythias (*Forsythia* spp.), crape myrtle (*Lagerstroemia indica*),

and witch hazel (*Hamamelis virginiana*). Ravenna grass (*Erianthus ravennae*) and moor grass (*Molinia caerulea*) also grow to 9 feet or more, while various types of Japanese silver grass (*Miscanthus* spp.) fill in spaces 4 to 6 feet high.

HOW TO DESIGN A COUNTRY BORDER

To design your country border, first mark its outline on the ground, using stakes and string or a garden hose so that you can alter its shape if necessary. The outside edge of the border does not have to be straight. It can curve to conform to the space needs of the plantings, but its contours should flow with other curves in the yard. Curved edges are less formal than straight, but no matter what the shape, the overall effect should be one that invites the viewer to stop and look.

Leave your markers in place and look at the design from an upstairs window, from places inside the house where you most frequently sit, and from your deck or places in the yard from which you will be viewing the border most often, to make sure that it is the shape and size you want and that the proportions are right. A lengthwise view will give more color impact than a border viewed from the front.

If you will generally view your border from the front, it is probably better to make it deeper. A 3-foot-deep border is the minimum, and such a border will

---

Seasons of Bloom

When planning almost any type of garden, draw up a monthly chart and indicate on it the time when each plant will be in bloom. Using this chart, you can prolong interest in the garden throughout the season and make sure you have something to draw attention at all times.

In a small garden, for example, a focal color grouping for June might consist of blue delphiniums, yellow coreopsis, and white pinks. If your border is large enough, repeat this color grouping in two or three other places. Since the rest of the garden is mostly foliage at this time, the observer's eye will be drawn to the colorful focal point.

---

depend heavily on annuals for continuous color. If it is twice that depth, you have the room to add more color from perennials in a seasonal succession and create a layered effect using short, medium, and tall plants such as ornamental grasses, tall shrubs, or small trees. As a general rule of thumb, the tallest plant should be about one-half the depth of the bed.

Mark which parts of the border are in sun and which are in shade. Once you are sure the boundaries are right and you know there is sufficient sun to grow the plants you like, measure the dimensions and make a scale drawing on graph paper. Mark fixed elements such as paths, walls, or fences first on the drawing. These should be installed before any planting is done.

A backdrop, such as a wall, fence, or trellis, gives a border structure, establishes its rear boundary, and makes the border easier to maintain (and to design) than a freestanding bed, which must be presentable from all sides at all times.

The backdrop to my first border remains my favorite: a row of pear trees espaliered onto a simple fence, 6 feet tall, which separated the garden from an orchard beyond. The pear trees put on a show of delicate bloom each spring, and after blooming, their branches leafed out and hid the wooden fence supporting them. As the trees matured, their branches became the fence. At the end of each summer the trees were heavy with fruit. We had to prune the trees every two months during the growing season to maintain their fence shape, but that was a chore that my husband and I both enjoyed. The overall effect was charming and unusual, and well worth the extra work.

Always include an access pathway along the back of the bed, wide enough to accommodate a wheelbarrow if possible, so that plants can be tended from the rear as well as the front. If your border is more than 6 feet wide, place stepping stones strategically in the bed itself so you can stand comfortably to do your staking, deadheading, and maintenance. In a very wide border you will need a path running along the midsection of the border, or several small access paths of stepping stones that lead to the center of the bed.

Flower borders running along either side of a pathway do not always have a backdrop. For example, a pathway to the front door, flanked by borders, can offer the nicest kind of country welcome, and it gives the gardener pleasure with each coming and going.

If you want deciduous or evergreen shrubs or small trees in the border for year-round interest, mark them on your drawing and plant them before you begin planting perennial flowers. Many popular border shrubs, such as prickly blue-gray junipers (*Juniperus* spp.) laden with smoky blue berries, or glossy-leaved, red-berried hollies (*Ilex* spp.), are at their best in winter. The furry, unopened buds of star magnolia (*Magnolia stellata*), for example, make a subtle statement that something is alive in the winter landscape, just as its white flowers in earliest spring brighten the still drab-looking border with a promise of

more to come. Scarlet to pink fall leaf color and the bare, winged bark of the burning bush (*Euonymus alata*) after its leaves have fallen are interesting to look at when the rest of the landscape is bare. The twisted, corkscrewlike branches of Harry Lauder's walking stick (*Corylus avellana* 'Contorta') and its pendulous catkins really show up when there is snow on the ground.

Design the herbaceous plantings next, allowing at least 1½ square feet per plant, and more for large perennials (like peonies, which need 3 square feet). Do this on paper first, with the help of garden catalogs and a good reference book (see "Recommended Reading" on page 251). As with a cottage garden, perennial plants form the skeletal structure of the border. Once they are in place, flesh out the garden with annuals and bulbs.

Group plants of one kind together in clusters of three or five to enhance their impact and prevent the design from appearing too "jumpy," making sure you allow space for these plants at maturity. Make a season-of-bloom chart (see "Seasons of Bloom" on page 148), including any existing plants as well as those you know you want to add month by month.

CHOOSING PLANTS FOR A BORDER

To create drama and liven things up, use bold architectural plants with strong vertical or horizontal planes. Try using a striking shape as a focal point. Biennial angelica (*Angelica archangelica*), which resembles a gigantic celery plant, reaches a height of 5 feet when it blooms every other year, and the shape of the plant and its blossoms are so dramatic in my garden that my eye is drawn irresistibly to it.

Pay particular attention to the foliage, as good foliage is truly the anchor of a good border. Plants like peonies and astilbes, with handsome foliage that lasts long after their flowers have faded, make the border look full. Lady's-mantle (*Alchemilla mollis*), hostas, pinks (*Dianthus* spp.), and ornamental grasses also have foliage that can stand alone.

Plants have vertical, horizontal, or rounded forms; they can be billowy or have straplike foliage. Generally, plants with opposite characteristics complement each other and should be planted together, while those with similar habits and foliage diminish one another. Siberian iris (*Iris sibirica*) and daylilies (*Hemerocallis* spp.), both of which have rushlike leaves, for example, look very unimpressive side by side, while daylilies with round-leaved Shasta daisies (*Chrysanthemum × superbum*) tend to bring out the best in each other.

Ornamental grasses are finding their way into borders because of their dramatic effect and naturalistic look. They also have low maintenance requirements and are tolerant of dry spells, which makes them an environmentally sound choice as well. Grasses (see "Ornamental Grasses" on page 153) such as maiden grass (*Miscanthus sinensis* 'Gracillimus'), fountain grasses (*Pennisetum* spp.), and reed grasses (*Calamagrostis* spp.), fill in the spaces left by those perennials that die back after bloom. Poppies (*Papaver* spp.), columbines (*Aquilegia* spp.), and Jacob's ladders (*Polemonium* spp.) have foliage that dies back soon after the bloom period has passed, and you should alternate these plants with grasses or other plants that retain their foliage.

Consider the colors you want to have in your border. Beware of a garden that is all pastel or monochromatic, because it can easily be boring. Add a very rich shade of color, like the purple 'Hella Lacy' aster (*Aster novae-angliae* 'Hella Lacy'), to a pastel grouping of lavender Russian sage (*Perovskia atriplicifolia*), Frikart's aster (*Aster × frikartii*), white boltonia (*Boltonia asteroides*), pink butterfly bush (*Buddleia alternifolia*), and the pink rose, 'The Fairy'. Use color in drifts and in soft, flowing curves, rather than in a grid, weaving different colored drifts together. The larger the border, the bigger or longer the drifts can be, and the more they can be repeated.

When plant colors are discordant or their characteristics are too similar, use silver-foliaged plants to soften the flow between colors. Pinks, lavender cotton, rue, ornamental grasses, or any of several artemisias ~ silver mound, 'Silver King', or 'Powis Castle' ~ all work well in this buffering role.

The final embellishments are annuals and bulbs, which go in between the perennial plants. Plan your bulb design by using a tracing paper overlay on top of your scale drawing. Plant spring-flowering bulbs in fall and summer-flowering bulbs in spring. The spring bulbs will provide color and reach their peak long before the perennial plants have filled out their space, and summer-flowering bulbs can usually make their way up through the perennial foliage.

Add annuals as fillers during the first year or two ~ impatiens, alyssum, ageratums, pansies, snapdragons, salvias, heliotropes, zinnias, stocks (*Matthiola* spp.), or any other favorites. Annuals furnish color all season, while most perennials bloom for only a few weeks.

A DESIGN FOR A COUNTRY BORDER

In Nancy DuBrule's design for a country border on page 152, the fixed elements include an access path along the back of the 6-foot-wide border and a backdrop of a stone wall with a flowering shrub border behind it. The stone wall stands out against the shrubs, and they add extra color to the garden.

Nancy uses foliage plants to add substance to the border all season. Candytuft (*Iberis sempervirens*) and peonies (*Paeonia* spp.), used symmetrically in the border, are foliage "anchors" that stay green throughout the season. Two silver-leaved beach wormwoods (*Artemisia stellerana*) are placed symmetrically in the front of the border, and 'Powis Castle' artemisia sits in the middle of the bed just behind a 'Palace Purple' heuchera, all of which have outstanding foliage that remains colorful and in good condition all summer.

Fountain grass (*Pennisetum alopecuroides*) and cushion spurge (*Euphorbia epithymoides*) both have lasting foliage, and the combination of the dainty leaves of the *Dianthus plumarius* 'Old Spice' with the bearded iris behind it (at the right front of the border) balances the candytuft, spurge, and Siberian iris (*Iris sibirica*) on the left. The two gold-and-silver chrysanthemums (*Chrysanthemum pacificum*) at each end of the garden feature outstanding variegated foliage. While they do have yellow button flowers in fall, similar to tansy's, they are most striking for their leaves' silver edging and backing.

Two spaces have been left open for annuals such as blue salvia, zinnias, or snapdragons. Different color groupings of plants that bloom at the same time draw the eye to various spots: peach-leaved bellflower (*Campanula persicifolia*) and 'Coronation Gold' yarrow in the very center of the border; 'Morden Pink' loosestrife (*Lythrum virgatum* 'Morden

Pink'), Frikart's aster (*Aster* × *frikartii*), and 'Russian Violet' phlox with 'Moonbeam' coreopsis (*Coreopsis verticillata* 'Moonbeam') close by in the left section of the border.

Peonies and red valerian (*Centranthus ruber*), and a little farther down, Siberian irises and delphiniums, all bloom together in the right-hand section. Certain plants that appear later have been placed next to early plants that die back to their basal foliage. 'Powis Castle' artemisia and white boltonia (*Boltonia asteroides*), for instance, will hide the faded delphiniums, and annuals will fill in around the peach-leaved bellflower.

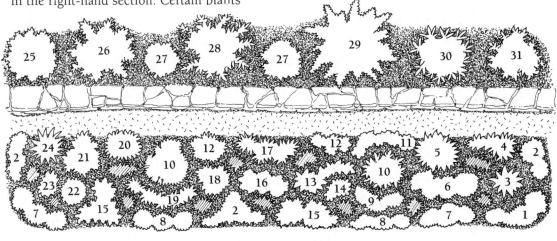

Scale

10 feet

A Country Border

1. *Dianthus* 'Old Spice' (pinks) 2. *Chrysanthemum pacificum* (gold and silver chrysanthemum) 3. *Iris* bearded hybrids (German iris) 4. *Phlox paniculata* 'Russian Velvet' (garden phlox) 5. *Lythrum virgatum* 'Morden Pink' (loosestrife) 6. *Aster* × *frikartii* (Frikart's aster) 7. *Iberis sempervirens* (candytuft) 8. *Artemisia stellerana* (beach wormwood) 9. *Coreopsis verticillata* 'Moonbeam' (coreopsis) 10. *Paeonia* cv. (peony) 11. *Thalictrum rochebrunianum* (meadow rue) 12. Assorted annuals 13. *Anemone hybrida* (white Japanese anemone) 14. *Sedum* × 'Autumn Joy' (sedum) 15. *Heuchera micrantha* 'Palace Purple' (heuchera) 16. *Achillea* × 'Coronation Gold' (gold yarrow) 17. *Campanula persicifolia* (peach-leaved bellflower) 18. *Pennisetum alopecuroides* (Chinese fountain grass) 19. *Centranthus ruber* (red valerian) 20. *Boltonia asteroides* (white boltonia) 21. *Delphinium* × *elatum* (blue delphinium) 22. *Artemisia* × 'Powis Castle' (artemisia) 23. *Euphorbia epithymoides* (cushion spurge) 24. *Iris sibirica* (Siberian iris) 25. *Abelia* × *grandifolia* (abelia) 26. *Chaenomeles speciosa* (quince) 27. *Rosa rubrifolia* (redleaf rose) 28. *Buddleia davidii* (purple buddleia) 29. *Spiraea prunifolia* (bridalwreath spiraea) 30. *Rhododendron mucronulatum* (Korean rhododendron) 31. *Rosa* 'Betty Prior' (rose)

Ornamental Grasses

GIANT-SIZED

Arundo donax (giant reed): Grows 15–20 feet. Bamboolike form creates airy screen. Tolerates moist soil. Needs full sun and good drainage. Zones 6–10. P

Cortaderia selloana (pampas grass): Grows to 4 feet. Bears immense white plumes that reach 12 feet. Needs full sun and good drainage. Zones 8–10. P

Miscanthus floridulus (giant Chinese silver grass): Grows 8–9 feet. With frost, turns peach-colored. Cascading ribbonlike foliage. Blooms in September. Prefers sun. Zones 4–9. P

Miscanthus sinensis (Japanese silver grass): Grows 4–8 feet. Silky red florets open in mid-August. Effective as a screen from June to February. Prefers sun. Zones 5–9. P

Miscanthus sinensis var. *strictus* (porcupine grass): Grows to 4 feet. Bright green with yellow horizontal bands. Prefers moist, fertile soil in full sun. Zones 4–9. P

MEDIUM-SIZED

Calamagrostis acutiflora 'Stricta' (feather reed grass): Grows to 5 feet. Flower plumes appear in June. Very robust. Needs full sun. Zones 5–9. P

Miscanthus sinensis 'Purpurascens' (flame grass): Grows to 3–4 feet. Broad, dark green blades. In fall, it turns brilliant red-orange. Thrives in full sun. Zone 5–6. P

Molinia caerulea subsp. *arundinacea* 'Windspiel' (windplay tall moor grass): Height varies depending on conditions. Long flower stalks appear in July. Zones 5–9. P

Panicum virgatum (switch grass): Grows 5–6 feet. Apple green. Blooms in August. Tolerates a variety of soils and situations. Zones 5–9. P

Pennisetum alopecuroides (fountain grass): Grows 2–3 feet. Blooms in July with pinkish flower remaining on plants until December. Cascading foliage. Especially effective in sunny areas. Zones 5–9. P

Spartina pectinata 'Aureomarginata' (golden-edged prairie cord grass): Grows to 4 feet. Bright green in summer and clear yellow in fall. Coarse, leathery plant. Tolerates sun and light shade, moist or dry conditions. Zones 4–9. P

SMALL

Carex buchananii (leather leaf sedge): Grows to 2 feet. Cinnamon bronze color all year. Blooms in June. Best in moist soil in full sun. Zones 7–9. P

Carex morrowii 'Variegata' (silver variegated Japanese sedge): Grows to 1 foot. Flowers form in March. Needs shade. Zones 5–9. P

Carex muskingumensis (palm sedge): Grows 2–3 feet. Effective from June until winter. Grows in light or full shade. Zones 4–9. P

Elymus arenarius (European dune grass or lyme grass): Grows to 2 feet. Blooms in late June. Spreads easily for beach plantings. Tolerates light shade and full sun. Zones 4–10. P

Imperata cylindrica 'Red Baron' (Japanese blood grass): Grows to 18 inches. Slow rhizomatous habit. Prefers half to full shade. Zones 6–9. P

Key
P: Perennial

Vines

Vines add a new dimension to cottage gardens. When choosing a perennial vine, be sure to understand the pruning techniques for that particular plant because they often determine whether a plant will blossom profusely. Also, learn about the vigor and mature size of the climbing plant and be sure to install a proper trellis, arbor, or pergola. Many of the vines listed below are very vigorous and need strong support in a permanent installation. Consider mixing different vines together on the same trellis, or growing vines up and through deciduous or evergreen shrubs, for added color in your garden.

ANNUAL VINES

Ipomoea tricolor (morning glory): Flowers are blue, white, rose pink, bicolor, opening in the morning and closing in the heat of the day. Fast-growing and vigorous.

Lathyrus odoratus (sweet pea): Blue-green foliage and fragrant pink, white, or lavender blossoms that make good cut flowers. Blooms best in cool weather.

Phaseolus coccineus (scarlet runner bean): Vigorous vine with bright red flowers and edible young bean pods.

Tropaeolum majus (garden nasturtium): Trailing types of nasturtium will climb fences, trellises, or other supports. Edible flowers in bright carnival colors; the foliage is also edible.

PERENNIAL VINES

Campsis radicans (trumpet vine): A summer-blooming vine with orange flowers (a yellow cultivar is *C. radicans* 'Flava'). Provide a strong support for this fast-growing vine. Zones 4–10.

Clematis spp. (clematis): There are hundreds of cultivars of clematis. The large-flowered types bloom in spring, summer, and fall and are available in almost every color. The small-flowering types are summer- or fall-bloomers and include sweet autumn clematis (*C. maximowicziana*), which is covered with star-shaped, fragrant white flowers in late summer and fall, and virgin's bower (*C. virginiana*), which blooms all summer. Both add an airy touch to the garden. Zones 3–10.

Lonicera spp. (honeysuckles): Fragrant white, pink, yellow, or red flowers, blooming all summer. *L.* × *heckrottii* (goldflame honeysuckle) has pink flowers with yellow throats. *L. sempervirens* 'Dropmore Scarlet' (trumpet honeysuckle) has brilliant red-orange flowers that attract hummingbirds. Zones 5–10, depending on species.

Rosa spp. (climbing roses): Climbing roses are the mainstay of the old-fashioned cottage garden. They come in almost every color and many are quite fragrant. Some types bloom only in early summer, but newer hybrids bloom all summer and fall. Zones 3–10, depending on species.

Wisteria spp. (wisterias): Fragrant hanging clusters of purple or white flowers in late spring. Vines are very vigorous. Chinese wisteria (*W. sinensis*) is fragrant and is more frequently planted than Japanese wisteria (*W. floribunda*), which is slightly hardier (to Zone 4) than the Chinese species. Zones 5–8.

Chapter Four

Country Herb Gardens

 One of the easiest ways to give your garden a country look is to grow herbs among your other plants. Wherever they are planted, herbs evoke a time when the garden was a rich source of flavorings, fragrances, medicines, cosmetics, teas, dyes, and ornaments for the home. You can interplant culinary herbs in the vegetable patch, for example, or tuck fragrant or medicinal herbs into a sunny border among the perennials.

Generally, herbs are tougher than other garden plants. Many originated in rough Mediterranean surroundings like Provence, in the south of France, where marjoram, oregano, thyme, and lavender grow on the dry, rocky hillsides. If they have plenty of sunshine and a well-drained soil with a pH above 6.5, most perennial herbs will survive year after year with little attention. Annual herbs, once established, withstand drought and insect attacks better than most

vegetables and flowers. In fact, the hotter and drier the weather, the stronger the taste and smell of herbs, and the concentrated aromatic oils make them more repellent to most insect pests. This alone makes herbs easier to grow, especially if you are using organic methods of insect control.

Whatever its size, shape, or composition, an herb garden is a place for growing useful plants in a decorative way. In fact, the usefulness of the plants is probably the most obvious difference between an herb garden and all other types of ornamental gardens. The Herb Society of America defines an herb as "a useful plant." Sal Gilbertie, owner of Gilbertie's Herb Nursery in Westport, Connecticut, elaborates on this useful definition: "A soft-stemmed plant grown for its fragrance or flavor, or for its value to health and beauty." Very often, herbs are further separated into five categories: culinary, medicinal, historical, dyeing, and fragrant or cosmetic.

Besides the many uses of the plants themselves, there are other benefits to gardening with herbs. It takes less time to establish an herb garden. Many herbs are prolific growers and, because they are less often disturbed by insects or diseases, they can fill out a garden in just one season, unlike a perennial border, which usually takes two or three years to become established and fill the same area. Such quick results are very satisfying, especially if you are starting a new garden.

Because most herbs are so resilient, they are less demanding on our resources. In parts of the country where conserving water is advisable, replacing a grass lawn with an herbal lawn results in real energy savings. Low-growing mother-of-thyme (*Thymus serpyllum*) will cover a sun-baked site that has infertile soil, where grass might have to be fussed over with irrigation, herbicides, and fertilizer to grow at all.

HERB LORE

Herbs have been important to human beings throughout history. People gathered them from the wild to fill everyday needs and to figure in traditional ceremonies and holiday celebrations. Over 4,000 years ago, the ancient Egyptians and Chinese had herbal schools where the various medicinal properties and uses of herbs were taught. The Greek philosophers, physicians, and astronomers knew about herbs; "to smell the thyme" was an expression used in Greece to describe an elegant literary style.

One of the earliest existing illustrated herbals was written by Dioscorides, an army doctor in the Roman legion in the first century AD. He recorded the healing qualities of over 500 plants in *De Materia Medica*, which herbal historians still study today. Benedictine monks who cared for the sick with decoctions of plants from their own gardens have also left us herbals. These books contain much information about the varied ways they used herbs. Tansy (*Tanacetum vulgare*), for instance, was used as a tonic and a sedative, to keep flies away, to stop meat from going bad, and ~ because it represented eternal life ~ to embalm the dead.

Old sayings have passed down through generations about almost every herb:

- Where rosemary flourishes, the lady rules.

- Stuff mugwort into your pillow to have dreams that reveal your future.

- Lovage root in the bath water will make you more lovable.

- A decoction of valerian root will restore domestic harmony.

- Trefoil, vervain, St.-John's-wort, dill hinder witches of their will.

- A sprig of thyme and a sprig of rosemary, one in each shoe, promises a girl that she will dream of her beloved.

A Simple Raised Herb Garden

Growing herbs in a raised bed has several advantages. First, it ensures the good drainage that most herbs require. Second, it brings the plants, many of which are fragrant, closer to garden visitors. And finally, a raised bed creates an architectural feature; it's an easy way to add interest to a flat garden.

You can construct a simple raised bed and fill it in a weekend. Allow the soil to settle for at least five days, and by the following weekend it will be ready to plant.

A U-shaped bed with walls about 1½ feet high works well because it gives you easy access to the entire planting area and is more interesting than a simple rectangle. A U-shaped bed made on an 8-foot-square plot with a 2-foot-wide, 4-foot-long central path will give you 56 square feet of planting area. That's plenty of room to grow a wide range of culinary herbs, with space left over for a few flowers and perhaps a small birdbath, sundial, or statue. Mother-of-thyme (*Thymus serpyllum*) planted near the perimeter to spill over the sides will make a delightfully fragrant edging.

Construct the bed using 4-by-4 posts at corners and every 3 to 4 feet as needed along the sides. Attach a plywood "membrane" to the interior perimeter of the bed to keep the exterior boards from popping off from the weight of the soil, and to protect the exterior from decay. Use rot-resistant cedar boards, attached horizontally, for the exterior. Cap these double walls with more cedar boards to keep rainwater from seeping between the wall layers. Miter the corners to make them look finished.

Turn over the soil and fill the bed to the top with a mixture of topsoil, sand, and leaf mold in equal parts, plus soil amendments as indicated by a pH test. Filling the bed is a lot easier if you construct a ramp so you can roll your wheelbarrow or garden cart right up to the top of the bed to empty it of soil. A second person on hand to steady the wheelbarrow is a great help.

In the central path, lay down landscape fabric as a weed barrier and top it with 2 inches of pea gravel to make a care-free walkway. Add a few strategically placed chairs near your herb garden, and it will be a delightful place to take morning coffee while you watch the garden awaken, or to sit with a friend in the afternoon, sharing tea and conversation.

DESIGNING AN HERB GARDEN

Visually, an herb garden, with its foliage shades of green, gray, blue-green, variegated white and green, purple, and gold, is engaging and subtle. It often invites an ordered, though not necessarily formal, layout that weaves and blends these colors and textures into a pleasing tapestry. You can create a formal herb garden with a country look simply by laying an old ladder on the ground and planting herbs in between the rungs.

Or you can make a garden as complex as a butterfly design, with one wing of culinary herbs and the other of fragrant herbs, each outlined in a low clipped herb, such as germander (*Teucrium chamaedrys*) or lavender (*Lavandula* spp.). You might plant the "spots" on the butterfly's wings with herbal tea plants, such as agrimony (*Agrimonia eupatoria*), chamomile (*Chamaemelum nobile*), and pennyroyal (*Mentha pulegium*).

If this is your first herb garden, keep the lines simple; don't try an elaborate design until you know more about herbs and how much attention they require. A small herb garden, about 100 square feet, can hold all the cooking and decorative herbs that you could want, and still leave room for other backyard plants.

Make sure the size of your herb garden is in scale with the rest of the landscape elements. The plants you choose should also be in scale with the space allotted to them. A 6-foot-tall angelica (*Angelica archangelica*) in bloom would overwhelm a 6 by 6-foot garden, but a potted bay tree (*Laurus nobilis*) could be clipped and kept in scale.

If your herb garden is a freestanding bed, place the larger plants at the center and the smaller plants towards the front, making sure that the bed looks attractive from all sides. Similarly, keep a freestanding garden of more than one bed balanced by including herbs of varying heights in all sections of the garden.

As a general rule, place several plants of the same herb together. Mixing lots of different individual plants creates a jumbled, busy appearance, whereas planting in masses produces a more cohesive design.

Because of the limited palette of herbs, any colors other than green, gray-green, or yellow-green have a powerful impact in an herb garden. A deep red, old-fashioned rose among gray and silvery foliage plants, or a white rose in a garden of blue and lavender sages is an eye-catching accent (see "Six Roses for Herb Gardens" on page 166).

If your garden has a particular theme, position it on your property accordingly. Put a fragrant garden beneath the windows of a room you use often, for example, or next to a frequently used path or patio where its scents can be appreci-

Nine Herbs for a Cook's Garden

All good cooks want to have fresh herbs right outside their kitchen door, available for picking when they're needed. The following herbs make up a basic collection of culinary herbs that cooks find indispensable. All can be either dried or frozen for later use.

PERENNIALS

Common chives (*Allium schoenoprasum*): To 18 inches. Harvest foliage by snipping leaves with scissors; blossoms also edible. Full sun and well-drained soil. Zones 3–9.

Garlic (*Allium sativum*): To 2 feet. Plant cloves of garlic in fall; harvest in summer after flowering, when leaves droop over and begin to die; lift bulbs and dry with tops attached in a warm, dark, well-ventilated location. When dry, trim roots and foliage. Replant more individual cloves each fall. Full sun. Zones 3–9.

Oregano (*Origanum vulgare* subsp. *hirtum*, also called *O. heracleoticum*): To 18 inches. Harvest leaves in summer; flowers appear in mid- to late summer. Will grow in any soil; vigorous and invasive. Full sun or partial shade. Zones 3–10.

Rosemary (*Rosmarinus officinalis*): Grows 2–4 feet. Harvest no more than one-third of the plant at a time. Tender perennial. To over-winter north of Zone 7, plant in a clay pot, sink it into the garden in summer, then bring indoors in winter. If a white mold (powdery mildew) appears on foliage, increase air circulation and spray weekly with a baking soda solution (2 tbsp. per gallon of water). Full sun. Zones 7–10.

Sage (*Salvia officinalis*): To 30 inches. Harvest leaves throughout the growing season; don't cut back too hard after the end of August. Sage forms a woody sub-shrub; shear each spring by about one-third to encourage new growth. Full sun and well-drained soil. Zones 3–9.

Thyme (*Thymus vulgaris*): To 8 inches. Harvest as needed throughout the growing season, taking up to one-half of the plant before flowering. Shear each spring by one-third to encourage new growth and prevent matting of foliage. Full sun and well-drained soil. Zones 3–9.

ANNUALS AND BIENNIALS

Start the following herbs from seed, or purchase plants:

Basil (*Ocimum basilicum*): Grows 1–4 feet, depending on the cultivar. Harvest foliage as needed. Do not put plants out in the garden until all danger of frost is past and soil has warmed up. Pinch out the first flowers to encourage the plant to branch out and become bushy. Basil needs full sun and warm temperatures.

Dill (*Anethum graveolens*): Grows 2–5 feet. Goes to seed easily in hot weather. Harvest foliage as needed. If growing dill for foliage, grow 'Dukat' dill, remove flowers as they form, and sow a fresh crop every 2–4 weeks during the growing season. For dill seed, allow flowers and seeds to form. Dill self-sows easily. Full sun.

Parsley (*Petroselinum crispum*): To 18 inches. Plant seedlings or sow seed directly into garden in early spring. Harvest as needed. Will tolerate most soils. Flat-leaved (or Italian) parsley (*P. crispum* var. *neapolitanum*) has more flavor; curly-leaved parsley (*P. crispum* var. *crispum*) is more decorative. Plants can tolerate light frost. Full sun or partial shade.

ated. Site a culinary garden near the kitchen door for the convenience of the cook. If the shape is interesting, such as a knot garden, place the garden where it can be seen from a higher level ~ from inside the house or a raised patio or deck.

Before you start planting, design the shape of the garden on graph paper. Use a scale of 1 inch = 1 foot and place the plants on your graph-paper design. As a general rule, symmetry equals formality, while asymmetry gives a more informal "country" look. If the garden is to be formal, allow enough space for the plants to be separate from one another when full-grown. In an informal garden the plants can be more crowded, blending together and blurring the outlines of the garden. In either case, make the paths at least 3 feet wide to allow you to kneel comfortably while clipping and trimming the edges, to allow a wheelbarrow in for easy maintenance, and to permit visitors to enjoy the plants at close range.

At this planning stage, gather all the data you can find on your chosen plants: the overall size, description, cultural requirements, time of bloom (if significant), and folklore about the herbs if that is what attracts you to them. Make a season of bloom chart (see page 148) on a large sheet of paper. Group plants with similar cultural requirements together, such as those requiring extra lime (lavender and thyme), or those that grow best in shade (sweet woodruff, lovage, sweet cicely).

In another list, organize your plants according to their foliage color: silver-gray, green-gray, blue-green, dark green, yellow-green, bronze, purple, or variegated. On your plan, group plants with the same foliage color together for a subtle, harmonious effect. In a small area, such as among the paving stones of a patio, you can create this effect very simply by planting four different thymes to form a soft, low carpet.

If you want a symmetrical design, divide your garden into identical beds and repeat the same color groupings in each bed, with the same or with different herbs. You could mix gray silver mound artemisia (*Artemisia schmidtiana*), gray-green woolly thyme (*Thymus pseudolanuginosus*), blue-green rue (*Ruta graveolens*), and dark bronze perilla (*Perilla frutescens* 'Atropurpurea' or 'Crispa') together in one bed; and gray-lavender cotton (*Santolina chamaecyparissus*), gray-green common thyme (*T. vulgaris*), blue-green chives (*Allium schoenoprasum*), and purple-leafed basil (*Ocimum bacilicum* 'Dark Opal' or 'Purple Ruffles') in another.

When you have completed your design on paper, transfer it to the garden site and mark its outline with stakes and string, or draw it directly onto the ground with powdered lime or white flour. After you've prepared the soil, but before putting in plants, install any permanent elements, such as board frames for raised beds, brick or stone paths, fencing, or a hedge.

Consider which herbs are invasive and need to be contained, like mint, which overwhelms most other plants. Contain these plants by sinking boards 10 inches into the ground around them, or grow them in containers like large clay pots or wooden half-barrels. Balance such containers with thymes, sages, or basils grouped together in similar wooden or clay planters. Herbs seem to thrive in pots, provided they are diligently watered.

HOW TO GROW HERBS

Well-drained soil, near-neutral pH, and eight hours of sun are ideal conditions for growing herbs. Too little sun produces leggy, less flavorful herbs. Acid soils with a pH of less than 5.0 will need lime. If so, apply it several weeks before you intend to plant, to give it time to work (see "Adjusting the pH of Your Soil" on page 175). Remove stones from the soil during digging, and add 6 inches of compost (as well as lime and any other amendments as indicated in a soil test), before planting.

If you want to improve drainage, build beds for your herbs (see "A Simple Raised Herb Garden" on page 157).

Planting

The easiest way to start an herb garden is to buy all the plants in pots. If you don't live near an herb grower or garden center, you can grow most herbs from seed (seed packets are also less expensive than plants). Sow seed directly in the ground at the time indicated on the seed-packet directions, to a depth equal to roughly three times their thickness. Cover the bed with a thin layer of sand, and firm the surface down with your hand or a board. Keep the bed damp with a misting spray until seeds germinate and seedlings are growing vigorously. (Young herbs need plenty of water, but once established, they can tolerate drought conditions.)

Since many herb seeds are slow to germinate, cover the soil very lightly with salt hay or burlap to avoid a washout during heavy rain, and to keep the soil moist between waterings. Do not sow an entire packet of seed all at once ~ it will give you more herbs of one kind than you need. Save some, and if a storm washes out the first planting, you will be able to start over again.

For parsley, dill, and summer savory, make "mini-greenhouses." Cut a half-gallon milk carton in half lengthwise (rinse it first with a mild bleach solution). Fill it three-quarters full with potting soil, sprinkle seeds evenly over the surface, and cover them with a thin layer of sharp sand (the kind used in a child's sandbox, available in garden centers or hardware stores). Sink the cartons halfway into the ground and cover with a plastic wrap secured with a rubber band.

Once the seedlings have sprouted and have one set of true leaves, remove the plastic. Then, thin the seedlings to well-spaced individual plants (3 to 4 inches apart) or small clumps of four to five plants, each spaced 6 inches apart. You may also transplant seedlings from this mini-greenhouse directly into the garden as soon as the weather permits. The benefit of this method is that you produce sturdy seedlings that are already hardened off to the early spring cold. It really speeds up the process and allows you to establish these herbs in your garden much sooner.

French tarragon seeds are sterile, and the flavors of horseradish, oregano, and mint will be variable from seed. So buy these herbs from a garden center or ask for divisions of established plants from a friend. Divide them by digging up the plant in spring and then pulling or cutting the roots apart into separate plants.

Sage, rosemary, and bay will grow from seed, but it is far easier to grow them from cuttings. Cut a 3- to 4-inch sprig of new growth from an established plant with a clean knife, strip any leaves or branches from the lower third of the cutting, and poke the bottom into a pot filled with a moist mixture of sharp sand and peat in equal amounts. Mist the cuttings each day, and water before the medium gets too dry. After two weeks, pull on the cutting very gently to see if there are any roots beginning to sprout. Once roots are established, harden off the cuttings and plant them.

Some seeds are finicky or unpredictable. Sweet woodruff (*Galium odoratum*), for example, can take up to a year to germinate. And, once you've grown dill (*Anethum graveolens*) in your garden, it self-sows when and where it wants, often appearing where you least expect it.

As a general rule, sow biennial herbs in late summer to allow the plants to become established and be ready to bloom the following year. If you sow a biennial like parsley in spring, however, you can pick its foliage until frost kills it back. The following spring, the parsley will put up new foliage and flower stalks. Once it flowers, parsley becomes bitter. If seed is set, the plant will dry out and die, and you can collect the seed to start a whole new generation of plants or allow it to self-sow.

Maintenance

Many herbs are slow growers as seedlings, so keep your herb bed weeded in the beginning to allow plants to grow without too much competition. Once established, most herbs like to be dry (though not dried out), so don't be too quick to water them. Do not use a thick mulch, as it will keep the soil too moist and promote fungal diseases. For aesthetic purposes, a light covering of buckwheat or cocoa bean hulls is good.

Herbs with Ornamental Foliage

Artemisia or wormwood (*Artemisia* spp.): Beautiful silver foliage. Needs full sun and well-drained soil. Non-invasive types for herb gardens include: *A.* × 'Powis Castle', 2½–3 feet, finely cut, aromatic silver foliage, Zones 6–10; silvermound artemisia, *A. schmidtiana*, 15–18 inches tall, lacy silver foliage, and a mounding habit; *A. stellerana* 'Silver Brocade', 1–2 feet tall, broad, felted silver foliage, spreads slowly along the ground and makes a good edging plant. Zones 3–8. P

Blessed or sacred thistle (*Cnicus benedictus):* 2 feet tall with leaves 2–3 feet wide. Spiny, broad basal leaves veined with white. Flowers are purple thistles borne on 3- to 4-inch stalks in late summer. B

Culinary sage (*Salvia officinalis).* 12–30 inches. Has attractive pebbly gray-green foliage. Full sun and excellent drainage. Zones 3–9. P

Golden feverfew (*Chrysanthemum parthenium* 'Aureum'): 12–20 inches. Lacy golden foliage and small white daisy flowers all summer long. Short-lived, but self-sows readily. Zones 3–9. P

Golden oregano (*Origanum vulgare* 'Aureum'): 12–18 inches. Golden yellow foliage. Needs sun or partial shade and average soil. Zones 3–10. P

Lavender cotton (*Santolina chamaecyparissus):* 12–18 inches. Silver-gray foliage forms a low shrub with yellow button flowers in midsummer. Full sun. Zones 5–8. P

Purple basil (*Ocimum basilicum* 'Purple Ruffles', 'Dark Opal'): 18–24 inches. Dark purple leaves, same spicy taste as green-leaved basil. Full sun. A

Rue (*Ruta graveolens):* 2 feet. Bright blue-green, finely divided, rounded foliage forms compact bushes. Full sun. Zones 4–9. P

Thymes (*Thymus* spp.): 3–15 inches, depending on the species or cultivar. *T.* × *citriodorus* 'Aureus Variegatus' (golden variegated lemon thyme): 8 to 10 inches. Bears green leaves edged with gold. *T.* × *citriodorus* 'Argenteus' (silver thyme): 8–10 inches. Bears green leaves edged silver. Silver thyme is slightly more tender than most thymes and needs protection north of Zone 6. *T. pseudolanuginosus* (woolly thyme): 3–5 inches. Bears soft, woolly gray-green foliage. All need full sun and sandy soil. Zones 3–9. P

Variegated calamint (*Calamintha grandiflora* 'Variegata'): 2 feet. Green leaves with cream markings; small pink flowers all summer. Full sun and good drainage. Zones 3–9. P

White-leaved everlasting (*Helichrysum angustifolium):* 2–4 feet. Silver foliage, when crushed, smells strongly of curry. Zones 8–10. Tender P

Key
A: Annual
B: Biennial
P: Perennial

The time to mulch herbs for the winter is in the late fall. After three successive nights below freezing, cut back the dead stalks and cover the garden with a mulch of salt hay. Remove the hay the following spring in early April.

INVASIVE HERBS

You may be surprised at how quickly some herbs grow. In fact, a plant that may begin the first year as your great gardening success story can return to haunt you in following years as an invasive plant threatening to take over your garden! Many people think that invasive is good: "It will be easy to grow, and I'll get lots of free plants." But with invasive herbs, it's easy to have too much of a good thing.

With aggressive self-sowers, such as borage (*Borago officinalis*), lemon balm (*Melissa officinalis*), or garlic chives (*Allium tuberosum*), cut off their flowers or thin them before they go to seed. But if they are perennials, it is not always a simple matter of dividing these plants when the time comes. Many members of the mint family, including mint, bee balm, catnip, and lemon balm, will resprout vigorously from even a tiny piece of root or creeping stem left in the ground. Once established, you may never be able to remove all of it from the garden.

Other invasive herbs include artemisias, sweet woodruff (*Galium officinalis*), and horseradish (*Armoracia rusticana*).

A SIMPLE HERB GARDEN DESIGN

You can easily adapt Nancy DuBrule's design for a backdoor kitchen herb garden to your own landscape (see plan on opposite page). It has all the classic herb garden features: pathways, sectioned beds, tender perennial herbs (rosemary, scented geraniums) in clay pots to sink into the garden in summer and bring inside in winter, and a barrel to contain the invasive mint.

FLOWERS FOR THE HERB GARDEN

The herb garden is an ideal place to grow flowers, because the grays, greens, and blues of the herb foliage and their often unobtrusive blossoms make a perfect backdrop for bold, bright colors as well as pastels. Poppies (*Papaver* spp.) are good choices for an herb garden ~ the orientals' fuzzy, toothed leaves look herblike, and their brilliantly colored tissue-paper flowers seem to glow against the subtle foliage colors of the herbs. Annual poppies to grow with herbs are the corn poppy (*P. rhoeas*) and the related Shirley poppies. California poppies (*Eschscholzia californica*) also mix nicely with herbs and like the same hot, sunny conditions.

Other flowers that look good with herbs include hollyhocks (*Alcea* spp.), especially the old-fashioned tall, single ones (still available from a few seed catalogs); pansies

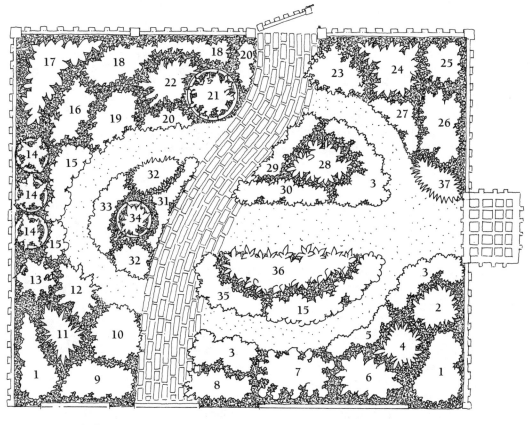

Scale

6 feet

N

1. Dill (*Anethum graveolens*)
2. Perilla (*Perilla frutescens*)
3. Curly parsley (*Petroselinum crispum* var. *crispum*) 4. Gray sage (*Salvia leucophylla*) 5. Silver thyme (*Thymus × citriodorus* 'Argenteus') 6. Borage (*Borago officinalis*) 7. Arugula (*Eruca vesicaria* var. *sativa*) 8. Tansy (*Tanacetum vulgare*) 9. Italian parsley (*Petroselinum crispum* var. *neapolitanum*) 10. 'Lemon Gem' marigold (*Tagetes signata*) 11. Egyptian topping onions (*Allium cepa*) 12.

Chervil (*Anthriscus cerefolium*)
13. Peppermint geranium (*Pelargonium tomentosum*) 14. Rosemary (*Rosmarinus officinalis*) (sunk in pots) 15. Nasturtiums (*Tropaeolum majus*) 16. 'Dark Opal' basil (*Ocimum basilicum* 'Dark Opal') 17. Fennel (*Foeniculum vulgare*) 18. *Monarda didyma* (red bee balm) 19. Greek oregano (*Origanum vulgare*) 20. Roman chamomile (*Chamaemelum nobile*) 21. Mint (*Mentha* spp.) (in barrel) 22. Tarragon (*Artemisia dracunculus*) 23. Lemon scented geranium (*Pelargonium crispum*) (sunk in pots) 24. Pineapple sage (*Salvia*

elegans) 25. Lovage (*Levisticum officinale*) 26. Coriander (*Coriandrum sativum*) 27. Salad cress (*Barbarea verna*) 28. Golden variegated sage (*Salvia officinalis* 'Aurea') 29. German chamomile (*Matricaria recutita*) 30. Golden oregano (*Origanum vulgare* 'Aureus') 31. Salad burnet (*Poterium sanguisorba*) 32. Chives (*Allium schoenoprasum*) 33. Golden thyme (*Thymus × citriodorus* 'Aureus') 34. Bay (*Laurus nobilis*) (sunk in pot) 35. Culinary thyme (*Thymus vulgaris*) 36. Basil (*Ocimum basilicum*) 37. Garlic chives (*Allium tuberosum*)

Six Roses for Herb Gardens

Roses pair well with herbs. Like herbs, they prefer full sun and warm temperatures. The foliage of many herbs, particularly gray foliage, is a pleasing backdrop that shows off rose blossoms like the jewels they are. Here are half a dozen roses to include in an herb garden:

SPECIES ROSES

Rosa gallica (French rose) has a well-earned place in the herb garden. Its variety, the apothecary's rose (*Rosa gallica* var. *officinalis*), is an ancient plant; its petals were used medicinally (hence the epithet *officinalis*). The fragrant scarlet flowers are 2½ inches wide, with showy gold stamens forming a sunburst at the centers. Hardy to Zone 4.

Rosa rugosa (rugosa rose) is unusually carefree. Handsome bright green wrinkled foliage that turns red in fall is characteristic of this group. These hardy and sturdy shrubs bloom repeatedly throughout the summer. Of the many rugosa cultivars, two of the best are 'Blanc Double de Coubert', with white double flowers and showy large, round, bright red-orange hips, and 'Roseraie de l'Haÿ' (sometimes listed as 'Rose à Parfum de l'Haÿ'), with deep pinkish red flowers that are highly fragrant. Hardy to Zone 3.

SINGLE ROSES

'Comte de Chambord' is a Portland rose that forms a compact 4-foot-tall plant and bears fragrant pink double flowers produced repeatedly throughout the summer. Hardy to Zone 4.

'Constance Spry' is a "pillar" rose ~ essentially a large shrub rose whose stems are too relaxed to stand up on their own. Position it where you can tie its 8-foot stems to a fence, trellis, or post. Its large, scented flowers are a deep pink. Hardy to Zone 4.

'The Fairy', a polyantha rose, produces abundant sprays of small, double flowers all season long on a 2-foot-tall upright shrub, until frost ends the gardening year. Its blossoms are a delightful medium pink, just the right color to display in a vase with velvety lamb's-ears or artemisia. Hardy to Zone 4.

and violas, which also have edible flowers; cheery, bright yellow-flowered coreopsis (*Coreopsis* spp.); daylilies, especially cultivars with simple, smooth-edged blossoms (these are edible, too); and Shasta daisies (*Chrysanthemum* × *superbum*). Lamb's-ears (*Stachys byzantina*) looks very "herby", as does Russian sage (*Perovskia atriplicifolia*),

named for its foliage, which has a sagelike smell.

The rounded, sometimes sprawling forms of the hardy geraniums (*Geranium* spp.) seem made for the herb garden, and the flowers ~ from white through pastel pink to vivid carmine and purple ~ are especially attractive surrounded by herbs.

Mountain bluet (*Centaurea montana*) and coneflowers (*Rudbeckia* spp.) have cheerful, informal flowers that are particularly well-suited to an herb garden. Pinks (*Dianthus* spp.) are an obvious choice, with their mats of spiky, gray-green foliage and clove-scented flowers.

Bearded iris are splendid in the herb garden ~ they like the loose, gritty, lean soil and hot sun that most herbs need, and their bold, swordlike leaves make a good foil for the billowing, lacy foliage of many herbs, keeping the herb garden from looking too rumpled. Foxgloves (*Digitalis* spp.) are another good choice, as are the sweet-smelling annual white flowering tobaccos (*Nicotiana* spp.); the tall flower spikes of both plants add much-needed spire shapes to the herb garden. Woody plants that make good backdrops for the herb garden are fragrant Carolina allspice (*Calycanthus floridus*) and dwarf fruit trees ~ potted fruit trees have been featured in herb gardens throughout history.

HARVESTING AND PRESERVING HERBS

Harvesting and preserving herbs makes it possible to enjoy the flavors and beauty of the garden year round. For culinary uses, you can dry, freeze, or combine herbs with vinegar, mustard seed, salt, or sugar. For teas and herbal medicines, air-dry or freeze herbs.

Decorative Seedpods

Don't overlook the decorative value of seedpods in the garden. The following herbs have decorative seedpods: fennel (*Foeniculum vulgare*), sweet cicely (*Myrrhis odorata*), teasels (*Dipsacus* spp.), garlic chives (*Allium tuberosum*), sages (*Salvia* spp.), oreganos (*Origanum* spp.), artemisia 'Silver King' and 'Silver Queen' (*Artemisia ludoviciana* 'Silver King' and 'Silver Queen'), safflower (*Carthamus tinctorius*), sweet wormwood or sweet annie (*Artemisia annua*), and basil (*Ocimum basilicum*).

Drying

If you are harvesting your herbs for drying, you can cut up to three-quarters of the stems from the plant. Choose a sunny morning after the dew has dried. Wash off clinging soil, and dry herbs by rolling them in a clean towel. For the brightest foliage color, use the refrigerator-drying method: Rinse the freshly picked herbs, wrap them in paper towels, and store them in the refrigerator for a day. Then strip the leaves from the stems and return them to their paper-towel wrapping and the refrigerator. After ten days, the herb leaves will be dry and green.

Pesto

Basil pesto is the best-known of various herb pestos or "pastes" used in Italian cooking on pasta, salads, and even vegetables, or stirred into soups. Try using sage, parsley, or oregano instead of basil.

½ cup olive oil
1 tablespoon pine nuts or walnuts
1–2 cloves garlic, minced
2 cups tightly packed fresh basil
    leaves
Parmesan cheese, to taste

Blend oil, nuts, and garlic in a food processor for 30 seconds. Add basil leaves and blend until smooth. Freeze in half-pint container. For use in smaller quantities, freeze in ice cube tray, then take cubes out of tray after they are frozen and store in a plastic bag in freezer. Thaw as needed. Add grated parmesan cheese to the pesto sauce just before serving.

For larger quantities, tie herbs in small bunches and hang in a dark but well-ventilated place. I use the fan in our dark, dry attic to keep the air circulating when I am drying herbs and flowers. This technique, called air-drying, is particularly well-suited for herbs that were grown in dry, sandy soil and have little moisture in their leaves or flower petals. It also works well with long-stemmed, small-leaved herbs like marjoram, sage, savory, mint, and oregano.

If herbs have fine, tiny stems and foliage, tying them into bunches can be a tedious, impractical chore. Instead, it is easier, quicker, and much more efficient to dry them on a screen. Screen-drying is also practical for large-leaved herbs that would mat together and rot if hung in bunches, such as lamb's-ears (*Stachys byzantina*) or lovage (*Levisticum officinale*). To screen-dry herbs, strip the leaves from the stems and place them on a fine-mesh screen. You can make a drying screen yourself by tacking nylon hardware cloth to an old picture or window screen frame. Set the screen on bricks or stacks of books so that air can circulate beneath as well as over it. Thyme, parsley, chervil, lovage, and rosemary dry well on a screen, as do small flowers.

The shorter the drying time, the more color and flavor is retained. For this reason, pick herbs on dry rather than humid days; and use a fan, if necessary, to circulate air. As a last resort, finish the drying process in a 150 to 200°F oven. In any case, it is important to remove every last bit of moisture so that the leaves are dry and crumbly to keep molds from forming on the dried herbs.

Freezing

Frozen herbs retain much of their taste

for several months, and you can use them in soups, stews, and sauces. Wash freshly cut sprigs of basil, dill, thyme, or any other herb that you'd like to have on hand, and dry by rolling them in a clean dish towel. Put 2 cups of sprigs in a pint-sized plastic freezer bag.

Frozen herbs lose their bright color, but the flavor of frozen basil, for example, is much stronger than that of dried basil, and if you use it within six months, it is almost as good in a tomato sauce as the fresh herb. Freeze pesto sauce (see recipe on opposite page) for use throughout the year.

Frozen chopped chives or parsley lose little color, and can be used as garnishes on cooked food. I always keep a plastic container of these herbs in the freezer to add a last-minute touch of green to rice, soup, or any anemic-looking winter fare. Blend frozen mint in a blender with vinegar and sugar and simmer briefly for a mint sauce to serve with lamb. Sprinkle chopped sprigs of dill, still frozen, over potato salad, omelettes, and frittatas ~ the taste is considerably more pronounced than that of dried dill.

CULINARY USES OF HERBS

Herbs, fresh or dried, are essential to a good cook. Fresh herbs are not as intense as dried and should be used in larger quantities in a recipe. The French are masters at using herbs in their cuisine, and

Herb Mustard

The following is Martha Paul's basic recipe for a simple herb-flavored Dijon-style mustard.

2 cups dry white wine
1 large onion, chopped
4 cloves garlic, minced
1 cup dry mustard
3½ tablespoons honey
1 tablespoon light vegetable oil
2 teaspoons salt
2 tablespoons dried herbs of your choice, such as tarragon, rosemary, lemon thyme, or herbes de Provence (a mixture of thyme, rosemary, lavender, and savory)

Combine the wine, onion, and garlic in a saucepan and heat to a boil. Simmer for 5 minutes. Remove from heat, allow to cool and strain; discard strained solids. Add dry mustard and stir until smooth. Add honey, oil, and salt and return to heat. Heat slowly until the mixture is thickened, stirring constantly (keep your face turned away from the steam). Cool in a covered bowl. Once the mixture is cool, stir in dried herbs. Allow the mustard to age for at least two weeks. Do not refrigerate, as this tends to slow the flavoring process. Makes 2 cups.

French cooking has introduced several terms connected with herbs, here are definitions of the most common:

Bouquet garni: An assortment of fresh herbs tied in a bunch and added to a simmering stew or soup until the desired flavor is achieved. You may use a tablespoon of dried herbs tied in a square of cheesecloth to make a small bundle in the same way. Bay leaf, thyme, parsley, and chervil are traditional bouquet garni herbs (using chervil instead of parsley is distinctively French), but you may add other herbs to taste.

Court bouillon: A fish stock made of fish bones and heads, seasoned with bouquet garni and a dash of tarragon vinegar.

Fines herbes: A combination of one herb from each of the mint, onion, and parsley families, finely chopped, and either used as a fresh garnish or mixed in as a last-minute seasoning.

Herbes de Provence: An aromatic blend of varying composition, but usually including dried thyme, rosemary, lavender, and savory. Used in marinades and grilling.

Marinade: A sauce of wine or wine vinegar, herbs, salt, and pepper used for flavoring and tenderizing meat.

Ravigote: A mixture of tarragon, chervil, chives, and burnet mixed with a vinaigrette salad dressing.

How to Make Herb Teas

A cup of herb tea is a healthy pick-me-up or quiet-me-down. Any kind of mint tea is said to soothe an upset stomach. Rosemary tea, made with ginger and honey, is said to improve the mind and strengthen the memory. Chamomile tea, made from the flowers only, is soothing and good for digestion.

You can use fresh or dried herbs to make herb tea. To make tea with fresh herbs such as mint or lemon verbena, strip the leaves off three or four sprigs (about 4 tablespoons) and put them into a 2-cup teapot. Fill the pot with boiling water and allow it to steep for at least 10 minutes. (It may take longer to achieve the desired taste, or you may have to add more leaves to the pot next time if you like a stronger flavor.)

For winter teas made with dried herbs, pick the herbs in summer and dry them thoroughly, leaving the foliage on the stems. Strip off the dry leaves and store in glass jars out of sunlight. Check the jars after a day to see that no moisture has collected on the inside of the jar. (Moisture causes mildew ~ if you can see moisture in the jar, you'll have to compost the herbs.) Since dried herbs tend to look alike, be sure to label the jars. Try mixing two or more of the dried herbs to make your own special blend. For a tea, use 1 tablespoon of dried herbs to 1 cup of boiling water.

Sun tea is perhaps the simplest herb tea to make, and a refreshing beverage to have on hand in the garden as you work. Start by filling a glass jug with a gallon of cold water. Add 2 cups of fresh peppermint, spearmint, orange mint, or apple mint leaves and flowers to the jug and put it in direct sun for at least four hours. The longer it stays in the sun, the stronger it will get. Then serve with ice and fresh sprigs of mint. To vary the taste, mix chamomile flowers, scented geranium leaves ~ especially peppermint-scented geranium (*Pelargonium tomentosum*), lemon-scented geranium (*P. crispum*), or lime-scented geranium (*P.* × *nervosum*) ~ and rose petals with the mint.

Use bee balm (*Monarda didyma*) to make Oswego tea, a fragrant beverage that originated with the Oswego Indians, who used it medicinally to cure sore throats and colds.

USING HERBS IN
THE HOUSE

It is sometimes difficult to separate facts about herbs from the folklore that has grown up around them, but we do know they can be safely used in the home in many ways that are practical and decorative. While southernwood (*Artemisia abrotanum*) under the mattress may not always evoke the sensual passion sought by believers in folklore, it does repel moths from woolen garments when placed in cloth bags in the closet or drawer.

Herbs offer some benign alternatives to a number of household products. Try using southernwood instead of napthene mothballs. Instead of cans of flea powder for pets, use fresh sprigs of winter

How to Make
Herbal
Sachets

Sachets are small fabric pouches or envelopes filled with mixtures of crushed, dried flower petals. As a child I made sachets with my grandmother, using lavender from her garden and scraps of muslin, batiste, or handkerchief linen. I cut out two identical pieces of cloth and sewed their right sides together, leaving a small opening. Then I turned them inside out and stuffed them with cotton, added a heaping teaspoon of powdered lavender to the cotton, and sewed up the opening. Today you can buy fragrant dried flower petals and orris root powder fixative from herb shops, health food stores, or specialty garden catalogs like Nichols (see "Sources" on page 248).

Make fragrant moth-repellent bags of southernwood (*Artemisia abrotanum*), mint, rosemary, or lavender. Use any thin fabric like gingham or muslin. Cut a 10-inch square of fabric and put 6 tablespoons of crushed, dried herb in the center. Gather up the corners and tie the fabric together over the herbs with thin ribbon or string. Suspend the bag in the closet with your linens or woolens to keep away the moths.

How to Make Pomanders

In ancient times, pomander balls were beautiful spice cases made of precious gold, silver, china, or ivory, and decorated with jewels. They were worn on a chain around the neck or waist. Today, we use pomanders, made with apples, oranges, lemons, or limes, less to perfume the person and more to freshen the air of a room.

To make a pomander ball, select unblemished fruit with a firm, thick skin and no soft spots. Stud the fruit evenly and closely with cloves. (It helps to use an ice pick or toothpick to make holes for the cloves before pushing them into citrus fruits.) When the fruit is completely covered, roll it in a mixture of equal parts of orris root, cinnamon, cloves, and nutmeg. You will need roughly 2 tablespoons of the spice mixture to coat each fruit.

Turn the fruit each day until, after several weeks, it shrinks and becomes dry and light. Attach a star anise on the bottom of the fruit with a straight pin. Tie the pomanders with satin ribbon to hang in closets, or put several in an open bowl alone or on a bed of dried lavender to give fragrance to a room.

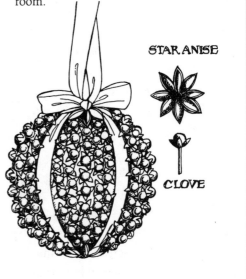

STAR ANISE

CLOVE

savory in the pet's pillow for the same result. A clove of garlic in a dog's food is said to prevent worms.

Potpourris and pomanders made of oranges studded with cloves and fixed with orris root (which has a spicy fragrance) keep rooms and closets pleasant-smelling during winter ~ a good alternative to spray deodorizers. Sachets of lemon-scented geranium or lavender will perfume a linen closet or a drawer of lingerie.

Chapter Five
Edible Landscaping

 What speaks more explicitly of "country" than a vegetable garden planted inside a morning glory-covered fence, with a flowering fruit tree at each corner?

Whether vegetables are grown in separate beds or with the flowers, an edible landscape offers a great opportunity for various personal statements. Both a single garden bed and an entire yard landscaped with edibles qualify as "edible landscapes." If you can't decide between flowers and food, why not grow both?

For almost half a century, the average American has grown only a few tomatoes at home, because fruits and vegetables can be so easily and inexpensively purchased. While the front yard may be the sunniest place available for a garden, few people dig it up and plant vegetables and flowers like the English cottager. Only during World War II, when "victory gardens" were a practical expression of patriotism, did a

high percentage of Americans grow food in their yards or in neighborhood plots.

By contrast, edible landscapes are found in less-developed countries the world over, where a living larder of food, conveniently grown just outside the door, is a necessity. These gardens are self-sustaining systems that have evolved over centuries. They supply rural households with most of their basic dietary needs, as well as materials for building and for making cooking utensils, baskets, mats, hats, and much more, right outside the front door. These edible landscapes are utilitarian and culturally distinctive, and their effect on our natural resources is minimal.

As part of her strong belief in "landscaping for a small planet," Rosalind Creasy wrote *The Complete Book of Edible Landscaping*, a book that explains how to plan a mixed garden of flowers and vegetables. A typical Creasy design is an imaginative mix of flowers, herbs, and vegetables. It could include feathery asparagus fern foliage (*Asparagus officinalis*) and tall red okra (*Abelmoschus esculentus* 'Red Giant') at the back. In front of this backdrop, there could be red-stemmed 'Rhubarb' chard (*Beta vulgaris*), peppers, bush cucumbers, and zucchini. Butterfly weed (*Asclepias tuberosa*), black-eyed Susans (*Rudbeckia hirta*), marigolds (*Tagetes* spp.), phlox (*Phlox* spp.), and lobelias (*Lobelia* spp.) might intermingle with the vegetables and herbs ~ basil, chamomile, chives, and thyme. The color range is yellow, orange, and light blue, with accents of red, but the look is very different from a perennial flower border.

An edible landscape, such as one of Creasy's designs, imitates the diversity found in nature; and like nature, it has checks and balances that help minimize the use of pesticides and herbicides. John Jeavons' book *How To Grow More Vegetables Than You Ever Thought Possible on Less Land Than You Can Imagine* explains the merits of the balanced ecosystem that is an edible landscape, where pests and predators coexist because the favorite food of each is there. As long as each plant is given the proper niche, it will thrive.

One plant's shadow, for example, is another's shade. Lettuce thrives in the shade of pea vines in the heat of late June. Broccoli sown in late July for fall eating survives the summer heat in the shadows cast by staked tomatoes. If the soil is healthy, the plants will be, too, but just to make sure, Jeavons suggests planting a little extra for the insects.

Some assistance can be had from predators. A tiny house wren will pick off 500 plant-eating caterpillars to feed her young in just one afternoon, and a northern oriole can eat 17 hairy caterpillars in a minute. The best insect balancer of all is the diversity of plants. If we are the "gentle shepherds" (Jeavons' words) who provide the right conditions for plant growth, the rest of the ecosystem falls into place.

PLANNING YOUR EDIBLE LANDSCAPE

Before planting, take measurements of your yard and draw its outline on paper. Include your house, any outbuildings like a garage or tool shed, significant trees and shrubs, and driveway and parking areas. I usually eyeball measurements for any small projects in our yard because it takes less time; but with larger projects, or if you are starting from scratch, make a scale drawing to be sure the results will be what you want.

If your yard is in some shade, note where the sun is at 9 AM, noon, 3 PM, and 5 PM. You need at least six hours of sun to grow most vegetables successfully, and while there are flowers that bloom even in deep shade, less than six hours of sun will limit your choices considerably. The sun is farthest north from the southern horizon on the summer solstice, June 21, the longest day of the year. It is lowest on the horizon on December 21, the shortest day. If you know where the sun shines in your yard on each of these days, you can approximate where the sun will be during the rest of the year.

Maybe you want to put your garden against a hedge or fence, far from the house and safe from intrusion by human activity; or perhaps you want it right next to a patio where it can be enjoyed. Having the drawing on paper will help you figure out how to use the space most attractively and efficiently. It will also enable you to measure the square footage of the garden so you can estimate fertilizer requirements and how many plants will be needed to fill the space. My first garden measured 25 by 30 feet, and I found that 750 square feet allowed me the space I needed without overwhelming me with work. If you have never had a garden before, begin with a 4 by 25-foot bed. With carefully planned successions, 15 different vegetables can be grown in this 100-square-foot plot, with space left for a few flowers as well.

If you are interested primarily in growing vegetables, include disease resistance among your criteria in making selections, as well as space requirements, days to maturity, and taste. All cucumbers may look the same, for instance, but those that resist wilt will not collapse in the middle of the summer from a disease transmitted by the striped cucumber beetle. The number of days to maturity from sowing the

Adjusting the pH of Your Soil

Soil should be tested to determine its pH, that is, to what degree it is acid or alkaline. A pH of 7.0 is neutral; above that number is alkaline soil and below it is considered acid soil. Most vegetables and flowers grow best in soil with a pH of 6.0 to 7.0.

In acid soils, adding lime is necessary in order to grow many perennials and vegetables. The best kinds of lime to use are dolomitic (containing magnesium) or ground limestone.

Caution: Do not apply lime at the same time as cow manure ~ the combination causes nitrogen to be released from the manure as ammonia gas, depleting this valuable plant nutrient.

To raise the pH one unit, use lime at the rate of 5 pounds per 100 square feet.

The fastest way to lower the pH of alkaline soil is with sulfur. A treatment once every two months is sufficient; be sure to follow instructions carefully.

To lower the pH one-half to one unit, use elemental sulfur at the rate of $\frac{1}{2}$ pound per 100 square feet.

seed or setting out seedlings is the key to making good selections. Mix early-, mid-, and late-season cultivars of peas, carrots, and lettuce so that they don't come all at once.

If you want unusual cultivars that are not available locally, start your own from seed, using an overhead fluorescent light over a basement table or a portable two- or three-tiered table with built-in lighting, available from garden supply centers or garden equipment catalogs. Otherwise, order those seeds that may be planted directly in the garden (such as beans, squash, carrots, beets, spinach, and other leafy greens) and buy seedlings of tender or cool-weather plants from a local garden supply store. If you buy tender plants (such as tomatoes, eggplant, peppers, and melons) as seedlings and transplant them into your garden at the right time, you can harvest them earlier than if you wait for the soil to warm up. The same is true for plants that grow best in cool weather, like cabbages, kale, and celery.

Plan where each vegetable will grow. Tall plants belong at the north side of the garden so they won't cast shade on shorter crops. If you plant in beds, rather than in rows, space each plant equidistant from its neighbors on all sides to fill the space efficiently and to shade out weeds.

Make a schedule for each bed, with dates for planting your initial crop and any succession plantings. To plant in succession simply means that as soon as one crop is finished, you pull it out and put another in its space, so that during the growing season the ground is never sitting idle. For example, you might begin in early April with peas, lettuce, spinach, strawberries, pansies, and onion sets. Follow these with main-season crops like tomatoes, squash, corn, eggplant, peppers, and beans. Plan for late harvests of cauliflower, leeks, Brussels sprouts, parsley, spinach, Swiss chard, and kale. In most areas of the country, gardeners can get two crops from every patch of ground, and three or four crops in warmer areas.

In an edible landscape, succession planting is essential to achieving a spring-to-fall supply of color and food. Replace vegetables or flowers that produce for only part of the season with either another food crop or flowers: kale after bush beans, for instance, or staked tomatoes after spring tulips, fall lettuce after radishes and pansies, or fall-blooming pansies after lettuce, and so on. (Start seed for fall pansies in early June and set plants in the garden in August. Pansies will flower through December as far north as Zone 5.)

Succession planting takes planning. You'll be more successful if you have seedlings in flats or in a nursery plot, ready to move into empty spaces. To determine the planting date, count backwards from the first frost date, then add two or three weeks to allow for harvesting.

GETTING STARTED WITH SEEDS

Growing plants from seed is something every gardener should do. It's easy and fun, and for less money you can raise a much greater number of plants than if you buy transplants. Another major benefit is the variety ~ instead of a handful of choices, you can select from hundreds of cultivars of tomatoes or dozens of lettuces. Gardeners who start plants from seed have the whole of the horticultural world at their fingertips.

You can make seed-starting as simple or as fancy as you desire. Besides the seeds, you'll need containers, a germinating medium, and a sunny windowsill or other light source. Your containers and light source can be as minimal as recycled yogurt cartons in a tray on a windowsill. At the fancy end are prefabricated, multi-level carts on wheels, complete with grow lights, timers, trays, and pots. It's possible to grow perfectly respectable seedlings on a windowsill; it's also possible to have mediocre results with a fancy setup. Success depends largely on the care and conditions you provide.

Commercially prepared sterile germinating mix is worth every penny you spend on it. It is free of weed seeds and disease organisms, and it is specially blended to provide the perfect drainage seedlings demand. Using a sterile medium

will help you avoid a fungal disease called damping-off, which attacks seedlings, causing them to keel over at the soil line. To further minimize the risk of damping-off, put a thin layer of pure, finely milled vermiculite over the starting mix, and be sure your seed-starting area has good air circulation.

Fill containers nearly to the top with seed-starting mix, and set them in pans of tepid water until the mix is thoroughly moistened. Sow seed at the spacing recommended on the packet, and cover with more pre-moistened germinating mix or vermiculite. Set the trays in a warm spot ~ under lights, on a germination mat, or on top of the refrigerator ~ until the seeds sprout.

Some plants require warm temperatures for germination. Some require complete darkness, and therefore need to be covered with a piece of cardboard or several layers of newspaper. All the information you need to germinate the seed successfully should be either on the seed packet or in the catalog you ordered from.

Once the seeds germinate, you may need to move them to different temperature or light conditions. If you're using fluorescent lights, adjust them so that the bulbs are no more than 2 to 4 inches away from the seedlings.

Be vigilant about watering. Keep the seedlings moist but not wet. Always use tepid water; cold water can set seedlings

Plants That Attract Good Bugs

Although many gardeners firmly believe in the value of companion planting ~ growing a particular type of plant among or near others to control pests ~ there's a lack of scientific evidence to support claims of the effectiveness of such practices. Including plants that support beneficial insects has been proven to be effective, however.

There are many beneficial insects, which include such familiar garden wildlife as lady beetles and praying mantids. Aphid lions (*Chrysopa*), parasitic wasps (*Trichogramma* and *Encarsia*), and parasitic nematodes (*Steinernema alaseri*) are a few of the lesser-known predators. It's possible to buy some types of predatory insects, but the best way to have (and keep) them in your garden is to grow insectary plants ~ those that provide food or shelter for the beneficial insects.

There's no need to plant the host plants right up against the crop you're trying to protect. Simply growing these on your property will suffice. Here's a partial list of insectary plants, with the insects they attract. The insects the predators feed on are listed in brackets.

- *Achillea* spp. (yarrows): Attracts parasitic wasps [moths], hover flies.
- *Angelica archangelica* (angelica): Attracts lady beetles [aphids, scales], lacewings [aphids].
- *Iberis* spp. (candytufts): Attracts syrphid flies [aphids].
- *Ipomoea purpurea* (morning glory): Attracts lady beetles [aphids], predatory mites [spider mites].
- *Nemophila menziesii* (baby-blue-eyes): Attracts syrphid flies [aphids].
- *Oenothera biennis* (evening primrose): Attracts ground beetles [gypsy moths].
- *Solidago* spp. (goldenrods): Attracts lady beetles, predaceous beetles [various insects and mites], parasitic wasps [moths].

back by slowing or temporarily arresting their growth. Also, always water pots and flats from the bottom to lessen the danger of damping-off.

The first leaves (or leaf) on a new seedling are the seed leaves, or cotyledons. They may not look anything like the true leaves, which come next. If you've sown seeds in a flat, or sown several seeds to a pot, you'll need to thin or transplant them.

Do this once your seedlings have a couple of sets of true leaves. Always handle young seedlings by their leaves, never by their stems. If you damage a leaf, the plant should survive; but if you damage the stem, the plant may die.

Commercial seed-starting mixes generally contain nutrients for the new plants, but these are quickly depleted. By the time you thin or transplant seedlings, you should start feeding with a very weak compost tea, liquid seaweed, or other fertilizer solution on a weekly basis. Neglecting to fertilize until you set transplants into the garden will result in malnourished plants.

The final step is to gradually accustom your tender new plants to the great outdoors. Full sun, wind, and fluctuating outdoor temperatures are too violent for seedlings that have been indoors all their lives. Start by moving plants out into dappled light on a balmy, calm day for two hours.

Gradually increase the length of time and then the intensity of sun until your seedlings are in full sun for most of the day. If unseasonable weather threatens ~ either a cold snap or a heat wave ~ bring the plants indoors. Don't neglect this process, or try to rush it. You'll be rewarded by plants that suffer no setbacks, that adapt easily to their new positions in the ground, and that bear flowers or fruit with no delays.

GROWING FOOD PLANTS SUCCESSFULLY

One of the greatest rewards for any gardener is harvesting the fruits of your labor. Beans, summer squash, peppers, eggplant, tomatoes ~ and even annual flowers ~ need to be picked to encourage more flowers and subsequent fruit. If you allow the plants to produce seed, the flowering

Edible Flowers

Many of the flowers found in a mixed garden are edible, and using them in salads, soups, and desserts will turn a tasty dish into a feast for the eyes as well as the palate.

At Caprilands Herb Farm in Coventry, Connecticut, they serve salads that are dotted with nasturtium and borage flowers, calendula petals, and many other edible herb blossoms in season. The salads are true works of art, and are carried into the dining room in huge bowls and shown to everyone present before they are served.

Plant any of the following flowers to add to your salads:

Agastache foeniculum (anise hyssop)
Allium schoenoprasum (chive blossoms)
Allium tuberosum (garlic chive blossoms)
Borago officinalis (borage)
Calendula officinalis (calendula)
Coriandrum sativum (cilantro)
Ocimum basilicum (basil)
Tagetes signata (marigold)
Tropaeolum majus (nasturtium)
Viola odorata (violet)
Viola tricolor (Johnny-jump-up)

becomes less vigorous, or stops entirely.

Rotate crops each year to prevent a buildup of disease organisms or recurrent insect infestations. A garden layout of four separate beds, for example, makes it easy to move each vegetable or a combination of vegetables over one bed each year. Even in a tiny 4 by 25-foot plot you can rotate crops. From year to year, move the tomatoes and their relatives (peppers and eggplant), and the cole crops such as broccoli, cauliflower and kale. The smaller your garden, the more important it is to use disease-resistant cultivars, and to practice good sanitation. In the absence of beds, be creative in finding different space

Ideas for Edible Landscapes

1. If space is short in your vegetable garden, consider growing perennial vegetables with your perennial flowers. Plant asparagus in groups of three crowns at the back of a perennial border, where the ferny summer foliage will make a background to the other flowers. Rhubarb's handsome, bold leaves and bright red stems earn it a place with ornamentals, too.

2. If you use strawberries as an edging in flower borders, give some of the newer day-neutral cultivars a try. Day-neutral strawberries flower continuously from spring until frost, so you can harvest fruit all season long. 'Tristar' and 'Tribute' are two good cultivars that bear over three seasons.

3. Parsley makes a great edging or filler plant for flower beds. Grow both the plain-leaf Italian parsley, which has a better flavor and is more popular for cooking, and curly-leaf parsley, which is a fine garnish.

4. If your vegetable garden is divided into separate beds, you know that the pathways between the beds need care, too. Is it going to be lawn or mulch? Why not do both at once? By growing white clover in the paths, you get an attractive green cover that cools the air, like lawn. In addition, it fixes nitrogen. After you mow, the clippings make a nutrient-rich addition to the compost pile.

5. In recent years, there's been an explosion in the array of lettuces available to American gardeners. In addition to fine flavor, these special "greens" come in gorgeous colors and textures. They're truly ornamental. Some of the best for both taste and looks are 'Lollo Rossa', 'Lollo Biondo', 'Red Sallis', 'Red Salad Bowl', 'Royal Oak Leaf', 'Four Seasons', 'Reine des Glaces', and 'Little Gem'.

in the garden for plants that are stressed by disease or insect attack.

Diana Bristol of Bloomingfields Farm rotates ornamental kales out of her mixed garden into a bed of fall-blooming asters. Curly 'Blue Vates' and 'Ragged Jack' kale (both a handsome blue-gray) and deep purple 'Tuscan Black' cabbage look particularly healthy among the bright purple fall asters. She has found that by moving perennial vegetables or flowers ~ which sometimes become choked by weeds such as quackgrass (*Agropyron repens*) ~ to different places in the garden, and by keeping their former locations thoroughly weeded and only planted with annuals, she can rid the area of the pesky weed in a year or two.

Interplant short- and long-season crops to use limited space most efficiently, such as spinach and onions, or bush beans and carrots; or ones with complementary growing habits such as low-growing lettuce among the taller broccoli, or corn, beans, and winter squash all in the same plot. I often grow peas, lettuce, parsley, and cucumbers all in the same 15-inch-wide strip, with a trellis running down the north side. Peas, lettuce, and parsley are all planted in early to mid-April. When peas are well on their way up the trellis, about mid-May, I plant cucumber seeds. The young cucumbers start climbing the trellis as the peas ripen, and take over the space after the peas

have been picked. Fast-growing lettuce matures and is ready to pull out just as the slower-germinating parsley starts to need space to spread out.

To make the best use of your garden space use poles, trellises, and fences, and stagger plantings of the same vegetable, like beans, summer squash, and lettuce. May through August, plant short rows of beans and two new hills of squash every month, to avoid "zucchini overload" and to make sure you have a continuous supply. Squash vine borers are regular visitors, and the early squash plants almost always succumb. Bean beetles are less predictable, but if they have established a foothold by midsummer, pull out the sad-looking row and concentrate on protecting a newer row that will give you beans in September and October. To produce a steady crop, sow one-foot rows of lettuce two or three times in June and tuck the seedlings into any open space that has some shade.

Mulch to keep weeds down and to maintain moisture in the soil at a constant level. I cannot always water my garden regularly, and I've found that root crops become tough and misshapen when the soil dries out. Blossom-end rot on tomatoes, which causes the fruits to develop soft spots and eventually rot, occurs during prolonged periods of drought or heavy rainfall. Use a mulch of salt hay or shredded bark over newspaper to keep the amount of moisture in the soil constant

A Mesclun Salad Garden

If you enjoy salads, grow a bed of mesclun; it makes a perfect green salad with just oil and vinegar. Mesclun, also known as misticanza, saladini, or salad greens mix, refers to a mixture of different greens grown in the same bed, which are harvested young by cutting them with scissors rather than pulling out the whole plant. The idea is to have the greens continue to grow new leaves for repeated cuttings.

Mesclun components include many cultivars of lettuce, and an assortment of other greens such as mustard, arugula, chicory, mache, endive, cress, and radicchio. Many nurseries now sell various mixes of their own. I grow mesclun in a round bed, 10 feet in diameter, which I divide into four sections with rows of shallots and stepping stones. In each quarter, I plant a different mix.

To grow mesclun, cast the seed thickly over a prepared bed and cover it with ¼ inch of soil. Ideally, you should sow a short row, 3 to 4 feet, of each mesclun mixture once a week in spring, so that the greens won't all be ready to cut at the same time. Either way, tamp the seed down with a board to make sure it is in contact with the soil, and keep the soil moist until the seed germinates and the seedlings have a good start.

The young plants will form a lush covering, in varying shades of green and deep red. Thin them out at 3 inches for a salad of very young 'baby' leaves, or wait until the greens are 5 to 6 inches high to begin cutting for salads. Whenever you cut, water with a dilution of organic fish and seaweed fertilizer. The mesclun will grow back for a second and third cutting before it eventually becomes bitter.

and cut down on watering time in general.

If you have any empty spaces, fill them with lettuce seedlings, annual flower seedlings, or any self-sown seedlings from elsewhere in the garden, or use them as nurseries to grow your own seedlings for fall crops of broccoli, kale, kohlrabi, collards, or Chinese cabbage.

FOOD PLANTS FOR A FLOWER GARDEN

There are certain food plants that combine particularly well with flowers in a mixed border because of their attractive foliage or fruits. Here are some recommended plants for a flower border:

Eggplant (*Solanum melongena* var. *esculentum*): 'Little Fingers' is a cultivar of baby eggplant that bears bunches of glossy, finger-shaped eggplant that last well. 'Violette di Firenze' has larger fruits that are a rich lavender, sometimes striped with white.

Hot peppers (*Capsicum annuum*): 'Serrano' bears 2-inch green and red fruits on 2- to 3-foot plants. 'Cayenne' bears slightly larger fruits that turn yellow, then red, early in the season. The fruits hang in cascades, and the entire plant may be pulled and hung upside down in order to dry the peppers for winter use. 'Superchili' is a bushy plant that has a canopy of leaves about 1 foot tall, covered with shiny 2-inch green, yellow, and red pointed peppers. Full sun is essential for peppers to bear fruit.

Jerusalem artichoke (*Helianthus tuberosus*): Unrelated to globe artichoke (*Cynara scolymus*), these are rangy plants, growing to 12 feet tall, topped with yellow sunflower-like blossoms from the end of August through October. They are very invasive, but their edible tuberous roots can be dug to keep them under control. The tubers are commonly sold as "sunchokes."

Kale (*Brassica oleracea*): The handsome edible leaves of kale come in several different shades of green to blue-green, and their textured leaves are tightly crinkled to smooth. 'Blue Surf' and 'Verdura' each have blue-green curly leaves, and are good foliage plants for late summer mixed borders. 'Russian Red' grows to 3 feet and has

stems and leaf veins that turn red as the weather cools. The taste of kale improves with colder weather.

Okra (*Abelmoschus esculentus*): This heat-loving plant grows 4 to 6 feet tall, has hibiscus-like blossoms, cream-colored with red throats, and edible long green pods. The cultivar 'Burgundy' has red stems, yellow-and-red flowers, and edible red pods. Too much nitrogen in the soil will produce leaves and no flowers.

'Rhubarb' chard: This cultivar of Swiss chard (*Beta vulgaris*) is a handsome vegetable that grows to 2 feet. It has deep red stems and deep green, savoyed leaves with red veins.

AN EDIBLE LANDSCAPE DESIGN

Taking her cue from Rosalind Creasy, Nancy DuBrule has designed a decorative landscape with a great number of food plants that is at the same time a beautiful flower garden, with color from April straight through the fall. This design is appropriate for the eastern parts of Zones 4 to 7.

The layout of this garden, shown on page 184, is a generic one that can be used in many backyards. Obviously it helps to have the garden facing south, as in the plan, but with a few changes in placement of plant material the design could be shifted to face east or west.

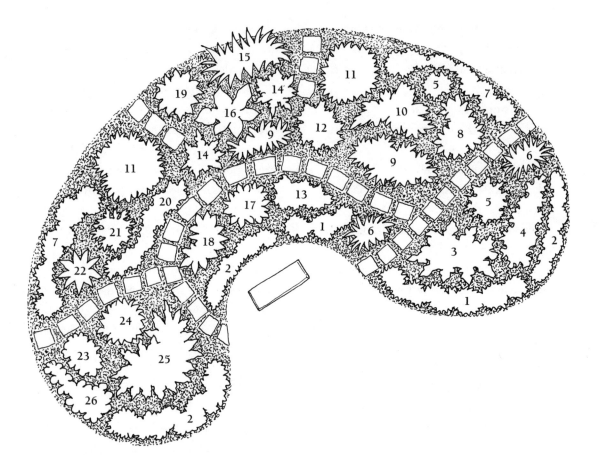

An Edible Landscape

1. *Coreopsis verticillata* 'Moonbeam' (yellow coreopsis) **2.** *Lobelia erinus* (blue edging lobelia) **3.** *Brassica oleracea* (broccoli) with *Centaurea cyanus* (bachelors' buttons) **4.** *Lactuca sativa* ('Red Oakleaf' lettuce) with *Viola × wittrockiana* (pansies) **5.** *Chrysanthemum × morifolium* 'Grenadine' (deep pink mum) **6.** *Allium tuberosum* (garlic chives) **7.** *Coreopsis rosea*

(pink coreopsis) **8.** *Ocimum basilicum* 'Cinnamon' (cinnamon basil) **9.** *Tulipa* cvs. (tulips) with *Cleome hasslerana* 'Alba' (white cleome) **10.** *Foeniculum vulgare* var. *purpureum* (bronze fennel) **11.** *Vaccinium corymbosum* (blueberry bush) **12.** *Aster novae-angliae* 'Hella Lacy' (aster) **13.** *Aster × frikartii* (Frikart's aster) **14.** *Lycopersicum esculentum* (tomato) **15.** *Hemerocallis fulva* (orange daylily) **16.** *Helianthus giganteus* (giant sunflower) **17.** *Ocimum basilicum*

'Dark Opal' (purple basil) **18.** *Solanum melongena* var. *esculentum* (baby eggplant) **19.** *Borago officinalis* (borage) **20.** *Chrysanthemum rubellum* 'Clara Curtis' (chrysanthemum) **21.** *Levisticum officinale* (lovage) **22.** *Iris* bearded hybrids (bearded iris) **23.** *Sedum ×* 'Autumn Joy' (sedum) **24.** *Caryopteris × clandonensis* (caryopteris) **25.** *Beta vulgaris* (ruby chard) **26.** *Tropaeolum majus* 'Cream Beauty' (white nasturtium)

Fruit Trees for an Edible Landscape

Fruit trees present more of a challenge to an organic gardener than berries because there are just so many more diseases and pests to contend with. There are apple scab, brown rot, fireblight, and powdery mildew for starters, with the plum curculio, codling moth, apple maggot, and peach tree borer waiting in the wings. Fortunately, they are not all found in one place, but it's safe to say that insects enjoy the taste of fruit as much as we do.

The best approach to take is a preventive one right from the start. The first thing to do is to choose the cultivars that are best adapted to your growing conditions and that show resistance to or tolerance of regional pests and diseases. A call to the fruit tree specialist at your local Cooperative Extension office can put you on the trail of the best apples, pears, plums, cherries, and so on for your locale. Since fruit trees are grafted ~ the fruit-producing crown is different from the lower portion that produces roots ~ it pays to ask about rootstocks, too. Rootstocks don't only affect the ultimate size of the tree. Some rootstocks are better adapted to particular soil types, and some resist soilborne diseases.

If your town has a farmer's market, don't pass up a chance to talk to local fruit growers about which cultivars do best.

Even if the grower doesn't use organic methods, he or she will still know which cultivars present the fewest problems.

Your county agent of the Cooperative Extension Service, or your state's Agricultural Experiment Station will tell you which cultivars are disease-resistant. They will give you basic information on growing fruit trees in your area, like which diseases and pests are prevalent where you live and which of the most recently developed disease-resistant cultivars would be right for you. If these are not available at local garden centers or nurseries, you can order them through the mail. Write to the New York State Fruit Testing Cooperative Association, Geneva, NY 14456, for their catalog of the newest resistant cultivars, enclosing a $10 membership fee.

If you plan to grow apple trees, write to Applesource, Tom Vorbeck, Route One, Chapin, IL 62628, for a list of old-time apple varieties. You can select six cultivars from the list, and Applesource will send you a box of 12 apples, two each of the six you select, so that you can choose which ones you might want to grow. If you really get into fruit growing, you may want to join the North American Fruit Explorers (NAFEX), also by writing Tom Vorbeck. With over 2,000 members, NAFEX publishes a journal, *Pomona*, four times a year that will put you in touch with other fruit growers to share information and experiences.

Preventive Measures for Fruit Trees

The following steps will discourage disease, insects, and damage to fruit trees from wildlife:

- Feed the trees each spring by applying 4 to 6 inches of compost out to their drip lines.
- Wrap tree trunks with white plastic tree wrap or hardware cloth (screening) in winter, down to 2 to 3 inches below the soil surface, to protect them from mice and rabbits nibbling at the bark. Unwrap them in summer.
- Keep the area beneath the trees free of leaf and fruit debris, which can harbor insect eggs and disease spores.
- Spray with liquid seaweed every month to keep the trees well supplied with essential trace minerals.
- Consult Rodale's *Chemical-Free Yard & Garden* for methods to control insects and diseases that become a problem.

Once you've chosen good cultivars, give the trees the right growing conditions and adopt good sanitation practices to help the young trees develop a tolerance for diseases and pests. Begin by having the soil tested to make sure its chemistry is in balance. Be sure to let the tester of your soil know that you plan to grow fruit trees; you will need to know if there are sufficient minerals (boron and calcium in particular) in the soil. Give the trees a diverse habitat to live in, one where beneficial insects are encouraged to live (such as an edible landscape).

For an edible landscape, choose trees that have been grafted onto dwarfing rootstocks, known as "dwarfs," or trees whose small size is in their genes; these are called "miniatures." Miniatures, also known as genetic dwarfs, have been selected from among hundreds of cultivars for their diminutive size, and then grafted onto standard rootstocks. This makes them extremely strong and productive. Dwarfs will grow from 6 to 10 feet tall, while miniatures take many years to reach a maximum of 6 feet. These little trees will produce as much fruit or more for the space they occupy as standard trees, and will be more in scale in a mixed garden. Because they are so short, you won't need a ladder for pruning, picking, or inspecting for insects or diseases, and should you have to spray, a small tree is much more accessible than a large one.

If you find trees that you want at a local nursery, be sure to check not only for their hardiness at low temperatures, but also their tolerance to heat. Seldom do catalogs or growers warn against putting a fruit

Identifying Bees

BUMBLE BEE   HONEY BEE

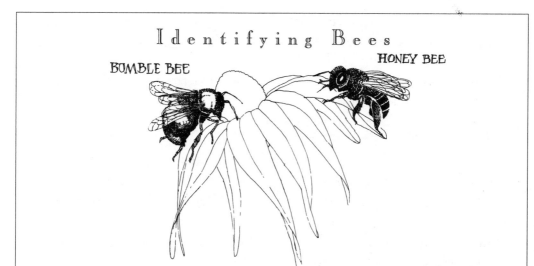

Bees, both honey (*Apis mellifera*) and bumble (*Bombus* spp.), belong in a garden. They are important pollinators and are quite different from their more aggressive cousins, the yellowjackets (*Vespula polistes*). We owe the beauty of flowers to the bees, for the fragrance, color, and forms of flowers were all developed to attract bees and other pollinators. Yellow, blue-green, blue, mauve, purple, and ultra-violet red flowers (like the Flanders poppy) are bee favorites, and bees prefer flowers in clusters so they can fill their pollen baskets on each trip. All bees feed on pollen and nectar from flowers.

Many people confuse bees and yellowjackets. Honeybees have golden brownish bodies covered with hair, so pollen will stick to them when they touch it. They live in hives, in tree holes, or in buildings. Bumblebees have hairy bodies, too, but are larger, with wide yellow and black stripes. Yellow-jackets and hornets have smooth, more brightly colored, yellow-and-black-striped bodies. They are predators and scavengers, eating other insects, garbage, or fallen fruit. They live in nests in the ground or build aerial nests. While the essential work of bees in pollinating flowers is well-known, yellowjackets are given little credit for the helpful roles they perform as insect predators and scavengers of decomposing material.

Bees pay little attention to the gardener unless both of them are headed for the same flower. Bees have barbed stingers which are left in their victim. A bee stings once and only as a last resort, because she knows it means death for her. A yellowjacket, on the other hand, can sting repeatedly because its stinger has no barb. Towards the end of summer their craving for a diet of sweets grows, and it is during this time that they are most apt to sting people.

tree too far south, which, according to Tom Vorbeck, can prevent fruit trees from producing fruit.

In the Northeast, you can have continuous bloom and fruit for many months. Cherries bloom early and bear fruit in May and June. Peaches bloom in May and bear fruit from mid-July through early September. Pears and plums bloom in May also, and bear their fruit in August and September. Apple trees blossom last and their fruit is ready for picking from late August through early November. Cherries and peaches are self-pollinating, but the other fruits need another cultivar close by in order to cross-pollinate ~ you must buy more than one tree if you want fruit.

If you find espaliered trees already started at a nursery, you should seriously consider including them in your garden design. The term "espalier" originated in northern Europe, where fruit trees were grown against south-facing walls which provided enough shelter and warmth to ripen the fruit in cold regions. It refers to a tree that is trained flat against a fence, trellis, or wall, and pruned to have the greatest amount of fruit in the least space.

Espaliered trees require persistent pruning, but they are so dramatic and so space-efficient that they are well worth the effort. Pear trees are good to begin with, because they blossom every year, and pruning will result in bigger fruit and more vigorous trees.

BERRIES FOR EDIBLE LANDSCAPES

In season, berries are part of our daily fare, and what we don't eat goes into the freezer. Berries are easier to raise organically than apples, peaches, plums, or pears, all of which can be vulnerable to insect damage unless sprayed. We share our strawberries with chipmunks and squirrels, and the blueberries with bluejays and cardinals, but there always seems to be enough for us all.

Strawberries

Except for the dainty alpine strawberry (*Fragaria vesca*), strawberries (*Fragaria × ananassa*) require more work than other berries. The alpines (or *fraises des bois*) are wild, perennial strawberries which remain in the same place for years, producing a smattering of white flowers and tiny berries throughout the season. There are never really enough to make a meal unless you use them extensively, perhaps as an edging for a large border. By contrast, you should pick regular strawberries daily to prevent mildew, and trim the runners which shoot off in every direction during the summer.

Replace strawberry plants every two or three years. It's not hard to find replacements from among the daughter and granddaughter plants that grow from runners. Give each strawberry plant 2 to

3 tablespoons of bonemeal each spring, and replenish the bed with rock phosphate when you replace the plants.

Raspberries

Easier to grow than strawberries, raspberries (*Rubus* spp.) need only seasonal pruning and a generous helping of compost each spring. When you plant them, incorporate plenty of compost and rock phosphate into the soil. They tend to spread but can be trained on fan-shaped wooden trellises or cordoned with a wire fence alongside the vegetable garden.

Raspberries are quick to mildew in persistently wet or oppressively humid weather, and the fruit gets visibly smaller when the weather is hot and dry. Pick them daily during hot, humid weather to keep mildew down to a minimum, and water with a hose left at the base of the canes for several minutes after a prolonged dry period, or install a drip irrigation system when you plant them.

Japanese beetles like raspberries, but they can be controlled by spreading milky spore disease powder over lawn and garden areas, or by hand-picking the beetles into a jar and then drowning them by filling it with water.

Blueberries

Blueberries (*Vaccinium* spp.) (see "Blueberries ~ The Best-Looking Fruit," on page 190) need even less attention than

strawberries and raspberries. Their most important requirement is an acid soil (pH 4.5 to 5.5). We give our blueberries an annual shovelful of compost, and a pine needle mulch. In return we have all the fruit we can eat, and fruit to give away as well. The blueberries stay well on the bushes, meaning you can delay picking them until it's convenient. Most are not self-pollinating, so you need to plant more than one cultivar to get berries.

In addition to lowbush Maine blues (*Vaccinium angustifolium*) and highbush blues (*V. corymbosum*) that can grow to 10 feet, there are hybrid crosses between them ~ called half-high blueberries ~ that are only a few feet in height. They make good end-posts for a mixed border. Blueberries can be underplanted with poppies, ferns, vinca, or any plant tolerant of acidic soil.

Currants and Gooseberries

Currants and gooseberries (*Ribes* spp.) are among the few fruit-bearing plants that actually thrive in the shade or in very cold climates. These fruits thrive in the cool, misty air of England, but many nurseries offer them for sale in the United States. Both are hardy bush fruits that grow well up into Zone 3, and are sometimes happiest on the north side of the house, in filtered sun and shade. I have wanted to grow red currants for years because I use currant jelly in special dishes like red cabbage and venison stew, and my husband

Blueberries ~ The Best-Looking Fruit

Most fruit plants are ornamental ~ the tree fruits have pretty spring blossoms, grape leaves are attractive and the vines can cover a pergola or arbor, a potted fig tree makes a good patio feature ~ but blueberries are perhaps the handsomest fruit plant.

These shrubs, which grow from 18 inches to over 12 feet high (depending on the type), have leaves that range from powdery blue to light or dark green. In the fall, foliage turns yellow, orange, or scarlet, and many cultivars have brightly colored stems in winter as well. Because the fruits ripen over a period of weeks, a cluster will have berries that are mint green, lavender, or indigo, depending on their maturity, all with a powdery bloom. In fact, blueberries are so good-looking that they can easily hold their own in foundation plantings, and are perfect in a mixed border, as long as their cultural needs are met. All this, and sweet, flavorful fruit too!

Gardeners over a wide area can grow blueberries, as long as you give them an acid soil ~ a pH of 4.5 to 5.5 is best ~ and regular moisture. The best type of blueberry for you depends on where you live. In the South, rabbiteye types thrive, as well as rabbiteye-highbush hybrids. In Zones 3 to 7, grow highbush or lowbush blueberries. Highbush blueberries are the most popular, producing many large fruits. Lowbush blueberries are essentially cultivars or hybrids of wild plants, and they have an intense, wild flavor that many people prefer.

---

dreams of scones with clotted cream and currant jelly. But we have never planted currants, because they are alternate hosts for a disease called white pine blister rust which could kill the white pine that grows on our property.

Some states (and areas within some states) will not allow *Ribes* species to be shipped in. Rust has been successfully kept from spreading in recent years by close inspections of the bushes for any sign of disease before shipping. A call to your local Cooperative Extension office will tell you whether or not you garden in a restricted area.

Both fruits grow on neat, compact bushes that grow 4 to 5 feet tall and have attractive leaves and fruit. Gooseberries are shades of green and pink, and currants are red, purple, and black. A particularly pretty cultivar of American black currant is *Ribes odoratum* 'Crandall', which is cov-

Two Very Berry Recipes

Red Currant Jelly

6 cups currants, washed and stemmed
½ cup water
sugar

Boil currants and water gently in saucepan for about 10 minutes, or until fruit is soft and juicy. Put mixture into dampened and wrung-out jelly bag to drain. Do not squeeze. Measure juice and pour into pan. Bring to boil and skim. Add an equal amount of sugar. Cook, skimming and stirring constantly, until jelly sheets on the side of a spoon. Pour into sterilized glass jars and screw on sterilized lids. Turn jars upside down for 5 minutes and then back upright to seal.

Gooseberry Fool

4 cups gooseberries
6 tablespoons butter
1 cup sugar or to taste
2 cups heavy cream

Both stems and petals must be removed from the gooseberries before they can be eaten or cooked.

Put gooseberries in heavy saucepan. Add butter in small pieces and heat slowly, stirring. When butter is melted, cover pan and stew berries for about 10 minutes until soft. Stir in sugar to taste. Cool for 3 to 4 hours. Whip cream until stiff and fold in gooseberry mixture. Turn into large glass bowl and chill. Makes 6 servings.

ered with yellow trumpet-shaped flowers. Also, the jostaberry (*Ribes nidigrolaria*), a cross between a gooseberry and black currant, is pretty as well as thornless, pungent-smelling, and rust-resistant.

Because they are susceptible to mildew, all *Ribes* need good air circulation, so a windy location helps rather than hinders their health. In an exposed yard, or on a hill, use them as a windbreak for less hardy plants. There are some mildew-resistant cultivars, such as the 'Careless' gooseberry and 'Cherry' red currant.

While they take abuse and neglect better than most bush fruits, good care will pay off. They grow best in a rich clay loam with a pH of 6.0 to 6.5. They are heavy surface feeders, so add compost or organic fertilizer each spring to keep them at their best.

Ideally, plant gooseberries and currants in the fall to give the roots a chance to get well established. They should be planted 5 feet apart, a little deeper than they were growing in the nursery. Bart Hall-Beyer, a fruit grower/agronomist from Quebec, suggests dipping the roots in liquid seaweed before planting, and trimming back the tops by one-third. Mulch to their circumference, but leave a space around the base of the bush to keep mice from nibbling at the bark from under cover. Fruiting canes bear well for three years. After the first season, prune out to 3 or 4 canes. After the second season, save the first-year canes and 3 to 4 from the second year. The final size should be 10 to 12 canes, with 3 to 4 from each of the first, second, and third year's growth. After three years of fruiting, the canes should be cut down to the ground.

Powdery mildew, anthracnose, and leaf spot all affect these fruits, but you can keep them under control with sulfur or baking soda sprays. Control aphids with insecticidal soap, and pick off fruit flies and sawflies by hand or spray with rotenone. There are several cultivars available that have strong disease resistance, such as 'Mountain' and 'Glendale' gooseberries.

Gooseberries and currants should be harvested when fully ripe for fresh eating, and slightly underripe, when their pectin content is highest, for jam and jelly.

Set against the soft tones of a bluestone patio, the spiky forms and textures of these herbs and rock garden plants are shown at their best. Creeping phlox and pink and white thymes spread between the flagstones, while in the distance an arbor of scented roses and clematis shelters a wooden seat.

↑

A collection of thymes and
other low-growing plants
create a delightfully scented
path when planted between
paving stones. Along the
edge of the stones against the
fence, gray lavender cotton
(Santolina chamaecyparissus)
and lavender provide additional fragrance.

↑

Functioning historically as sources of medicinal, culinary, and cosmetic materials for the home, herb gardens followed very practical, formal plans that over time evolved into intricate and contrived knot garden designs. These gardens were more ornamental than useful, and made the most of the subtle textures and hues of herbs. This seventeenth-century-style design mixes "blue" ropes of common rue (Ruta graveolens) with a green rope of germander (Teucrium chamaedrys).

Gravel is a particularly
good choice for a path in an
herb garden. It provides good
drainage, it retains and
reflects the warmth that
most of these sun-loving
plants enjoy, and it provides
a neutral backdrop contrast
that highlights the plants.
Here, creeping thyme spills
over the edge of a raised bed.

A mix of lavender cultivars
forms a fragrant corner in a bed.

Plant individual herbs in groups of at least three or four so that they form compact masses. Contrasts in foliage are far more effective this way than if individual plants are scattered throughout a bed. In this garden, golden sage (Salvia officinalis 'Aurea') and lady's-mantle (Alchemilla mollis) form a subtle mix of textures.

Silver-gray artemisias, such
as 'Silver King' artemisia,
earn their place in the herb
garden as neutral foliage
plants that relieve the all-
green palette without being
intrusive. Here, artemisia is
paired with self-sown feathery
dill in a garden containing
various culinary and
medicinal herbs.

Put low-growing herbs, such
as silvermound artemisia,
lamb's-ears, and thyme, next
to a path at the very front of
a border where their colors
and textures can be appreci-
ated. Sweet alyssum (Lobularia
maritima), in bloom, is a nice
summer accent.

The traditional cottage garden provided all kinds of herbs, flowers, and food for the home. The modern edible landscape is really only a refinement of the cottager's yard. This garden shows how attractive and interesting mixed plantings can be. Spires of hollyhocks and delphiniums rise above lush, leafy rows of string beans, chives, basil, and fennel.

Vegetables do not need to be planted in rows. This tiny circular salad garden was turned into a decorative feature by dividing it into quarters and planting a different mesclun mix in each quadrant.

Rhubarb is often as undervalued in the garden as it is in the kitchen. In spring, long before most fruit is ripe, its stalks can be baked in pies, stewed, or used in jams and jellies. In the mixed garden, its ruby red stalks add color, but the dramatic foliage is its most important ornamental feature.

Once freed from the rigid lines of a traditional vegetable garden, mixed plantings can be every bit as exciting as any other garden, mixing colors and textures in much the same way. Feathery gray silvermound artemisia and blue fescue grass provide a counterpoint to the lettuce and parsley in this garden.

Mixing two very different lettuces, 'Ruby Red' and 'Salad Bowl', forms a very appealing color contrast.

↑

This tiny mixed garden makes the most of its space by growing upwards.

↑

Highly ornamental lemon cucumbers and purple pole beans form a colorful covering for a wall.

Cherry trees grown for their →
fruit will also provide a beautiful show of blossoms in spring. Sour cherry trees are generally hardier and more disease-resistant than sweet cherry trees and will bear a crop for pies or preserves in late June.

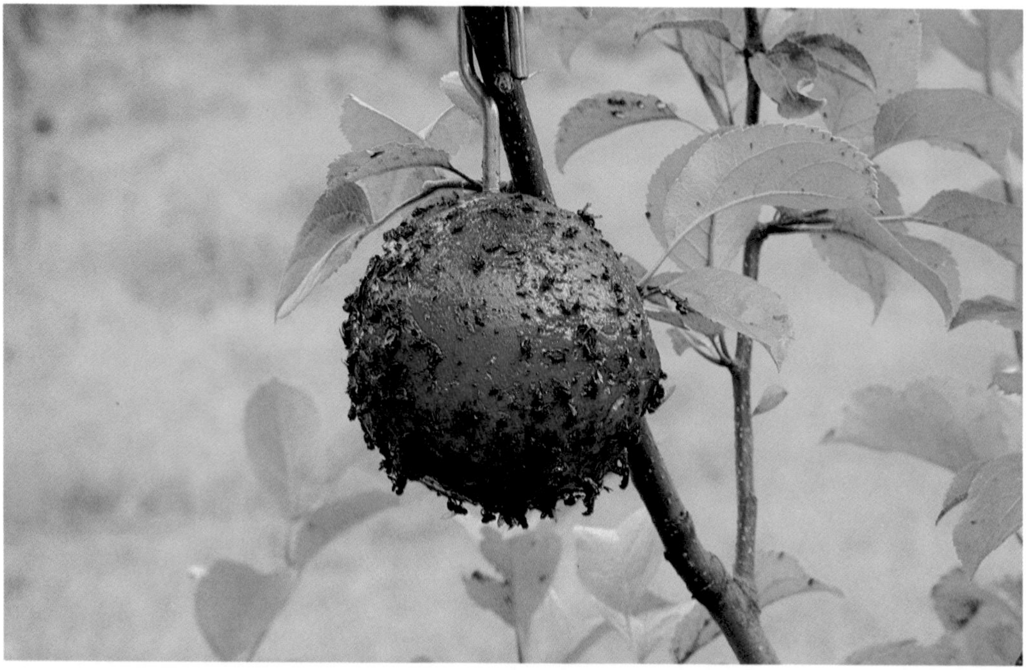

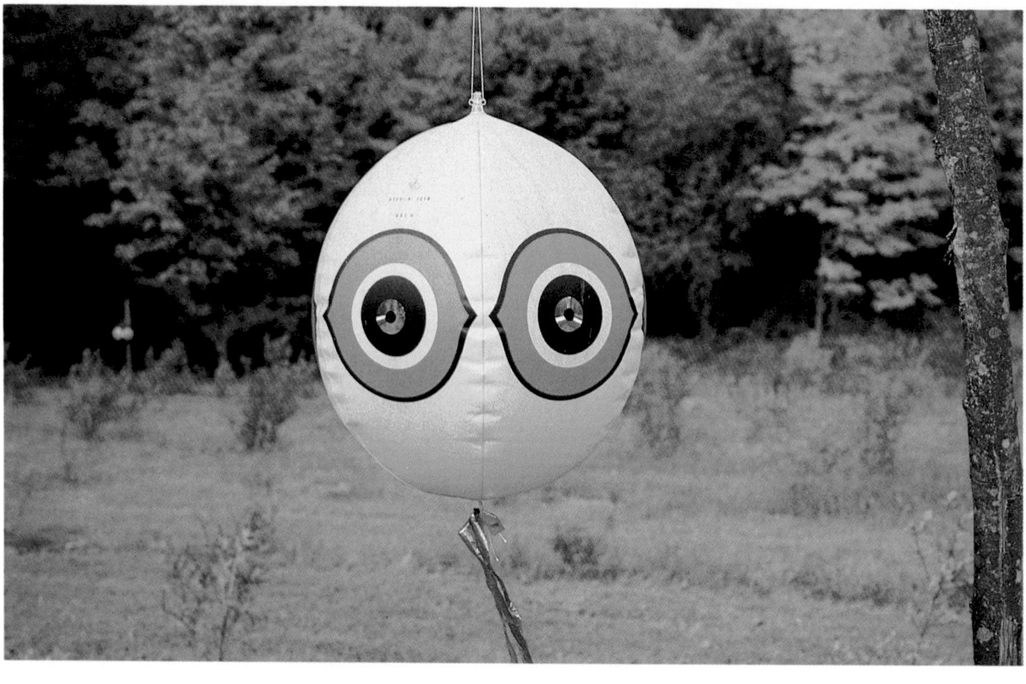

◄ Pest control is a vital part of a mixed garden. Planting insect- and disease-resistant cultivars, using good garden hygiene, and identifying problem pests as soon as they appear help to minimize damage. Fruit gardens are especially vulnerable to attack, and netting or other defenses, such as the sticky apple maggot trap, top, or the "scare eyes" to frighten hungry birds, bottom, are essential.

↑

Of all the resident insect-eaters you can attract to your garden, few are as effective as a bat, which can consume a thousand bugs a night. Adding a bat house will encourage bats to roost in your yard.

overleaf:

Scarlet runner beans are easy to grow. They produce edible beans and brilliantly colored flowers every bit as ornamental as any other flowering vine.

PART III

COUNTRY GARDEN PROJECTS

How to create and use country features in your backyard

Working with Wood

HOW TO BUILD A COUNTRY GATE

A gate is often the first thing you encounter when entering a garden, and the last thing you see when departing. Garden gates can serve many purposes. They can keep wild animals out or they can prevent your children and pets from wandering off into traffic. They can help maintain the privacy of your property yet not be too forbidding.

A lot of thought should go into the planning and building of such an important structure. The gateway shown here was designed to complement different fence systems. It can be incorporated into a wood fence or stone or masonry wall.

This gateway could also serve as a portal through a hedge or other natural barrier. Its quiet country style and practicality make it work almost anywhere. Increase the size of the gate, closing off the opening entirely, and you'll have a very secure and private entry. Decrease the gate height and you'll have an entry that is more inviting to the casual passerby. Or leave the gate as shown for a compromise between the two.

This gate was designed to be easy to build. It employs basic carpentry techniques and standard sizes of lumber. Although you can build it with hand tools and a sabre saw, a few more power tools, such as a hand-held circular saw and a drill, will make the job easier.

The materials you'll need can be found at any good lumber yard or home center. When you go to pick out your materials, take a few extra minutes to sort through the piles of wood. Try to find the straightest, most defect-free stock you can. Working with good materials makes any project go better.

The *Materials List* specifies the stock at its nominal size. This is the actual size of the wood when you purchase it. The

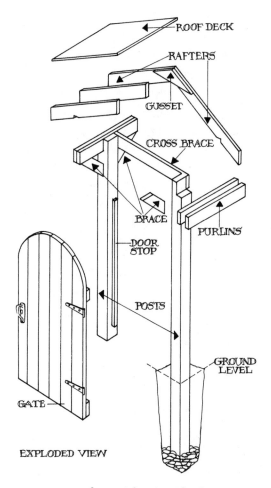

ROOF DECK

RAFTERS

GUSSET

CROSS BRACE

BRACE

PURLINS

DOOR STOP

POSTS

GROUND LEVEL

GATE

EXPLODED VIEW

to weather naturally, choose a species such as cedar or redwood which is naturally weather-resistant. If you plan to paint the gateway, regular spruce, pine, or fir lumber will serve you well.

As you go through the project, work carefully to make sure your cut wood dimensions do not change much from those given. Stop every now and then to double check your work, and to fix any minor problems before they become major headaches.

1. Dig the foundation holes. Mark the location of the foundation holes. The centers of the two holes should be 41 inches apart. With a spade and a post hole digger dig 4-foot-deep holes .

2. Notch the posts. Cut the posts to the length specified in the *Materials List*. Mark the freshly cut ends "top." This will mean the uncut ends, which probably have more preservative in them, will be in the ground. Lay out a notch at the top end of each post as shown in the *Notch Detail*. Cut the notches with a circular saw and/or a handsaw. Keep in mind that all the joinery will be exposed, so do a neat and careful job as you cut.

3. Set the posts. Fill the foundation holes with about 12 inches of gravel. Measure down 48 inches from the top and make a mark all the way around each post. This will serve as a guide so you can set each post at the correct height.

Place the posts in the holes with their

posts are cut from 6 by 6s. The braces from 2 by 4s and almost everything else from 2 by 6s. The only piece you'll need to do more to than cut to length is the gate stop, which is cut lengthwise to a 1½-inch width.

Depending on how you plan to finish the gateway, you can build it from almost any type of wood. The posts should be made from pressure-treated stock since they will be in contact with the ground. If you plan to leave the rest of the wood

Hardware & Materials List

PART	QUANTITY	DIMENSIONS
Posts	2	5½" x 5½" x 132"
Purlin Halves	4	1½" x 5½" x 33 ½"
Cross Braces	2	1½" x 5½" x 41"
Braces	4	1½" x 3½" x 17½"
Rafters	6	1½" x 5½" x 46"
Gussets	4	1½" x 5½" x 19½"
Roof Decks	2	¾" x 33½" x 42½"
Door Battens	2	1½" x 5½" x 35½"
Door Planks	6	1½" x 5½" x 78"
Door Brace	1	1½" x 5½" x 67½"
Doorstop	1	1½" x 1½" x 48"

HARDWARE
Gravel, as needed
Concrete, as needed
½" x 6" carriage bolts with
  nuts and washers, 4
16d nails, as needed
8d nails, as needed
Aluminum drip edge, 22'

Aluminum roofing nails to
  attach the drip edge, as
  needed
Asphalt shingles, 24 square
  feet
¾" roofing nails, as needed
Gate hinges, 2
Gate latch, 1

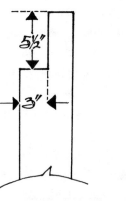

NOTCH DETAIL

notches facing out. Have two helpers hold the poles plumb. Measure the distance between the posts. It should be about 36 inches. Try to maintain this distance as carefully as possible. If necessary, cut two 36-inch spacers and nail them to the posts to hold the posts the correct distance apart. Hold a level even with the marks on the posts. It should indicate that the marks are level with each other. If they are not, add or subtract gravel from the holes to

FRONT VIEW

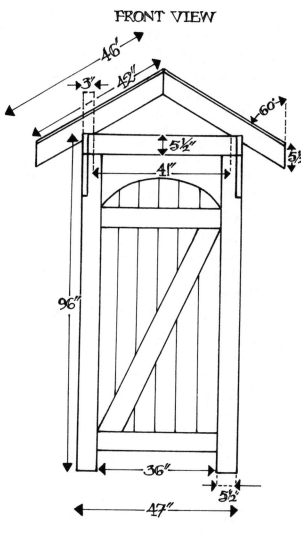

SIDE VIEW

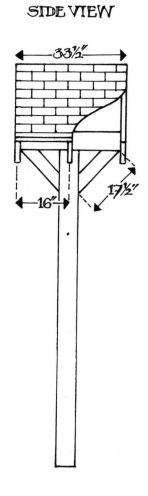

adjust the posts. Once you get the posts adjusted properly, backfill the holes.

What material you backfill with depends on what type of soil you have. If your soil compacts well, you can simply fill the holes with the soil you dug out of them. Fill the holes a little bit at a time, tamping the soil well as you go. Keep checking to be sure the posts remain plumb and parallel to one another.

If you're working with soil that does not compact well, such as sand, you'll have to backfill with concrete. Buy enough bags of premixed concrete to fill the holes, and follow the directions on the bag. Make sure the posts are plumb and parallel to each other, then let them set for a few days while the concrete cures.

4. Make the purlins. The purlins are built up from 2 layers of 2 by 6s. Cut the 2 by 6s to the length specified in the *Materials List*. Stack the boards in pairs, then nail them together with 8d nails. Make sure the ends and edges stay flush. Use about 12 nails per purlin.

5. Attach the purlins. Place a purlin in the notch at the top of one of the posts. Center it carefully from side to side. Drill through the purlin and post with a ½-inch drill bit. Bolt the purlin to the post with two carriage bolts. Place the nuts to the inside of the post. Repeat with the other purlin and post.

6. Cut and attach the braces. Cut off the ends of the braces at a 45-degree angle. Use 16d nails to attach the braces in place diagonally between the purlins as shown in the *Side View*.

7. Attach the cross braces. Measure the distance between the purlins on either

side of the posts. Cut the 2 by 6s for the cross braces to fit in these spaces. Nail the cross braces to the posts as shown in the *Exploded View*.

8. Make the rafters. Cut the rafters to the length specified in the *Materials List*. Cut the ends of the rafters at a 60-degree angle as shown in the *Front View*. Cut the gussets to the size specified in the *Materials List*. Then cut the gussets to the shape shown in the *Rafter Detail*. These angled cuts can be made easily with a hand saw or a saber saw.

Butt a pair of rafters together as shown in the *Rafter Detail*. Then place a gusset over the joint. Nail the gusset in place with 8d nails. Use about 10 nails per gusset. The outside pairs of rafters each get one gusset. The inside pair gets two, one on either side.

9. Notch the rafters. Lay out the notches on the rafters as shown in the

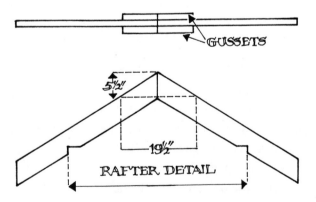

RAFTER DETAIL

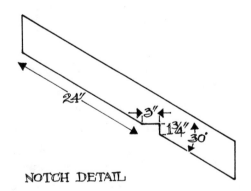

NOTCH DETAIL

Notch Detail. Measure the overall width of the gateway from purlin to purlin. This distance should match the distance from notch to notch on the rafters as shown in the *Rafter Detail.* Adjust the notch layout if necessary to make the notches align with the purlins. Cut the notches with a hand saw or a saber saw.

10. Install the rafters. Start with the center rafters. Position them on the purlins and center them over the posts. Toe nail them in place with 16d nails through the rafters into the purlins. Repeat with the outside rafters, make sure the rafters are flush with the ends of the purlins.

11. Attach the roof decking. Cut the plywood for the roof decks to the size specified in the *Materials List.* Position it on the rafters and nail it in place with 8d nails.

12. Attach the drip edge. Cut the aluminum drip edge to fit along the edges of the roof deck. Nail it in place with aluminum roofing nails.

13. Shingle the roof. Start by nailing a course of shingles along the lower edges of the roof. The tabs on this first course should point toward the peak. Then cover the first course with a second course. The tabs on the second course should point toward the ground.

After you get the first two courses nailed in place, draw a series of parallel lines horizontally across the roof decks. Space the lines 5 inches apart. Start measuring from the top edge of the shingles. Once you have the lines drawn, continue installing the shingles, one course at a time. The top edge of each course should align with one of the lines you drew on the deck. When you reach the peak, gently bend the shingles over the top and nail off the edge on the other side. Then cut a number of shingles into thirds and bend these over the peak, nailing them in place as you go.

14. Make the door. Measure the distance between the posts. Cut the door battens ½ inch shorter than this measurement. Place the batten on the floor, 58 inches apart. Lay out the door planks on top of them. One end of the planks should be flush with the edge of one of the battens. Arrange the planks so that the space between each of them is equal. Nail the planks to the battens with 8d nails, 6 nails per plank.

Turn the door over. Cut the door brace to fit between the battens as shown in the *Door Detail.* Nail the brace to the door with 8d nails, 2 nails per plank.

15. Cut the door to shape. Find the center of the door from side to side, 22 inches down from the top edge. From this point, swing a 22-inch radius arc across the top of the door. This can be done by tying a length of string to a pencil. Hold one end of the string at the center point while you draw with the pencil. Cut along your layout line with a saber saw.

16. Hang the door. Attach the hinges to the door near the top and bottom. Hold the door in the opening between the posts and attach the hinges to one of the posts. Cut the door stop to the dimensions specified in the *Materials List*. Hold the door in its closed position. Place the door stop against the post and door. Nail it in place with 16d nails. Install the latch.

17. Finish the gate. Paint or stain the gateway to match or complement your color scheme.

DOOR DETAIL

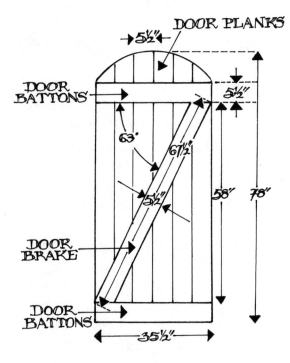

HOW TO MAKE A PICKET FENCE

While a fence is primarily a practical addition to a lawn or garden, there is no reason it has to look utilitarian. A beautiful fence can be every bit as functional as an ugly one.

There are a few things to consider before you start digging post holes. First, you should consult the zoning regulations for your area. These are usually available at your town hall or at the local library. You may find there are restrictions governing the height of the fence, its placement, or the materials from which it can be constructed. With this information in hand, you should talk to your neighbors and tell them what you have in mind. It may even be that your neighbor was contemplating putting up a fence as well and the two of you can share the expense and the work. Finally, make sure you know where the boundaries are.

Materials for a wooden fence are similar to those for any outdoor project. Choose woods that are highly weather-resistant and use hardware that has been coated to prevent rust. Cedar is one of the most readily available species of naturally weather-resistant wood. Locust is another excellent choice, if you can find it. Or you can go with pressure-treated stock which, of all the choices, is the longest lasting ~ often guaranteed for 30 years or more. For this reason, you might want to consider using treated wood for the posts even if you're going to use another species for the remainder of the fence. Just make sure you buy treated wood that is rated for ground contact.

The fence presented here is designed to use standard sizes of lumber. The posts are made from 4 by 4s, the stringers and gate parts are made from 2 by 4s, and the pickets are cut from 1 by 3s. The *Materials List* specifies enough parts to make one 8-foot length of fence and a gate. Once you determine the layout of your fence, you can make your own list according to your needs.

1. Lay out the fence. Lay out the fence on your lawn or in your garden. Use lime to draw directly on the ground. Leave gaps in the lines for any gates or other openings. Live with the layout for a week or so. Walk only through the "gates" during this time and see how livable your design is. Remember, it is much easier to change your ideas now than it will be once you've set a few posts.

When you are satisfied with the basic layout, use stakes and mason's cord to

SOME PICKET FENCE DESIGNS

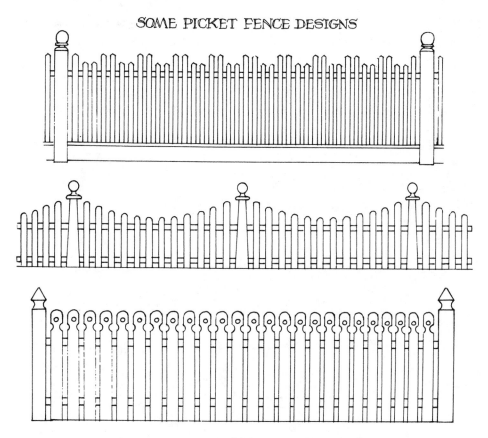

OVERALL VIEW

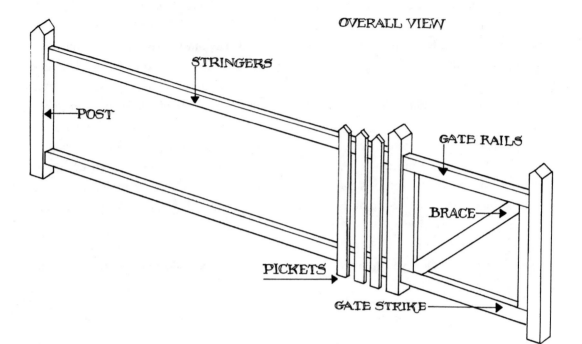

STRINGERS

POST

GATE RAILS

BRACE

PICKETS

GATE STRIKE

Hardware & Materials List

PART	QUANTITY	DIMENSIONS
Posts	3	3½" x 3½" x 63"
Stringers	2	1½" x 3½" x 92½"
Gate Rails	2	1½" x 3½" x 36"
Gate Stiles	2	1½" x 3½" x 33½"
Brace	1	1½" x 3½" x 39½"
Pickets	35	¾" x 2½" x 39"

GRAVEL, as needed

CONCRETE MIX, as
needed

HARDWARE
#8 x 3½" galvanized wood
screws, as needed
#8 x 1½" galvanized wood
screws, as needed
Gate hinges, 2
Gate latch, 1

finalize the dimensions and placement of the posts. Mason's cord works better for this task than regular twine or string because it won't stretch and sag.

Start by locating the corners. Drive a stake into the ground to mark each corner post. Then tie the mason's cord tautly between the stakes. If you need square corners, use a framing square as a guide. Measure along the cord and drive a stake into the ground every 8 feet to mark the placement of the intermediate posts.

2. Shape the posts. Cut the posts to the length specified in the *Materials List*. Before you set the posts in the ground, cut them to shape. The tops of the posts and the tops of the pickets are angled to shed water and to add some visual interest and character to the fence. Here is an opportunity to make your fence reflect your sense of aesthetics. You can choose one of the designs shown in the *Fence Design Ideas* or invent your own.

Make your selected pattern from 1/4-inch plywood or heavy cardboard. Then you can quickly trace the shape on all the posts. Cut the posts to shape with a saw. For straight cuts, a circular saw will work well. For curved cuts, a reciprocating saw or a band saw will do the job best.

Once you finish cutting all the posts to shape, measure down from the top and mark the ground line all the way around the post as shown in the *Post Detail*. This line will serve as a guide as you set the

posts in the ground.

3. Set the corner posts. Remove the corner stakes, and dig the holes for the corner posts with a spade and a posthole digger. Dig down about 30 inches. Fill the holes with about 9 inches of gravel as shown in *Setting the Posts*. The gravel acts as a footing and allows water to drain away from the posts. Place the posts in the holes and check to see that the guide line is even with the ground level. Add or subtract gravel to adjust the post height.

Once you have the height adjusted properly, hold a level against the posts to plumb them. Temporarily brace the posts to hold them in position while you backfill the holes. If your soil compacts well, you

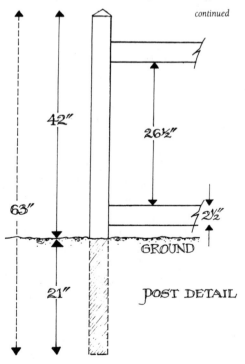

continued

POST DETAIL

Trees and Shrubs for Country Hedges

Hedges, like fences, form boundaries, either between neighbors or between areas of your own property. Which plants you choose for a hedge depends upon the mature size required, the amount of light available, and the degree of informality you want.

The ultimate result of any hedge planting will depend in a large part upon how it is pruned as it grows and matures. Electric hedge clippers are one of the most misused tools in the gardening world! Countless plants are damaged or destroyed when hedge clippers are used to shear plants that really should be hand pruned and allowed to grow in a natural shape. Save them for formal plantings of boxwood (*Buxus* spp.), yew (*Taxus* spp.), and privets (*Ligustrum* spp.).

Consider also not just how, but also when your hedge should be pruned. A pruning method that is more natural is to remove about a quarter to a third of the oldest flowering branches down to ground level, and then cut back long shoots by hand, carefully shaping the plant to a more loose, natural form.

If you are looking for less formal, looser plants for naturalistic country-style hedging, consider the following plants:

LOW-GROWING (3 TO 5 FEET TALL)

Caryopteris × *clandonensis* (bluebeard): Subshrub. Silvery gray leaves and sky blue flowers in late summer and fall. It will grow 3–4 feet per season, so prune in early spring to maintain it at the desired height. Zones 5–8.

Paeonia spp. (peonies): Bloom in late spring and early summer with enormous fragrant flowers; good for cutting. Attractive dark green foliage after blooming; some cultivars have handsome bronze to reddish fall color. Needs full sun. Zones 2–8. P

Spiraea spp. (spireas): Low-growing hedge plants. Summer-blooming spiraeas include 'Shirobana' Japanese spiraea (*Spiraea japonica* 'Shirobana') which has pink and white flowers and will tolerate sun or partial shade; and goldflame spirea (*S.* × *bumalda* 'Gold Flame'), with yellow foliage and lavender flowers in early summer, providing a foliage accent even when the flowers have faded. Summer-blooming spiraeas bloom on the current year's wood and can be cut back in early spring to encourage bushiness and control height. Will rebloom in fall if dead-headed after the first bloom. Zones 4–10.

MEDIUM-HEIGHT (5 TO 9 FEET TALL)

Clethra alnifolia (sweet pepperbush): Fragrant white flowers in midsummer. Will tolerate moist soil. Good soft hedging plant for the shade. There is a pink cultivar available ('Rosea') as well as a dwarf cultivar which only grows 4–5 feet tall. Zones 3–9.

Cornus alba 'Elegantissima' (Tartarian dogwood): Green and white variegated leaves; white, fairly insignificant flowers, brilliant red stems in the winter. Grown for its foliage and red branches. Forms a dense, wide hedge in full sun or dappled shade. Zones 3–7.

Euonymus alata 'Compactus' (dwarf burning bush): Grows 5–7 feet tall if left unsheared. Brilliant scarlet red fall color. Will tolerate sun or shade. Zones 3–7.

Shrub roses: These offer a wide choice for flowering, informal hedge plants. Use the rugosa or beach rose (*Rosa rugosa*) if you have lots of space and want a dense, thorny barrier. Rugosa rose hybrids offer the same hardiness and ease of care with a less vigorous habit of growth. Cultivars to try to include 'Therese Bugnet', with soft, double lavender blossoms and red stems; 'Pink Grootendoorst' with soft pink, fringed, carnation-like flowers; and 'Hansa', with violet-red fragrant flowers. There are many other shrub roses that offer hardiness, vigor, and all-summer bloom. My favorites are 'Simplicity' roses, available in pink or white ('White Simplicity') called "the hedge rose" by Jackson and Perkins. 'Bonica' is a Meidiland hybrid with soft, double pink flowers and beautiful red rose hips in the fall.

Syringa spp. (lilacs): The common lilac (*Syringa vulgaris*) grows 8–10 feet or more. Dwarf lilacs such as Meyer (*Syringa meyeri*), little leaf (*S. microphylla*), or 'Miss Kim' Manchurian (*S. patula* 'Miss Kim') all have fragrant lavender flowers on 5–7 foot compact plants that bloom a few weeks later than the common lilac. Lilacs are classic country garden plants, providing beautiful fragrance as well as color in the late spring. Zones 3–7.

Vaccinium corymbosum (highbush blueberry): Edible landscape hedge plant. Lovely white flowers in spring, delicious fruit in summer, and a gorgeous red fall color. Will grow in full sun or partial shade. Needs an acid soil. Zones 3–9.

TALL (10 FEET AND UP)

Hibiscus syriacus (rose-of-Sharon): Hardy flowering shrub with single or double flowers in many colors. Can be treated as a large specimen in the landscape, but can also be used as a tall hedge plant as it becomes very bushy and full. It blooms in late summer, therefore all pruning should be done in early spring. Zones 5–8.

Ilex × *meserveae* (blue holly): Will grow 8–15 feet depending on the cultivar, with dark blue-green glossy leaves. Dense, compact habit of growth, red berries on the female plants all winter. (You must plant a male and female plant to have berries.) These plants take well to shearing, but may also be allowed to grow into a more natural form and pruned selectively by hand. Will grow in sun or partial shade. Zones 5–9.

FENCE DESIGN IDEAS

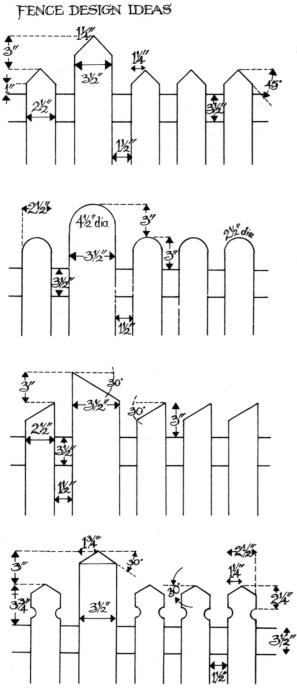

can simply backfill the hole with the soil that came out of it, tamping down well as you go. You can tamp with a length of 2 by 4 or even a stout stick. As you work, keep checking the post to make sure it stays vertical.

If the soil is very sandy and does not compact well, you should backfill the holes with concrete. Unless you are setting a great many posts, use pre-bagged concrete mixes. Simply dump the contents of the bag in a wheelbarrow and mix in the required amount of water. Then shovel the wet concrete into the hole. As you fill the hole, keep checking the post make sure it remains vertical.

4. Set the intermediate posts. If you are backfilling the corner posts with tamped soil, you can immediately start digging the holes for the intermediate posts. If you are using concrete, wait a few days for it to cure before setting the intermediate posts.

Double-check the spacing of the intermediate posts, and dig the holes as you did for the corner posts. String two lengths of mason's cord between the corner posts near the top and bottom to serve as a guide for aligning the intermediate posts. Cut a stringer to the length specified in the *Materials List* to aid you in positioning the posts. Plumb the posts and backfill.

5. Attach the stringers. Double-check the distance between the posts and cut the stringers to fit. Drill two angled holes

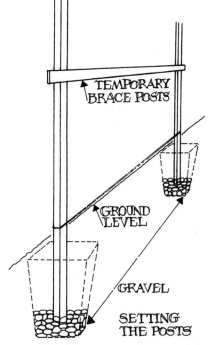

TEMPORARY
BRACE POSTS

GROUND
LEVEL

GRAVEL

SETTING
THE POSTS

through the ends of each stringer as shown in the *Stringer Detail*. Mark the stringer heights on each post as shown in the *Post Detail*. Hold the stringers in position and screw them to the posts.

6. Make the pickets. Cut all the pickets to the length specified in the *Materials List*. Be sure to cut enough pickets for the gate as well as a few extra just in case. Make your top shape pattern from ¼-inch plywood or heavy cardboard. Trace the shape on each picket and cut all the pickets to shape. This is most easily accomplished on a band saw but a saber saw or even a coping saw will work. If you plan to paint a finish on the pickets, posts, and stringers, do it now before you attach the pickets to the fence.

7. Attach the pickets. Make a spacer

from an extra picket. Cut it down to 1½ inches wide. Use this spacer to help locate the pickets along the stringers. Attach the pickets to the stringers with 1½-inch galvanized screws. A power screwdriver will make this task less tedious.

8. Make the gate. Cut the gate stiles, rails, and brace to the sizes specified in the *Materials List*. Notch the ends of the stiles and rails as shown in the *Gate Detail*. These notches can be cut with a dado blade on the table saw, or with a handsaw.

If you have a table saw, set up a dado blade that is as wide as possible. Set the height of the blade to one half the thickness of the stiles and rails. Guide the pieces past the blade with the miter gauge. Make several passes until the notch is wide enough. If you are cutting the notches by hand, lay out the cuts with a square and carefully cut along the lines.

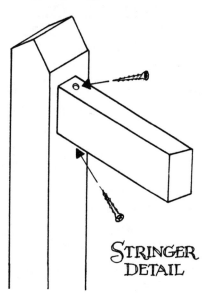

STRINGER
DETAIL

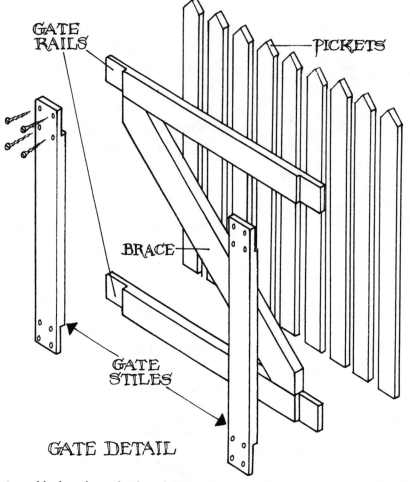

GATE
RAILS

PICKETS

BRACE

GATE
STILES

GATE DETAIL

Assemble the stiles and rails with 1½-inch galvanized screws as shown. Measure across the diagonals to make sure the gate frame is square. If the diagonals are equal, the frame is square. Adjust the frame if necessary.

Cut the corners off both ends of the brace to fit it into the frame. Drill holes through each end as shown and screw the brace in place with 3½-inch screws. Paint or finish the frame as you did the fence. When the paint dries, lay the frame down on the ground and attach the pickets. Use the spacer you cut for aligning the fence pickets to aid with the spacing. Screw the pickets to the gate with 1½-inch screws.

9. Hang the gate. Drill pilot holes into the gate and attach the hinges. Hold the gate up in its opening and mark the hinge locations on the post. Drill pilot holes in the post, then screw the gate in place. Adjust the position of the hinges if necessary to make the gate swing freely. Install the latch, then step back and admire the results of your work.

HOW TO BUILD A WOODEN PLANTER

Using planters in your country garden can open up a whole range of design options. They allow you to rearrange some of the landscape to create different spaces and different moods. They're a perfect setting for a cottage garden of old-fashioned annuals. And they're the perfect size to grow dwarf fruit trees or standard roses.

Beyond their ornamental uses, planters are excellent containers for vegetables, being in many ways like small raised beds. Build several, and you'll have a complete, if small, vegetable garden. This can save hours of tedious work preparing a plot for a garden, weeding it, and harvesting the crop. Since a planter is already elevated, you won't have to bend very far to tend to the plants, the amount of preparation is limited because of the size, and the weeds will be right at your fingertips.

If you have a limited amount of space, a planter may be the only way you can garden. Even if you have only a balcony, a planter can provide a place to grow vegetables, flowers, or whatever suits your ambitions.

This planter is made from standard sizes of common lumber. All you have to do is cut the boards to length. It is put together with screws for ease of assembly. Any wood can be used, but the best choice is cedar for its natural weather resistance. Pressure-treated wood will also work, but it is not as nice to work with. If portability is a real concern, cut the legs 2 inches short and screw on a set of heavy-duty casters. These will allow you to scoot the planter almost anywhere you want it.

1. Cut the parts to size. Cut the parts to the sizes specified in the *Materials List*. The legs are cut from a 4 by 4. The rest of the pieces are cut from $\frac{5}{4}$ (five quarters) by 6 decking. If $\frac{5}{4}$ stock is not available, you can use 1 by 6s instead.

2. Cut the tops of the legs to shape. The tops of the legs are pointed to help them shed water and to improve their appearance. Lay out the cuts as shown in the *Front View*. You can use a combination square to help draw the 45-degree angles. Cut the legs on the table saw or with a hand-held circular saw. If you are using a table saw, tilt the blade over to 45 degrees. Make the cuts by guiding each leg past the blade with the miter gauge. If you are using a circular saw, tilt the base on the saw to 45 degrees to make the angled cuts.

3. Attach the battens. Each of the four legs gets two battens screwed along its inside corner as shown in the *Exploded View*. Make a mark on the inside corner of a leg, 3 inches up from the bottom. Place one end of a batten on this mark and align the edge of the batten with the edge of the leg. Drill and countersink pilot holes, then screw the batten in place. Attach another

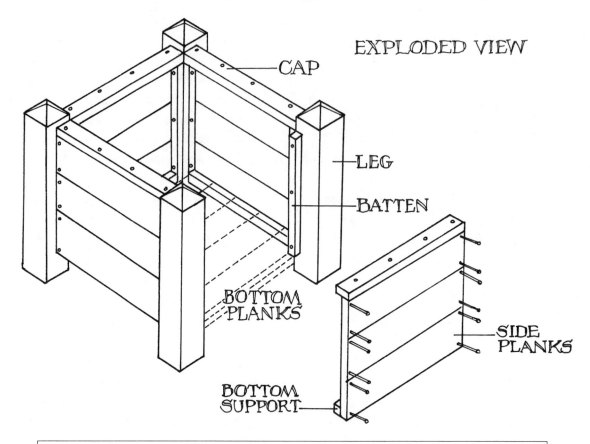

EXPLODED VIEW

CAP

LEG

BATTEN

SIDE PLANKS

BOTTOM PLANKS

BOTTOM SUPPORT

Hardware & Materials List

PART	QUANTITY	DIMENSIONS
Legs	4	3½" x 3½" x 23½"
Battens	8	1" x 1" x 16½"
Side Planks	12	1" x 5½" x 19"
Caps	4	1" x 2" x 19"
Bottom Supports	4	1" x 1" x 17"
Bottom Planks	4	1" x 5¼" x 20⅞"

HARDWARE
#6 x 1¾" galvanized wood
   screws, as needed
Casters, 4 (optional)

batten adjacent to the first. Repeat with the other three legs.

4. Attach the side planks. Select a pair of legs and fasten three planks between them. Start with one plank flush with the bottom end of the battens and work your way up. Hold each plank in place, drill and countersink pilot holes, then screw the plank to the battens; repeat with the other two planks. Repeat with the other pair of legs. Then connect the two sets with the remaining planks.

5. Attach the caps. Place a cap between two of the legs as shown in the *Top View*. Hold it in place so its outside edge is flush with the outside of the planks. Drill and countersink pilot holes along the cap into the side plank. Screw the cap in place. Repeat with the other three caps.

6. Attach the bottom supports. Fit the bottom supports in between the battens at the bottom edge of the side planks as shown in the *Exploded View*. Hold them in

place as you drill and countersink pilot holes into the side planks. Screw the supports to the planks.

7. Fit the bottom planks. The bottom planks just rest on the bottom supports. They should have a ⅛- to ¼-inch space in between them to allow for drainage. Cut them to fit down inside the planter. You will have to notch the two outside planks to fit around the legs. Cut these notches with a coping saw.

8. Finish the planter. As with most outdoor projects, you have a choice of finishes for your planter. The most durable exterior finish is paint. Use a good quality exterior primer followed by several coats of exterior trim paint. If you prefer to let the natural wood color show, apply several coats of exterior polyurethane. Or you can simply leave the planter to weather naturally.

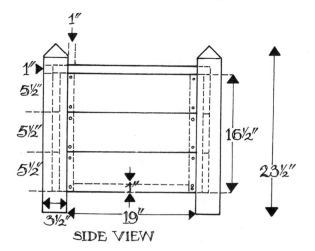

SIDE VIEW

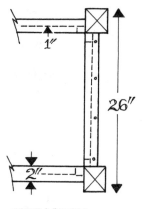

TOP VIEW

Choice Annuals and Others for Country Planters

There are many, many interesting annual flowers that can add a country feeling to the deck, porch, or patio. You do not have to be stuck in the traditional style of geraniums and petunias when planting a container garden.

Planters can ease the transition between the deck and the yard, or the outside and the inside. By growing a tree in a planter, you create almost a living piece of furniture or sculpture, with elements that are part of both the natural world and the man-made one. This sense of duality helps to bring the outside in and vice versa. And planters offer another advantage: Because they are portable, you can enjoy gardening year-round. If you're growing annuals, vegetables, or tender perennials, simply keep them outside during the warm months, then move them in for the cold ones.

Soil mix is important. Be sure it drains well and is not too heavy. A good mix is 2 parts soil, 1 part compost, 1 part perlite, and 1 part peat moss with a cup of bonemeal added per 5 gallons of soil mix. Be sure the soil is well-mixed and moistened before planting.

Water your planter garden often and fertilize with liquid seaweed or fish emulsion every two weeks to keep it growing happily. Remove all spent (faded) flowers two or three times a week for continued bloom. You can leave your wooden planters in the garden over winter, with plants cleaned out after hard frost, and stick evergreen branches and berries into the soil for an attractive display through the holiday season.

Make planting your container garden an exercise in creativity. When choosing plants, remember to consider the light available and their size and scale in relation to the container. Think of your planter as a miniature garden, an opportunity to design beautiful combinations of unusual annuals to brighten your summer days.

Try a planter of cheerful daisies. Marguerite daisies (*Chrysanthemum frutescens*) can reach 3 feet tall and are available in white, yellow, and lavender. There is also a white-flowering species with blue foliage (*C. vera*). As long as the spent flowers are removed, they will bloom until hard frost. The Swan River daisy (*Brachycome iberidifolia*) is a small blue, lavender, or white daisy with delicate, lacy foliage. It grows only 10 inches tall and is lovely softening and trailing over the edge of containers in full sun. The Dahlberg daisy (*Dyssodia tenuiloba*) is similar in foliage and habit with yellow flowers. Treasure flowers (*Gazania rigens*) are an excellent choice for areas that heat up in full sun. They have a rosette of basal foliage and colorful yellow, orange, pink, or cream flowers that open in the daytime and close at sunset. There is a silver-leaved cultivar available which is attractive for both flowers and foliage.

Other lacy, delicate, softening plants for containers include cupflower (*Nierembergia hippomanica*) with blueish-purple, upward-facing cup-like flowers and thin needlelike foliage. It grows to 12 inches tall and blooms in sun or partial shade. It is especially tolerant of seashore conditions. Cosmos (*Cosmos bipinnatus*) is usually considered too tall for containers, but the dwarf 'Sonata' cultivars are perfect for containers, growing only 20 inches tall with pink or white flowers. Look for dwarf cultivars of the fiery *Cosmos sulphureus*, too. Annual baby's-breath (*Gypsophila elegans*) adds a delicate touch with soft sprays of white flowers all summer long born on 15-inch plants.

Common heliotrope (*Heliotropium arborescens*) has rich purple, vanilla-scented flowers growing on plants 2 to 4 feet tall. It is actually a tender perennial; it blooms in the garden in full sun all summer until hard frost; then can be brought into the house and overwintered in a sunny window. For a striking contrast, combine it with blue mealy-cup sage (*Salvia farinacea*) and purple globe amaranth (*Gomphrena globosa*).

If your planter is in the shade, try flowering tobacco (*Nicotiana alata*). There are tall cultivars with night scented flowers, as well as the popular but less fragrant 'Nikki' cultivars ~ short compact plants with blooms in bright red, pink, purple, and white. For foliage effect, choose the polka-dot plant (*Hypoestes phyllostachya*) which thrives in the shade. It has green leaves spotted white, red, or pink and is often grown as a houseplant. Edging lobelia (*Lobelia erinus*) is effective cascading over the planter's edge; it grows best in shade. Besides the traditional rich blue 'Crystal Palace', there are many new cultivars available such as purple 'Rosamunde', 'Sapphire' (which is soft blue with a white eye), and pure white 'White Lady'.

Add a surprise element in your planter with alpine strawberries, also called *fraises des bois* (*Fragaria vesca* 'Alpine'). These tiny, sweet strawberries are produced all summer long on excellent low edging plants. For another unusual choice, try scented geraniums (*Pelargonium* spp.). There are hundreds of cultivars to choose from, offering fragrance from lemon and rose through chocolate and nutmeg, interesting leaf textures, and delicate sprays of flowers. The leaves are edible, and are often used in teas, in potpourri, and as cake decorations.

Perennials can also work well in planters if you choose plants that have either a long season of bloom or attractive, long-lasting foliage. Good perennials for planters include soft yellow 'Moonbeam' thread leaf coreopsis (*Coreopsis verticillata* 'Moonbeam'), which grows 15 inches tall and blooms all summer; heuchera 'Palace Purple', a foliage plant for partial or full shade with large burgundy leaves, and blue oat grass (*Helictotrichon sempervirens*), a tall ornamental grass with brilliant steel blue leaves that grows 24 inches tall.

HOW TO MAKE A GARDEN BENCH

A country garden is a wonderful place to wile away a lazy summer afternoon. And what better place to sit than on the garden bench shown here? A bench that even a novice woodworker can build with just a few tools and some spare time.

While the bench may look complicated at first, it is really very easy to put together. The whole thing is assembled with screws; there are no tricky or painstaking joints to cut. And all the parts are cut from stock lumber, so there is very little material preparation involved. The whole bench could be built entirely with hand tools, but a table saw and a saber saw will speed the process. Other than these two power tools, you'll need a tape measure, square, protractor, compass, drill, hand saw, block plane, and screwdriver.

There is one part that will prove challenging: To make the bench comfortable, some of the parts will have to be cut at angles other than 90 degrees. While this is a little bit more difficult than making things square, it is worth the added effort.

This bench can be made from almost any species of wood; however, the parts are designed to be cut from the standard sizes of lumber available at most lumberyards. The front legs are cut from a 4 by 4. The back legs are cut from a 2 by 8. The side and middle rails come from 2 by 6s, and the rest of the parts are made from ⁵⁄₄ (five-quarters) by 6 decking. If you intend the bench to be an outside piece, cedar, redwood, or pressure-treated pine would be appropriate. Otherwise, regular pine or fir lumber will do. The finish is up to you. You can leave the wood to weather naturally, or you can apply paint or an exterior wood finish like spar varnish or exterior polyurethane. For less weather-resistant woods, a finish will make your bench last longer, but for best results you'll have to touch it up every year.

1. Make the front legs. Lay out the front legs on the 4 by 4. Leave about 1 inch between the two legs. Mark the cut for the bottom of each leg square across the board. Mark the cut for the top of each leg at 88 degrees as shown in the *Front Leg Detail*. Cut the legs to length by cutting along the layout lines. This is most easily done with a handsaw, since few power saws have blades big enough to cut through a 4 by 4 in one pass.

Lay out the notches in the top of the legs. Be sure to make one right and one left leg. Cut the notches with the handsaw.

2. Make the back legs. Cut the 2 by 8 to the necessary length. With the aid of the protractor, lay out the shape of the back legs as shown in the *Back Leg Detail*. Cut out the legs with a saber saw. Smooth the sawed edges with a block plane. Cut

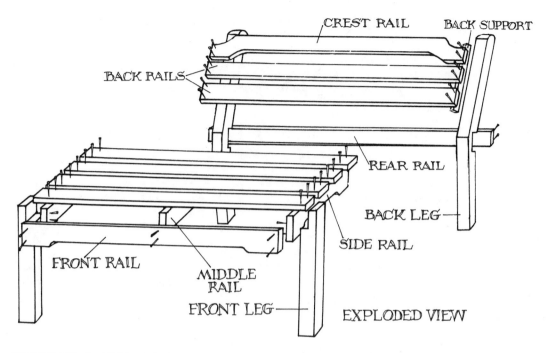

CREST RAIL

BACK SUPPORT

BACK RAILS

REAR RAIL

BACK LEG

SIDE RAIL

FRONT RAIL

MIDDLE RAIL

FRONT LEG

EXPLODED VIEW

Hardware & Materials List

PART	QUANTITY	DIMENSIONS
Front Legs	2	$3\frac{1}{2}$" x $3\frac{1}{2}$" x 17"
Back Legs	2	$1\frac{1}{2}$" x $7\frac{1}{2}$" x 35"
Side Rails	2	$1\frac{1}{2}$" x 4" x $17\frac{1}{4}$"
Front Rail	1	1" x 4" x 45"
Rear Rail	1	1" x 3" x 44"
Middle Rail	1	$1\frac{1}{2}$" x $2\frac{1}{2}$" x $17\frac{1}{4}$"
Back Supports	2	1" x 1" x 12"
Crest Rail	1	1" x $4\frac{1}{2}$" x 41"
Back Rails	2	1" x 3" x 41"
Seat Planks	4	1" x 4" x 47"

HARDWARE
#6 x $1\frac{3}{4}$" galvanized wood
  screws, as needed
#8 x $2\frac{1}{2}$" galvanized wood
  screws, as needed

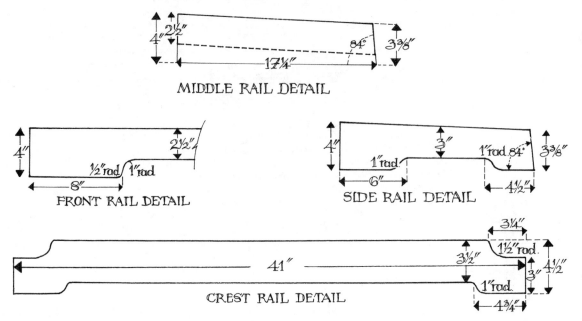

MIDDLE RAIL DETAIL

FRONT RAIL DETAIL

SIDE RAIL DETAIL

CREST RAIL DETAIL

out the notch in the legs with the saber saw as well.

3. Make the side and middle rails. To rough-cut the 2 by 6 for the side and middle rails about 1 inch longer than is called for in the *Materials List,* use a handsaw. Set the rip fence on the table saw for the width of the side rails, and rip all three pieces to width. Leave the middle rail as wide as the side rails for now.

Square one end of each rail by guiding it past the saw blade with the miter gauge. Reset the miter gauge to cut an 84-degree angle, and cut the other ends of the rails as shown in the *Side* and *Middle Rail* details.

Lay out the taper on the top edge of each piece as shown. Cut the tapers with a saber saw and smooth the sawed edges with a block plane.

Set the rip fence on the table saw to cut

the middle rail to the width given in the *Materials List*. Rip the middle rail to width. Be sure to guide the top edge of the rail against the fence while making the cut.

4. Cut the side rails to shape. Lay out the curved cutouts on the side rails as shown in the *Side Rail Detail*. Make the cuts with a saber saw. Sand the sawed edges to smooth them.

5. Attach the side rails to the legs. Place a side rail in the notch of a front leg. Align the rail so it is flush with the front of the leg. Hold it steady while you drill and countersink pilot holes for the screws. Screw the rail to the leg with 2½-inch screws. Align the rail on the back leg as shown in the *Back Leg Detail*. Hold it steady as you drill the screw holes and screw it in place. Repeat with the other legs and side rail.

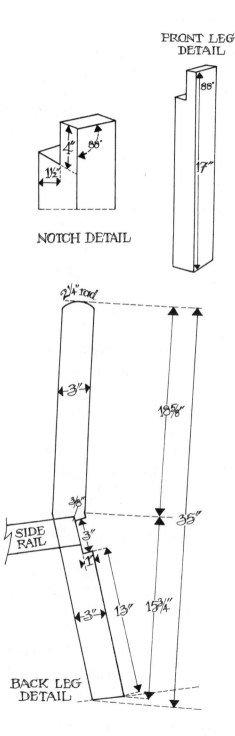

FRONT LEG
DETAIL

88°

17"

4"

88°

1½"

NOTCH DETAIL

2¼" rad

3"

18⅝"

3⅛"

SIDE
RAIL

3"

35"

1"

3"   13"   15¾"

BACK LEG
DETAIL

6. Make the front and rear rails. Cut the wood for the front and rear rails to the sizes specified in the *Materials List*. Lay out the curved cutouts on the front rail as shown in the *Front Rail Detail*. Make the cuts with a saber saw. Smooth the sawed edge with sandpaper and a block plane.

7. Attach the front and rear rails. Place the rear rail in the notches in the back legs. The ends of the rail should be flush with the sides of the legs. Drill and countersink pilot holes through the rail into the legs. Screw the rail to the legs with 2½-inch screws.

Hold the front rail in place along the front of the bench. Align it so the ends of the rail are flush with the outside of the legs. Hold it there while you drill and countersink pilot holes, then screw it in place.

8. Attach the middle rail. Place the middle rail between the front and rear rails then center it from side to side. Hold it so its top edge is flush with the top edges of the front and back rails. Drill and countersink pilot holes through the front and rear rails into the ends of the middle rail. Screw it in place with 2½-inch screws.

9. Make and attach the back supports. Cut the back supports to the size specified in the *Materials List*. Screw them to the back legs as shown in the *Side View*.

10. Make and attach the crest rail. Cut the stock for the crest rail to the size specified in the *Materials List*. Lay out its

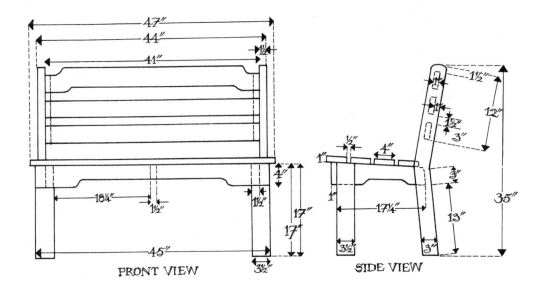

FRONT VIEW

SIDE VIEW

curved shape as shown in the *Crest Rail Detail*. Cut the rail to shape with a saber saw. Smooth the sawed edges with a block plane and sandpaper.

Position the rail between the back legs as shown in the *Front View*. The ends of the rail should be flush with the top of the back supports. Drill and countersink pilot holes through the rail into the supports. Screw the crest rail in place with 1¾-inch screws.

11. Make and attach the back rails. Cut the back rails to the size specified in the *Materials List*. Position the rails against the back support. Leave 1½ inches between the back rails as shown in the *Side View*. Hold the rails in place as you drill and countersink pilot holes. Screw the rails to the supports with 1¾-inch screws.

12. Make and attach the seat planks. Cut the seat planks to the size specified in the *Materials List*. Position the planks on the bench. The foremost plank should overhang the front rail by 1 inch. The others attach behind, with ½ inch in between. Use a saber saw to notch the rear plank to fit around the back legs. Drill and countersink pilot holes through the seat planks into the side and middle rails. Screw the planks to the bench with 1¾-inch screws.

13. Finish the bench. Go over the entire bench with sandpaper. Pay special attention to the back and seat. Finish the bench with your choice of paint or other exterior wood finish. Or, if you've built the bench from weather-resistant wood, leave it to weather naturally.

HOW TO BUILD
AN ARBOR

Few garden structures blend in with their surroundings as well as an arbor. An arbor can easily be adapted to cover a patio, bench, picnic table, or walkway. You may even want to build a bench or two into the arbor's sides.

The arbor presented here is very straightforward and easy to build. Build it as shown, or feel free to adapt it to suit your purposes. It will provide an excellent place to grow grapes, roses, clematis, wisteria, or other climbing plants. Some arbors have even been built to support weeping fruit trees such as the mulberry. Or try your hand with some annual climbers such as cucumbers, melons, or scarlet runner beans (*Phaseolus coccineus*). They will provide shade as well as a tasty crop for the dinner table.

To build this arbor, you'll need a basic set of hand tools including a hammer, measuring tape, square, saw, wrench, and drill. While you could do all the work with hand tools, there are a couple of power tools that will make the job easier. These include a circular saw, and a power hand drill. With this basic complement of tools, you should be able to put together your arbor in no time.

You can get the wood needed for this project at a good lumberyard or home improvement center. The posts should be made from pressure-treated 6 by 6s, since they will be in direct contact with the ground. The rest of the parts could be made from cedar or some other weather-resistant species. Or you might choose to build the whole arbor from treated stock. In many ways this might be the best option since painting or staining the arbor will be difficult once the vines take hold. The cross bars and rafters are made from 2 by 6s and the braces are cut from 2 by 4s. Look for straight stock as you shop. It is much easier to work with wood that is warp-free.

1. Dig the foundation holes. Determine the location of the arbor in your garden. Mark the centers of the foundation holes with stakes. The stakes should be 66 inches apart. Dig the holes to a depth of about 42 inches with a spade and post hole digger.

2. Notch the posts. Notch the top of the posts to receive the cross bars. Lay out the notches as shown in the *Post Detail*. Cut the notches with a handsaw or a circular saw. Measure down 48 inches from the top and make a mark all the way around each post. This mark will serve as a guide as you set the posts.

3. Set the posts. Fill the foundation holes with about 6 inches of gravel (you'll need approximately 60 pounds). Stand the posts upright in the holes with the notches facing away from each other. Have

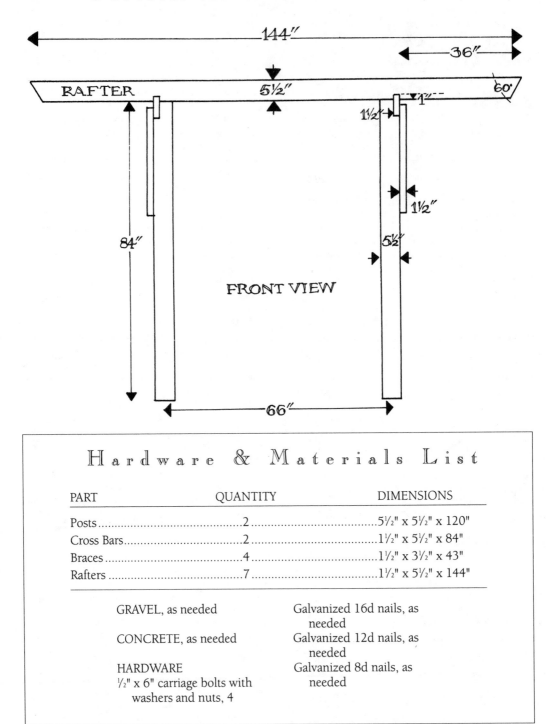

FRONT VIEW

Hardware & Materials List

PART	QUANTITY	DIMENSIONS
Posts	2	5½" x 5½" x 120"
Cross Bars	2	1½" x 5½" x 84"
Braces	4	1½" x 3½" x 43"
Rafters	7	1½" x 5½" x 144"

GRAVEL, as needed

CONCRETE, as needed

HARDWARE
½" x 6" carriage bolts with washers and nuts, 4

Galvanized 16d nails, as needed

Galvanized 12d nails, as needed

Galvanized 8d nails, as needed

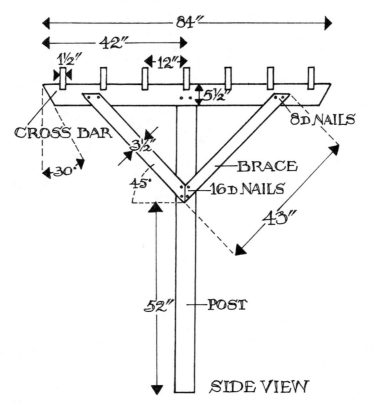

84"

42"

1½"

12"

5½"

8D NAILS

CROSS BAR

3½"

30°

45°

—BRACE

16D NAILS

43"

52" —POST

SIDE VIEW

two helpers hold them plumb. Stretch a line level between the posts at the reference marks. Add or subtract gravel from the holes until the reference marks are level with one another.

Backfill the holes. What you backfill with depends on what type of soil you're dealing with. If your soil compacts well, you can simply backfill with the soil that came out of the holes. Shovel it in around the posts a little bit at a time. Tamp it down well as you go. If your soil is very sandy and does not compact well, you'll have to backfill with concrete. Buy several bags of premixed concrete and mix it according to the directions on the bag. Shovel the con-

crete around the posts. Use a pole to help distribute the concrete and to work out any air pockets that might form.

4. Make the cross bars. Cut the cross bars to the length specified in the *Materials List*. Cut the ends at an angle as shown in the *Side View*. Lay out the notches in the top edge of the bars as shown in the *Cross Bar Detail*. Cut the notches out with a coping saw or a saber saw.

5. Attach the cross bars. The cross bars get bolted to the posts with carriage bolts. While they are still on the ground, drill two ½-holes in each cross bar as shown in the *Side View*. Then position a cross bar in the notch on one of the posts.

Center it from side to side and drill holes through the post, using the holes in the cross bar as a guide. Bolt the cross bar to the post. Repeat to attach the other cross bar to the other post.

6. Make the braces. Cut the braces to the length specified in the *Materials List*. Cut their ends off at a 45-degree angle as shown in the *Side View*.

7. Attach the braces. Measure 52 inches up from the ground and make a mark across the outside of both posts as shown in the *Side View*. Align the brace with the mark as shown, and nail them to the posts and to the cross bars with 16d and 8d nails, respectively.

8. Make the rafters. Cut the rafters to the length specified in the *Materials List*. Cut the ends of the rafters at a 60-degree angle as shown in the *Front View*.

9. Attach the rafters. Place the rafters in the notches in the cross bars. Center them from end to end. Use 12d nails to toenail through both sides of the rafters into the cross bars to anchor the rafters. (Drive the nails at a 45-degree angle

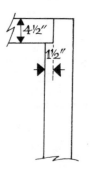

POST DETAIL

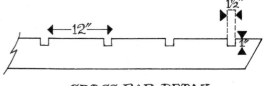

CROSS BAR DETAIL

through the rafters into the cross bars.)

10. Finish the arbor. Paint or stain the arbor to suit your tastes. Or leave it bare to weather naturally. This may be the best choice, because you won't have to worry about refinishing the arbor when it is covered with vines.

HOW TO MAKE A BAT HOUSE

Have you ever looked up into the twilight sky and seen a dark shadow flitting about? If so, then chances are you've seen a bat. These much-maligned creatures fly through the night feeding, then sleep during the daytime. Their natural habits, more than anything else, have given bats a bad reputation.

A bat house provides bats with a place to perch while they sleep during the day. In return for their lodging, your new tenants will patrol your garden during the night and help eliminate mosquitoes and other pesky insects.

In addition to consuming insects, bats also provide another free service. A few weeks after a colony of bats moves into your new bat house, you'll notice an accumulation of guano on the ground underneath it. This nitrogen-rich manure, once composted, makes a wonderful organic fertilizer.

The bat house shown here is similar in appearance to a skinny birdhouse but there are some important differences. Instead of having an entry hole, the house is bottomless. The bats can come and go through the bottom of the house, and their guano falls to the ground, eliminating the need to clean the house out. Inside, there are two compartments, each able to hold six to ten bats. The inside walls should be cut with a series of saw kerfs to give the bats a place to grip. The best place to locate the house is 12 to 15 feet up on the side of a tree or pole and within 1,000 feet of water. If your bat house isn't occupied within two years, try changing its location.

This bat house was designed to make use of standard sizes of lumber. The entire house can be made from a single 8-foot-long piece of 1 by 12.

1. Cut the parts to size. Cut the parts to the sizes specified in the *Materials List*. Note that the long dimension of the roof is listed as its width. Cut the roof so that the grain runs parallel to its short dimension. This will allow the roof to expand and contract with changes in humidity in harmony with the rest of the house. If you run the grain the other direction, the house might crack apart.

2. Bevel the front, partition, and roof. Tilt the blade on the table saw over to form a 60-degree angle with the table. Cut a 60-degree bevel on one end of the front, the partition, and the roof as shown in the *Side View*. Use the miter gauge to guide the pieces past the blade.

3. Cut the sides to shape. Reset the blade on the table saw at 90 degrees. Set the miter gauge at 60 degrees to the blade. Cut the sides to shape by guiding them past the blade with the angled miter gauge.

4. Score the inside surfaces. The inside surfaces of the front and back and both sides of the partition should be

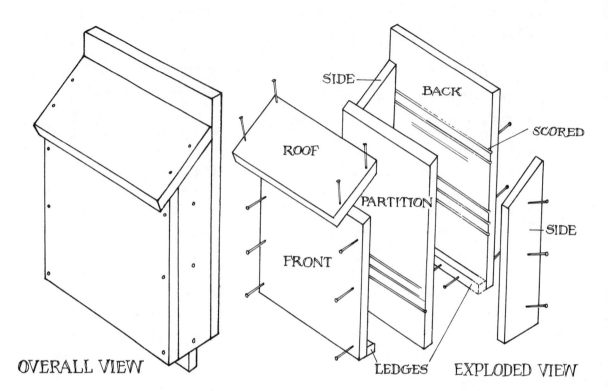

OVERALL VIEW

SIDE

ROOF

BACK

SCORED

PARTITION

FRONT

SIDE

LEDGES   EXPLODED VIEW

Hardware & Materials List

PART	QUANTITY	DIMENSIONS
Back	1	$\frac{3}{4}$" x $11\frac{1}{2}$" x 18"
Front	1	$\frac{3}{4}$" x $11\frac{1}{2}$" x $12\frac{7}{8}$"
Partition	1	$\frac{3}{4}$" x 10" x 16"
Roof	1	$\frac{3}{4}$" x $11\frac{1}{2}$" x $6\frac{3}{4}$"
Sides	2	$\frac{3}{4}$" x $3\frac{3}{4}$" x 15"
Ledges	2	$\frac{3}{4}$" x $\frac{3}{4}$" x 10"

HARDWARE
4d galvanized finish nails,
    as needed
12d galvanized finish nails, 2

This bat house was designed
to make use of standard
sizes of lumber. The entire
house can be made from a
single 8-foot, 1 x 12 piece.

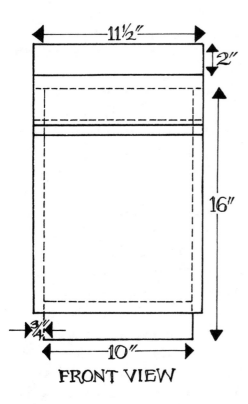

FRONT VIEW

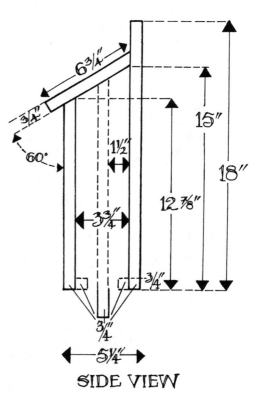

SIDE VIEW

lightly scored to give the bats a foothold, as shown in the *Exploded View*. Lower the blade on the table saw until it is barely above the table. Straighten the miter gauge and use it to guide the pieces past the blade. Space the kerfs about ½ inch apart.

5. Assemble the house. Center the ledges along the bottom edge of the front and back and nail them in position as shown in the *Exploded View*. Then nail the front and back to the sides with 4d finishing nails. All the pieces should be flush along the bottom. Slip the partition into the house and center it from front to back. It should be flush with the top of the sides. Use 4d finishing nails to nail it in place

through the sides and also to nail the roof in place.

6. Finish the house. Run a bead of caulk along the joint between the roof and the back to prevent water from seeping through. When the caulk dries, give the exterior of the house a coat of primer. Then paint the house a dark green, gray, or brown color to help it blend in with its surroundings.

7. Hang the house. Hang the house 12 to 15 feet in the air on the side of a tree or pole. Nail through the back with 12d nails to anchor it. Ideally it should face east or southeast to catch the warm morning sun.

HOW TO BUILD A BIRDHOUSE

Attracting birds to your garden has other immediate rewards. The mere presence of endearing and entertaining creatures may inspire you to take up ornithology, or birdwatching. This lifetime interest can be practiced almost anywhere and anytime. You can devote as little or as much energy to it as you wish, and the equipment needed is minimal. A good field guide and a pair of binoculars are all that are required. As your interest grows, you may even be inspired to build a variety of houses to see how many different species you can attract. There is nothing that can quite compare to the thrill of seeing a new arrival take up residence in one of your own creations. And even if you don't care to watch your new neighbors, it is hard to ignore their songs. What chorus could be finer on a bright spring morning?

Don't think that your new tenants will be a bunch of freeloaders, either. Birds require an enormous amount of energy to go about their lives. With migration, reproduction, and just staying warm to worry about, the average bird will eat many times its own weight during the course of a year. Depending on the species, its diet might include insects, weed seeds, even rodents and other small game. So if you attract a few birds to your garden, you can be sure to see a reduction in the number of pests without having to resort to more extreme measures.

The birdhouse shown is designed for the house wren, one of the more common cavity-nesting species. With some slight modifications, it could easily accommodate any of a number of other species. Should you become interested in constructing a variety of houses, the U.S. Fish and Wildlife Service Conservation Bulletin #14, *Homes for Birds* (publication #024–010–00524–4) lists the requirements for a variety of different species.

A birdhouse can be built from common materials with a few basic handtools. Cedar is an ideal choice for wood, because it is naturally weather-resistant, but it is sometimes hard to find and is generally fairly expensive. Pine, if it is well-finished and sealed against the elements, will last for many years and will make a fine birdhouse. Avoid pressure-treated wood: While it will last outside indefinitely, the chemicals with which it has been treated are toxic to birds.

The tools you will need include a tape measure, square, protractor, hammer, screwdriver, saw, and drill. A table saw or scroll saw will speed the process, but neither one is a necessity. Work carefully and measure things accurately, and you will have a beautiful birdhouse to grace your garden. But don't worry if it doesn't come out exactly as planned: The birds won't complain.

OVERALL VIEW

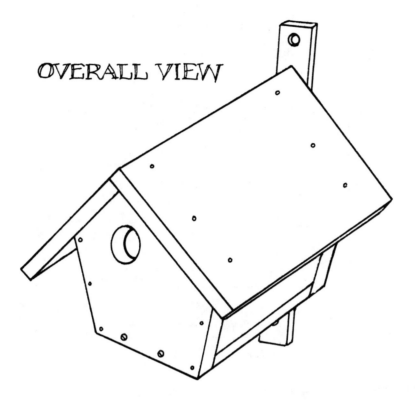

Hardware & Materials List

PART	QUANTITY	DIMENSIONS
Front/Back	2	$\frac{3}{4}$" x $7\frac{3}{4}$" x 8"
Sides	2	$\frac{3}{4}$" x $3\frac{5}{8}$" x 4"
Bottom	1	$\frac{3}{4}$" x 6" x 4"
Wide Roof	1	$\frac{3}{4}$" x 7" x $7\frac{1}{2}$"
Narrow Roof	1	$\frac{3}{4}$" x $6\frac{1}{4}$" x $7\frac{1}{2}$"
Hanger	1	$\frac{3}{4}$" x $1\frac{1}{2}$" x 12"

HARDWARE

#6 x $1\frac{1}{2}$" brass wood
    screws, 6
4d galvanized finish nails, as
    needed

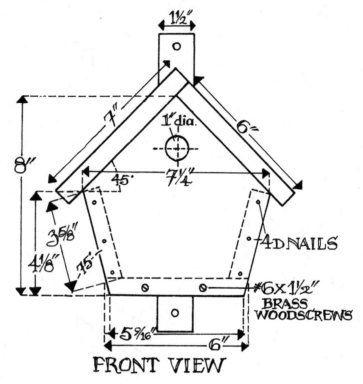

FRONT VIEW

1. Cut the parts to size. Cut the parts to the sizes specified in the *Materials List*. On all the pieces except the bottom, the grain should run parallel to the longest dimension given. On the bottom, the grain should run perpendicular to the longest dimension.

2. Make the front and back. Lay out the angled cuts on the front and back as shown in the *Front View*. Cut the pieces to shape. Mark the center of the entrance hole on the front with an awl. Drill the hole with a spade bit in an electric drill.

3. Bevel the sides and bottom. The lower edges of the sides and the short edges of the bottom are beveled to match the front and back. If you have a table saw, these cuts are easily made by tilting the

blade over to a 75-degree angle. Guide the pieces past the blade with the rip fence.

If you don't have a table saw, bevel the edges with a block plane. Make the angle you need at one end of the cut. Hold the piece in a vice and plane the edge. Keep comparing the bevel you are planing to the layout mark.

4. Assemble the front, back, and bottom. Drill and countersink two holes in the front and back for the screws that attach the front and back to the bottom. The approximate locations of the screws are shown in the *Front View*. Hold the bottom in a vice with its front edge up. Hold the front in place and drill pilot holes into the edge of the bottom using the holes in the front as guides. Screw the front to the bottom and repeat procedure to attach the back.

5. Attach the sides. Slide the sides into position between the front and back. The beveled edges should sit flat on the bottom. The upper edges should be just short of the outer corners of the front and back. This will help keep the house ventilated. If the sides meet or go past these upper corners, trim them until they are about ⅛ inch short. Nail the sides in place with 4d galvanized finishing nails. Predrill the nail holes if necessary to prevent the wood from splitting.

6. Make and attach the roof. Glue and nail the wide roof to the narrow roof to form an L-shape as shown in the *Overall View*. Use a waterproof glue such as

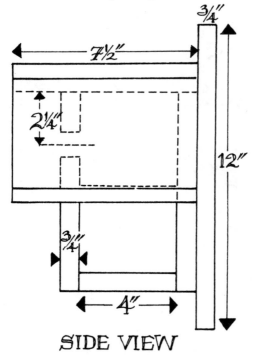

SIDE VIEW

Titebond II that will hold up outside. Spread glue along the top edges of the front and back and set the roof in place. It should be flush with the back and overhang in front. Nail it in place.

7. Attach the hanger. Turn the birdhouse face down on the bench. Place the hanger on the back and center it both horizontally and vertically. Drill and countersink two holes through the hanger and screw it to the back.

8. Finish the house. Finish the outside of the house with a good grade of exterior paint or stain. Dull browns, greens, and grays are good choices because they will blend in with the surrounding areas. Do not finish the inside of the house.

9. Hang the house. Find a tree or post on which to attach the house. The best positions are at the edges of wooded areas or along hedge rows. The house should be hung 6 to 10 feet off the ground. Hang it by screwing through the hanger into the tree or post.

10. Keep the house clean. During the course of a year, it is not unusual for several nests to be built in a house, one on top of the other. You don't need to worry about cleaning the house in between. At the end of the season, unscrew the bottom and clean out all the accumulated debris. Air the house for a day or so then reattach the bottom to prepare it for the next season. You can take it inside for the winter, but be sure to put it out again early next spring. Repaint as necessary.

PART IV

COUNTRY RESOURCES

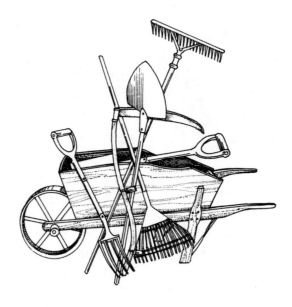

USDA PLANT
HARDINESS ZONE MAP

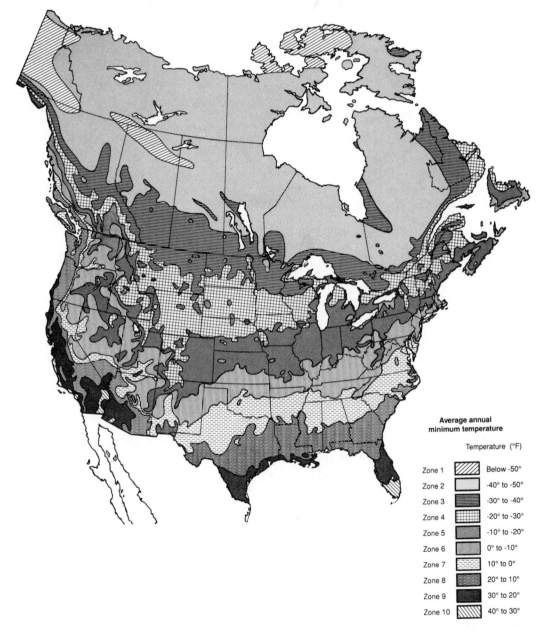

**Average annual
minimum temperature**

Temperature (°F)

Zone 1	Below -50°
Zone 2	-40° to -50°
Zone 3	-30° to -40°
Zone 4	-20° to -30°
Zone 5	-10° to -20°
Zone 6	0° to -10°
Zone 7	10° to 0°
Zone 8	20° to 10°
Zone 9	30° to 20°
Zone 10	40° to 30°

SOURCES

GARDEN SUPPLIES

Gardener's Supply Company
128 Intervale Rd.
Burlington, VT 05401

Gardens Alive!
Highway. 48
P.O. Box 149
Sunman, IN 47041

The Kinsman Company
River Rd.
Point Pleasant, PA 18950

Langenbach
P.O. Box 453
Blairstown, NJ 07825

The Necessary Catalogue
P.O. Box 305
New Castle, VA 24127

Walter Nicke Company
36 McLeod Ln.
P.O. Box 433
Topsfield, MA 01983

Peaceful Valley Farm Supply
11173 Peaceful Valley
Nevada City, CA 95959

Smith & Hawken
25 Corte Madera
Mill Valley, CA 94941

Ringer Corp.
9959 Valley View Rd.
Eden Prairie, MN 55344

SEEDS

W. Atlee Burpee & Co.
300 Park Ave.
Warminster, PA 18974

High Altitude Gardens
P.O. Box 4619
Ketchum, ID 83340

Johnny's Selected Seeds
Foss Hill Rd.
Albion, ME 04910

J.W. Jung Seed Co.
Randolph, WI 53957

Landreth Seed Co.
180-188 West Ostend St.
P.O. Box 6426
Baltimore, MD 21230

Park Seed Co. Inc.
P.O. Box 31
Greenwood, SC 29647

Plant Finders of America
106 Fayette Circle
Fort Wright, KY 41044

Seed Savers Exchange
Rural Route 3, Box 239
Decorah, IA 52101

Seeds Blum
Idaho City Stage
Boise, ID 83706

Seeds of Change
621 Old Santa Fe Trail, #10
Santa Fe, NM 87501

Southern Exposure Seed
 Exchange
P.O. Box 158
North Garden, VA 22959

Stokes Seeds
P.O. Box 548
Buffalo, NY 14240

Territorial Seed Company
P.O. Box 157
Cottage Grove, OR 97424

Thompson & Morgan
P.O. Box 1308
Jackson, NJ 08527

WILDFLOWERS AND NATIVE PLANTS

Abundant Life Seed
 Foundation
P.O. Box 772
Port Townsend, WA 98368

Allgrove Farm
P.O. Box 459
N. Wilmington, MA 01887

Brookside Wildflowers
Route 3, Box 740
Boone, NC 28607

Dallas Nature Center
Attn.: Randy Mock
7575 Wheatland Rd.
Dallas, TX 75249

LaFayette Home Nursery
R.R. 1, Box 1A
Lafayette, IL 61449

New England Wildflower
    Society
Garden in the Woods
Hemenway Rd.
Framingham, MA 01701

Panfield Nurseries, Inc.
322 Southdown Rd.
Huntington, NY 11743

Plants of The Southwest
Agua Fria, Rt. 6, Box 11-A
Santa Fe, NM 87501

Prairie Nursery
P.O. Box 306
Westfield, WI 53964

The Primrose Path
R.D. 2, Box 110
Scottdale, PA 15683

Vermont Wildflower Farm
P.O. Box 5
Charlotte, VT 05445

We-Du Nurseries
Route 5, Box 724
Marion, NC 28752

Wildseed, Inc.
P.O. Box 27751
Tempe, AZ 85285

Wildfinger Woodlands
P.O. Box 1091
Webster, NY 14580

Woodlanders
1128 Colleton Ave.
Aiken, SC 29801

BULBS

Peter de Jager Bulb Co.
188 Asbury St.
P.O. Box 2010
South Hamilton, MA 01982

McClure & Zimmerman
108 W. Winnebago
P.O. Box 368
Friesland, WI 53935

Michigan Bulb Co.
1950 Waldorf N.
Grand Rapids, MI 49550

Netherland Bulb Co., Inc.
13 McFadden Rd.
Easton, PA 18042

Quality Dutch Bulbs
50 Lake Dr.
P.O. Box 225
Hillsdale, NJ 07642

PERENNIALS

Bluestone Perennials, Inc.
7211 Middle Rd.
Madison, OH 44057

Kurt Bluemel, Inc.
2740 Greene Ln.
Baldwin, MD 21013

Carroll Gardens
444 East Main St.
P.O. Box 310
Westminster, MD 21157

Clifford's Perennial and Vine
Route 2, Box 320
East Troy, WI 53120

Companion Plants
7247 N. Coolville Ridge Rd.
Athens, OH 45701

Fieldstone Gardens, Inc.
620 Quaker Ln.
Vassalboro, ME 04989-9713

Holbrook Farm and Nursery
Route 2, Box 2238
Fletcher, NC 28732

Klehm Nursery
Rt. 5, Box 197
South Barrington, IL 60010

Milaeger's Gardens
4838 Douglas Ave.
Racine, WI 53402

Powell's Gardens
Route 3, Box 21
Princeton, NC 27569

André Viette Farm and
    Nursery
Route 1, Box 16
Fishersville, VA 22939

Wayside Gardens
1 Garden Ln.
Hodges, SC 29695

White Flower Farm
Litchfield, CT 06759

ROSES

The Antique Rose Emporium
Rt. 5, Box 143
Brenham, TX 77833

High Country Rosarium
1717 Downing St.
Denver, CO 80218

Jackson & Perkins
P.O. Box 1028
Medford, OR 97501

Roses of Yesterday and Today
802 Brown's Valley Rd.
Watsonville, CA 95076

HERBS

Abundant Life Seed
   Foundation
P.O. Box 772
Port Townsend, WA 98368

Caprilands Herb Farm
534 Silver St.
Coventry, CT 06238

The Cook's Garden
P.O. Box 65
Londonderry, VT 05148

Gilbertie's Herb Garden
7 Sylvan Ln.
Westport, CT 06880

Goodwin Creek Gardens
P.O. Box 83
Williams, OR 97544

Herb Gathering, Inc.
5742 Kenwood Ave.
Kansas City, MO 64110

Martha's Herbary
276 Main St.
Hampton, CT 06247

Meadowbrook Herb Garden
Route 138
Wyoming, RI 02898

Nichols Garden Nursery
1190 North Pacific Hwy.
Albany, OR 97321

The Sandy Mush Herb
   Nursery
Route 2, Surrett Cove Rd.
Leicester, NC 28748

Sunnybrook Farms Nursery
9448 Mayfield Rd.
P.O. Box 6
Chesterland, OH 44026

**ORNAMENTAL TREES
AND SHRUBS**

Forestfarm
990 Tetherow Rd.
Williams, OR 97544

Mellinger's Nursery
2310 West South Range Rd.
North Lima, OH 44452

Mountain Plant Kingdom
Dept. CLM 4125
Harrison Grade Rd.
Sebastopol, CA 95472

Roslyn Nursery
211 Burrs Ln.
Dix Hills, NY 11746

Springvale Farm Nursery
Mozier Hollow Rd.
Hamburg, IL 62045

**FRUITING TREES AND
SHRUBS**

Applesource
Rte. 1
Chapin, IL 62628

Arbor & Espalier Company
201 Buena Vista Ave. East
San Francisco, CA 94117

Carino Nurseries
P.O. Box 538
Indiana, PA 15701

Edible Landscaping
P.O. Box 77
Afton, VA 22920

Forestfarm
990 Tetherow Rd.
Williams, OR 97544

Girard Nurseries
P.O. Box 428
Geneva, OH 44041

Bart Hall-Beyer
R.R. 3
Scottstown, Quebec
Canada J0B 3B0

New York State Fruit Testing
   Cooperative Association
P.O. Box 462
Geneva, NY 14456

St. Lawrence Nurseries
R.R. 5, Box 324
Potsdam, NY 13676

Southmeadow Fruit Gardens
15310 Red Arrow Hwy.
Lakeside, MI 49116

Stark Brothers Nurseries &
   Orchards
Hwy. 54 West
Louisiana, MO 63353

Van Well Nursery
P.O. Box 1339
Wenatchee, WA 98807

RECOMMENDED READING

Armitage, Allan M. *Herbaceous Perennial Plants*. Watkinsville, Ga.: Varsity Press, 1989.

Ball, Jeff. *Rodale's Garden Problem Solver: Vegetables, Fruits, & Herbs*. Emmaus, Pa.: Rodale Press, 1988.

Bradley, Fern Marshall and Barbara W. Ellis, eds. *Rodale's All-New Encyclopedia of Organic Gardening*. Emmaus, Pa.: Rodale Press, 1992.

Carr, Anna et al. *Rodale's Chemical-Free Yard and Garden*. Emmaus, Pa.: Rodale Press, 1991.

Cox, Jeff and Marilyn. *Perennial Garden: Color Harmonies Through the Seasons*. Emmaus, Pa.: Rodale Press, 1985.

Creasy, Rosalind. *The Complete Book of Edible Landscaping*. San Francisco: Sierra Club Books, 1982.

Darr, Sheila, Helga Olkowski, and William Olkowski. *Common-Sense Pest Control*. New Town, Ct.: The Taunton Press, 1991.

Damrosch, Barbara. *The Garden Primer*. New York: Workman Publisher, 1988.

Druse, Ken. *The Natural Shade Gardener*. New York: Clarkson Potter Publishing, 1992.

Ellis, Barbara and Fern Marshall Bradley. *The Organic Gardener's Handbook of Natural Insect and Disease Control*. Emmaus, Pa.: Rodale Press, 1992.

Harper, Pamela and Fred McGourty. *Perennials: How to Select, Grow, & Enjoy*. Los Angeles: Price, Stern, Sloan, 1985.

Heriteau, Jacqueline and Henry M. Cathey. *The National Arboretum Book of Outstanding Garden Plants*. New York: Simon and Schuster, 1990.

Hylton, William H. and Claire Kowalchik, eds. *Rodale's Illustrated Encyclopedia of Herbs*. Emmaus, Pa.: Rodale Press, 1987.

Jabs, Carolyn. *The Heirloom Gardener*. San Francisco: Sierra Club Books, 1984.

Jeavons, John. *How to Grow More Vegetables Than You Ever Imagined on Less Land Than You Ever Thought Possible*. Berkeley, Calif.: Ten Speed Press, 1991.

Kourik, Robert. *Designing and Maintaining your Edible Landscape Naturally*. Santa Rosa, Calif.: Metamorphic Press, 1986.

Lloyd, Christopher, with Richard Bird. *The Cottage Garden*. New York: Prentice Hall, 1990.

Martin, Deborah L. and Grace Gershuny, eds. *The Rodale Book of Composting* [rev. ed.]. Emmaus, Pa.: Rodale Press, 1992.

National Gardening Association. *Gardening: The Complete Guide to Growing America's Favorite Fruits and Vegetables*. Reading, Mass.: Addison-Wellesley Publishing Co., 1986.

Ottesen, Carole. *Ornamental Grasses: The Amber Wave*. New York: McGraw-Hill Publishing Co., 1989.

_____. *The New American Garden: A Manifesto for Today's Gardener*. New York: Macmillan Co., 1987.

Page, Stephen and Joseph Smillie. *The Orchard Almanac* [2nd ed.] Rockport, Maine: Spraysaver Publications, 1988.

Roth, Susan A. *The Weekend Garden Guide*. Emmaus, Pa.: Rodale Press, 1991.

Schenk, George. *The Complete Shade Gardener*. Boston: Houghton Mifflin, 1985.

Sinnes, A. Cort. *How to Select and Care for Shrubs and Hedges*. San Francisco: Ortho Books, Chevron Chemical Co., 1980.

_____. *Shade Gardening*. San Francisco: Ortho Books, Chevron Chemical Co., 1982.

Taylor's Guide Staff. *Taylor's Guide to Groundcovers, Vines, and Grasses*. Boston: Houghton Mifflin, 1987.

_____. *Taylor's Guide to Shrubs*. Boston: Houghton Mifflin, 1987.

_____. *Taylor's Guide to Trees*. Boston: Houghton Mifflin, 1988.

_____. *Taylor's Guide to Perennials*. Boston: Houghton Mifflin, 1986

Thorpe, Patricia and Eve Sonneman. *America's Cottage Gardens*. New York: Random House, 1990.

Whitehead, Jeffrey. *The Hedge Book*. Charlotte, Vt.: Garden Way Publishing, 1992.

INDEX

Page numbers in bold indicate illustrations and photographs.

ACKNOWLEDGMENTS

We would like to fondly acknowledge the many passionate gardeners who created the gardens we wrote about and photographed. Thanks to the staff at Natureworks, and to Billy Woods, and Helen Pratt. Smallwood & Stewart extends its thanks to Ken Burton, Donald Barker, Ruth Lively, and Sarah Price for their invaluable contributions.